T0355053

BLESSED IS HE

Learning to Trust the Lord

Timothy L. Colwell

WESTBOW
PRESS®
A DIVISION OF THOMAS NELSON
& ZONDERVAN

WestBow Press books may be ordered through booksellers or by contacting:

WestBow Press
A Division of Thomas Nelson & Zondervan
1663 Liberty Drive
Bloomington, IN 47403
www.westbowpress.com
844-714-3454

Cover image provided by Jaime Colwell.

Scripture taken from the King James Version of the Bible.

Scripture quotations are from the ESV® Bible (The Holy Bible, English Standard Version®), copyright © 2001 by Crossway, a publishing ministry of Good News Publishers. Used by permission. All rights reserved.

This book was edited by Nicole Colwell of Colwell Creative Content. For help with your editing needs, she can be reached at colwellcreativecontent.biz or colwellcreativecontent@gmail.com.

ISBN: 978-1-6642-3431-4 (sc)
ISBN: 978-1-6642-3433-8 (hc)
ISBN: 978-1-6642-3432-1 (e)

Library of Congress Control Number: 2021909578

Print information available on the last page.

WestBow Press rev. date: 6/11/2021

Contents

Dedication

I dedicate this book to my parents, LeWayne and Susan Colwell. Their never-ending trust in God's faithfulness laid the foundation of my reliance upon the Lord. The love and faithful encouragement they showed inspired me to be the man I have become. At an early age, they taught me what it means to trust God and helped me see the importance of putting Him first in all I do. With loving persistence, they helped me to be willing to share the passion of my heart. Though I have spent much of my adult life with thousands of miles between us, their constant prayers have sustained me in ministry. Their faithfulness to Jesus Christ has been a great example to me. They are not perfect, but God used them to teach me, "Blessed is the man who trusts in the Lord..." (Jeremiah 17:7)

Foreward

The author's journey is captivating. He certainly comes across as one who doesn't have it all together, but earnestly desires to keep reaching to be/do better. His writing dispels the myth that missionaries are super-human and examples of being giant Christians. His vulnerability stands out.

Ted Baker- Pastor- Faro Bible Chapel- Faro, Yukon

If you are looking for a missionary biography of heroic adventures in Africa, boldly rescuing people from poverty in Asia, or proclaiming faith to unreached tribes in the Amazon, there are other books for you. On the other hand, this memoir of an "average" man and his family serving humbly and faithfully for years in one out-of-the way part of the world, reflecting on how a great God draws people to Himself and once in a while miraculously answers prayers of faith, I highly recommend Blessed Is He. Without fanfare, Tim Colwell shares how his faith grew from childhood and early adult years, leading him (and his family) to follow Christ in serving with SEND International in the Aboriginal community of Ross River, Yukon and how the Spirit works despite opposition to make disciples of all nations. Whether a new worker in ministry, one with some experience, or a Christian wrestling through the normal questions of everyday life in your workplace, community and family, this book will bless you!

Dr. Steven C. Ibbotson - Adjunct Professor-
Prairie College- Three Hills, Alberta

Theories. Not a bad thing and even quite useful at times. However, this isn't a book about theories. Tim Colwell has given us a glimpse of the "where the rubber meets the road" practical faith that has guided his life and ministry. I found myself nodding my head in agreement and encouraged in my faith as I joined Tim's walk with God through these pages.

Dr. Barry Rempel- SEND Missionary- York, South Carolina

In Mark 9:24 a father replied to Jesus, "I believe; help my unbelief." Have you every wondered how Jesus helps our unbelief? In this book by Tim Colwell you will read stories from the life of a missionary in Canada's Yukon Territory that will answer that question. Tim shares everyday life stories in which Jesus taught him to trust and increased his faith. These stories will encourage you as you learn to trust God in everything.

Dr. Gary Ridley- SEND U Missiologist- Palmer, Alaska

Preface

When I began to write in the spring of 2020, I never imagined where this project would take me. My original purpose in writing was to tell how God strengthened my trust in Him in one specific area of ministry. In 2009, God gave my wife Gwendy and I a burden to do more for the small community in which we have ministered since February 2001. He asked us to step out in faith and build a thirty-six-hundred-foot ministry center near the middle of our community. I had never seen or participated in a project to this magnitude. The way the Lord brought everything together increased my trust tremendously.

As I began to think over the events which led to the creation of the HOPE Centre, I realized how God began to strengthen the depth of my trust in Him long before the first nail was driven. He began to strengthen my faith long before we moved into Ross River, the community where we live.

Sure, He did a mighty work in bringing the people, resources, government officials, and materials together so the Centre could be built. But, He started working with us long before we sketched the first draft floor plan.

I knew there were times when God asked me to trust Him; like when He asked me to trust His Son Jesus to be my Savior. I knew He asked me to trust Him when I surrendered my life to be a missionary in Canada's Yukon Territory. He asked me to trust Him in choosing my life-partner. But, did He only desire my full trust in the big decisions of life? What about the day-to-day things, like where to go or who to talk to? Did He want my trust in those areas as well?

He has been working in me trying to get me to trust Him more from the day I took my first breath. The more I wrote, the more He opened my eyes to the other situations and life experiences He brought me through in order to strengthen my trust in Him.

It is my conviction that we do not trust God to the extent of which He is worthy. We trust Him until it gets uncomfortable and then we back away and try to handle things ourselves. Like Peter, who stepped out of the boat in the midst of the storm (Matthew 14:22-33), we take our eyes off Jesus and get caught up in the troubles around us. In doing this, we forget Who controls the storm. We forget what made us step out of the boat to begin with – the realization of the greatness of our God.

As I recalled the stories God has brought me through, I see trust as a journey. I did not get up one day and decide to trust the Lord fully. God has grown my trust little by little, day by day. I see Him working in the great and awesome experiences, but it is in the everyday experiences where He also makes my trust in Him grow. The more I trust Him, the more I see how trustworthy He is.

"The Lord is my strength and my shield; my heart trusted in him, and I am helped: therefore my heart greatly rejoiceth; and with my song will I praise him." (Psalm 28:7)

Acknowledgements

I want to thank the following people who have helped to make this book possible. First and foremost, it goes without saying, but who am I to write such a book if it were not for my Lord and Savior, Jesus Christ, who has continued to work with me to conform me into His image? My beautiful wife, Gwendy, of twenty-five years who has stood beside me for many of the adventures you are about to read about, and she continues to push me to strengthen my faith.

To Natalie for her countless hours of reading and rereading, editing and challenging me in writing. To Barry, Gary, Rachel, Sarah, Steven, Ted, and Veronica who willingly critiqued the book and helped find mistakes before I sent the manuscript to the publisher.

To our daughter, Jaime, to whom the Lord has given a great eye for details. Whether in looking for a misplaced period or taking the cover photograph, she has been a great help in the process. To our other children, Janelle, Jocelyn, Jessie, Jenna, and Joe who encouraged me to keep writing, endured months of Daddy talking about "the book," and willingly read through stories they have heard many times before.

It is wrong of me to write a book and not acknowledge the many people who have stood with us. While we may get to enjoy the benefits of being on the "front lines" as many like to say, we have not done the work alone. There are many who have stood with us in helping to reach Canada's Yukon with the Gospel.

When we began our missionary journey in July 1996, little did we know how many amazing and wonderful people we would meet. You are more than just partners in ministry; you are our friends. You have welcomed us into your home. You have fed us. You have taken us to your missionary cupboard. You have listened as we shared about the work. You cried with us. Laughed with us. Prayed with us. You have written letters. Sent birthday cards. Christmas gifts. You have welcomed our children into your Sunday School classes, AWANA youth groups, and special activities. You have treated us like your family.

Our faithful prayer partners – When we joined SEND, we were required to have thirty prayer partners who were committed to praying for the ministry. Many of the prayer partners who committed to pray for us in the early years have been praying for us for close to twenty-five years. We do not take the work they do on a daily basis lightly. They read our newsletters, emails, Facebook posts, and letters looking for our prayer needs. Then they faithfully pray for these requests, looking for the Lord to answer. They are the backbone of the work of the Lord. In 1 Thessalonians 5:17 we read,

"Pray without ceasing."

Thank you to those who have prayed fervently for this ministry.

Our financial supporters – Of course, the Lord's work needs money; not that the Lord needs our money, but He chooses to allow people to have a part in giving to His work. We would not be where we are today had it not been for those who have given sacrificially to help supply our monthly support. Whether it is the one who gives five dollars per month or the church who gives seven-hundred and fifty dollars per month, each gives as unto the Lord. Some gave once a year, some gave once a month. But each gave in faith, trusting the Lord to meet their needs as they supplied ours. In 2 Corinthians 9:7 we read,

"Each one must give as he has decided in his heart, not reluctantly or under compulsion, for God loves a cheerful giver." (ESV)

Thank you to all those who have given cheerfully
to see God's work moving forward.

Our Summer Missionaries and interns – Over the course of our time in the north, we have seen countless Summer Missionaries and countless interns who have served with us. Many of these come for only a summer and are seeking the Lord's direction for their future ministry. They have given their time, their talents, their gifts and abilities. They have befriended our children, making them a part of their lives. They have taught Vacation Bible School, helped with Kids Bible Club, served as counselors at Kamp Klondike, served coffee, and helped visit the elders. They have lived and ministered with us. They were a blessing and encouragement to us and our family. Romans 10:13-15 says,

> *"For whosoever shall call upon the name of the Lord shall be saved. How then shall they call on him in whom they have not believed? and how shall they believe in him of whom they have not heard? and how shall they hear without a preacher? And how shall they preach, except they be sent? as it is written, How beautiful are the feet of them that preach the gospel of peace, and bring glad tidings of good things!"*

Thank you to all who used your feet to help us share the
Gospel to those who would otherwise never hear it.

Our volunteers – Often there is work a missionary cannot do by themselves. Either there is not time or the work is too great. Over the years, we have had many amazing volunteers who have come and helped us with the work we could not get done ourselves. They have dug outhouse holes, washed windows, built buildings, and torn down buildings. They have scrubbed toilets, hung doors, painted and varnished. They have set up children's camps, sorted recyclables, organized craft supplies, and made thank you notes. They have cut and split firewood, replaced engines, changed oil, and so much more. They have done all this with joy. They have followed Paul's advice in Colossians 3:23,

> *"And whatsoever ye do, do it heartily, as to the Lord, and not unto men."*

Thank you to all who gave of your blood, sweat,
and tears to serve the Lord and help us.

Our co-workers – We have the privilege of belonging to a great mission organization, SEND International. Being a part of SEND has allowed us to work along-side some wonderful people. Sometimes it has been working and doing ministry with them in Ross River. At other times, it has been working together to train and prepare our Summer Missionaries. Sometimes it has been working together to do a joint service with a neighboring community. There are other times we are working together to give direction and leadership to the mission. Together, we have seen people discipled and turned into northern disciple-makers. In 1 Peter 4:10, we read,

> *"Each of you should use whatever gift you have received to serve others, as faithful stewards of God's grace in its various forms."*

Thank you to all our coworkers for using
your gifts to serve God faithfully.

Our community- For the past 20 years, we have served as in Ross River, Yukon. We came in as strangers and have developed deep friendships. They welcomed us and treated us like family. They taught us their traditions and helped us learn so much about living on the land. They took us camping in some of the most beautiful spots in the world. They helped us harvest berries in their favorite patches. They showed me how to call moose (if only I could learn how to sit still long enough to get one) and how to make dry meat. They helped the Yukon become more than where we live; it has become our home. In Mark 10:29-30 we read,

> *"Truly, I say to you, there is no one who has left house or brothers or sisters or mother or father or children or lands, for my sake and for the gospel, who will not receive a hundredfold now in this time, houses and brothers and sisters and mothers and children and lands, with persecutions, and in the age to come eternal life." (ESV)*

Thank you for allowing us to be a part of your community.
From the bottom of our heart, we say **THANK YOU.**

Introduction

"But blessed is the one who trusts in the Lord, whose confidence is in Him. They will be like a tree planted by the water that sends out its roots by the stream. It does not fear when heat comes; its leaves are always green. It has no worries in a year of drought and never fails to bear fruit." (Jeremiah 17:7-8)

The company is downsizing. You are about to lose your job. You have four young children at home. You have been fighting with your spouse for months. There seems to be no end in sight. Everything you have tried fails. You received an urgent call from the doctor, who confirmed your worst nightmare. You only have a few months to live.

We all face impossible situations when we know we have nowhere else to go but to the Lord. What about the daily trials and tribulations? To whom do we run? Do we handle things on our own?

Several years ago, my wife, Gwendy and I took our children on a sight-seeing trip to New York City (NYC). We both grew up in the country, several hours from the city that "never sleeps." Growing up, my family avoided the city. My parents taught me that this city was not a place to go. In the early years of my life, a person had to keep his hand on his wallet to avoid losing it to pick-pockets.

After we got married, we enjoyed going to the city. Even though we did not want to live there, we enjoyed the energy and excitement. We loved to walk to Times Square. Stroll through Central Park. The kids loved the Lego Store and riding the Staten Island Ferry.

On one particular visit, we decided to ride the City Sights tour bus. We were able to get on and off wherever we chose and see several things the kids wanted to see. Our last stop led us into Central Park to see the statue of Balto, the sled dog recognized for his contribution in helping to save Alaskans during a diphtheria outbreak in the 1920s.

We were watching the clock, since we knew we needed to be at the bus stop by five o'clock to catch the last bus, (or so we thought). As the hands on the clock drew close to the four o'clock hour, we made our way back to the street to walk back to where we would catch the bus. As we looked at the map, we realized the distance we needed to cover was immense. We had walked further than we thought. I felt the weight of our youngest, snuggled in the baby carrier on my back. Our children were already weary from the day's adventures.

As we trudged on to where we thought we were going, out of nowhere, a stranger came and asked where we needed to go. Now, my parents taught me not to talk to strangers, especially in a big city. One can never be too careful.

The man had a sincere look in his eyes and seemed to have a genuine interest in our well-being. He may have heard the girls complaining about having to walk so far. He may have seen the bewildered looks that told him we did not belong there. It may have been the way I stood, all hunched over under the weight of the child on my back. Somehow, he knew we needed help. Little did we know how much help we needed.

We told him we needed to get to the City Tour bus and needed to make it before the bus made its last round. He told us we were mistaken. The bus stopped running at five but went by our stop much earlier. We only had a couple of minutes to make it to that stop. We had to hurry if we were going to make it in time to ride. If we missed it, we would have to walk twenty-four blocks. Then he said, "I know where to go. Follow me."

What were we to do? What if this stranger was up to no good? We did not know him. He did not know us. Why did he care so much? We faced two choices. Were we going to follow the one we did not know? Or, were we going to try to make it on our own? We chose the crazy choice. We could have said, "It's ok. We've got this." We could have tried to make it on our own. But, he seemed like someone we could trust. We let a stranger lead us.

With the skill of a seasoned New Yorker, he wove his way through the city's busy sidewalks. Business people walked shoulder to shoulder as they headed home from their day of work. Traffic rushed by. Horns blasted.

The stranger never lost his focus. He guided us to our stop, making sure not to lose any of us in the process.

Gwendy with our children on Staten Island Ferry

When we arrived at the bus stop, the stranger disappeared. We looked around for him in order to express our appreciation, but he vanished from sight. He led us safely and efficiently to where we needed to be, then left without saying a word. We made it with a couple of minutes to spare, thanks to the stranger's help.

I do not look for angels under every tree. It is my belief that God sent us an angel to help us get to where we needed to go. How else could the man have known the struggle we faced?

His words echo in my ears. "I know the way. Follow me." Whether we are on the streets of NYC or in the country milking cows, we face daily difficulties and challenging situations. It may be our health. It may be the loss of a loved one. Our marriage may be a disaster. It could be financial uncertainty. It may even be a pandemic, affecting the world.

What do we do in these situations? Do we run and hide? Do we try to muscle our way through on our own? Or is there a better way? I am reminded of Jesus' words to Peter, Andrew, James, and John when he chose them to be His disciples. They sounded much like the stranger did on the busy streets of NYC. In Matthew 4:18-22 we read,

> *While walking by the Sea of Galilee, he saw two brothers, Simon (who is called Peter) and Andrew his brother, casting a net into the sea, for they were fishermen. And he said to them, "**Follow me**, and I will make you fishers of men." **Immediately** they left their nets and followed him. And going on from there he saw two other brothers, James the son of Zebedee and John his brother, in the boat with Zebedee their father, mending their nets, and he called them. **Immediately** they left the boat and their father and followed him. (ESV, emphasis added)*

At Jesus' command, these men left their comfortable, familiar lives. They left the certainty of their jobs to follow someone they knew little about. Today, Jesus still calls people to follow Him. Not only in the hard stuff, but in the everyday stuff. Christ is not some stranger from off the street. We know Who He is and what He can do. Yet, we often ignore His voice, that says, "I know the way, follow Me." We want to feel like we are in control.

In Jeremiah17:7, we read, "Blessed is the man who *TRUSTS* in the Lord." (emphasis added) The prophet Jeremiah makes a promise. The Lord blesses everyone who trusts in Him. In the Oxford University Press Online Dictionary we have the following two definitions for "blessed."

> *"Endowed with divine favor and protection.*
> *Bringing pleasure or relief as a welcome contrast*
> *to what one has previously experienced."1*

We desire to experience the divine favor and protection of the Lord. We want to know God hears our prayers and grants us our requests. When we face difficulties, we want relief and pleasure. None of us like to go through hard times. We want to be in the place where we know we have trusted the Lord and He has come through. What does it mean to trust in the Lord? How does a person get to the point where they are trusting the Lord in all areas of life?

In Genesis 22, we read the story of the Old Testament patriarch,

Abraham. God asked him to offer his one and only son, Isaac, as an offering. The problem was, God promised Abraham He would multiply his descendants as the stars in the heavens. (Genesis 12:2, 15:5) Abraham and his wife were old, well past child-bearing years. If he offered Isaac as an offering, he was doing away with the one God promised. It did not make sense to do what God asked. Yet, the Bible says, he went ahead, trusting the Lord to provide a Lamb. (Genesis 22:8)

Abraham knew what God asked him to do, but he also had an unwavering trust in the Lord to follow through on His promise. We gain more insight into how strong his trust was when we get to the Faith Hall of Fame listed in Hebrews 11. In verse 19, we read, "He considered that God was able even to raise him from the dead..." (ESV) How does a person develop such a deep faith in the Lord?

Over the past three decades of ministry, I have heard people say, "I believe in God." Trusting in the Lord is more than a mere belief that He exists. We can say we believe in God, yet would we be willing to go as far as Abraham, offering our own child on an altar if God told us to? Do we show a deep, unwavering trust in God, or are we trusting in ourselves? Many times, the way we live shows that God is not the one we trust. We trust what we can do for ourselves more than we trust what God can do for us.

Lest I sound arrogant and judgmental at the very start of this book, I must state, I do not write under the guise of having it all together. As the Apostle Paul wrote in Philippians 3:12, "Not that I have already attained this or am already perfect, but I press on to make it my own..." The Lord has been working with me for almost fifty years to help me trust Him better. It is a growing process. God is working moment by moment, through many different situations and circumstances to teach me how to trust Him completely.

I do not write this book feeling like I have "arrived" at full trust in God. I am like the father of the demon possessed boy in Mark 9. He brought his son to the disciples for healing. The disciples tried to help, but could not offer the boy what he needed, so the father brought the boy to Jesus. When Jesus saw the father and his son, He said, "If thou canst believe, all things are possible to him that believeth." The father's words are where I am so many times. His response to Jesus was, "Lord, I believe; help thou mine unbelief." He believed Christ had the power to heal his son, but lacked the trust that God would do it. I see myself trusting that God has the power, but doubting He will actually use the power to help me.

We do believe God can do something, but we doubt He will do something. I have learned that the more I trust the Lord even in the smallest things, the more He shows He is worthy of receiving all my trust. It is like working an arm or leg muscle. The more I work with a muscle, the stronger it becomes. The more I work out my trust muscle, the more my faith grows. God shows He is able to do "exceeding abundantly above all that we ask or think, according to the power that worketh in us." (Ephesians 3:20)

The stories and experiences shared in this book have helped me to have a stronger faith and trust in Him. I know in my mind that I can trust God, but I get frustrated by how small my trust is.

It is my hope and prayer as you read through the pages of this book that your faith and trust in the Lord Jesus Christ are strengthened and grown tremendously. I pray that your faith and trust develop from a tiny mustard seed into the tall mustard tree. I pray God uses the experiences He brought us through to encourage you in your trust in Him. I pray that you will see the blessing of God in your life.

Part I

LEARNING TO TRUST

"For no one can lay a foundation other than that which is laid, which is Jesus Christ." (1 Corinthians 3:11 ESV)

"Except the Lord build the house, they labour in vain that build it: except the Lord keep the city, the watchman waketh but in vain. It is vain for you to rise up early, to sit up late, to eat the bread of sorrows: for so he giveth his beloved sleep. Lo, children are an heritage of the Lord: and the fruit of the womb is his reward. As arrows are in the hand of a mighty man; so are children of the youth. Happy is the man that hath his quiver full of them: they shall not be ashamed, but they shall speak with the enemies in the gate." (Psalm 127:1-5)

Part I

LEARNING TO TRUST

Chapter 1

BREAKING OR BUILDING TRUST

"He that is faithful in that which is least is faithful also in much: and he that is unjust in the least is unjust also in much." (Luke 16:10)

I was in kindergarten when I learned the importance of being trustworthy. Dad and Mom were not rich by any stretch of the imagination. We had enough to live on, but we did not have enough to buy the things that a young boy might wish for. When I went to school, lunches were simple, yet adequate, if we ate them. Mom usually packed peanut butter and jelly sandwiches in my lunch. They were cheap and easy to prepare. The problem was, I did not care for them. Often, I left the sandwich uneaten in my lunch box. Since Dad and Mom did not like to see food wasted, it bothered them when I did not eat all my food. They encouraged me to eat, but to no avail. In vain, I tried to hide the fact I did not eat them. They still found out.

After many failed attempts to get me to eat my whole lunch, they tried to appeal to my love of sweets and made a deal with me. If I ate all my lunch for the whole week, we would go out for ice cream at the local ice-cream shop. As a kid, I loved ice cream. What kid does not? I still did not like peanut butter and jelly. What was a boy like me to do? I had an idea. Each day before mom could look in my lunchbox, I would sneak into the back room and dispose of my uneaten sandwich in the garbage. Then I placed my lunch box on the counter for the next day. When asked if I had finished all my lunch, I lied to them and told them I had eaten everything.

The first few evenings, I experienced no difficulty. On Wednesday night, my scheme came to a sudden end. I am not sure whether Mom found the sandwich in the garbage or if she had seen me sneaking around, but she caught me in my attempts to cover the truth. She pushed me for honesty and I spilled it all. Not only was there no ice cream for me, I also learned how important it was to tell the truth all the time. A sore seat stood as my reminder.

This lesson has stuck with me all my life. The foundation for how we trust others and how trustworthy we live is often taught to us early in life. The way we are treated as infants and toddlers has a profound impact on our ability to trust others. If someone breaks the trust we have in them, we find it hard to rebuild it again.

In ministry, I have seen kids in whom trust has not been built. They have learned how to lie, manipulate, and twist the truth to protect themselves. Many have done so in order to survive. They lie about their mom or dad being home to take care of them when they know their parents are out drinking. They say they have eaten food when they are starving and would love to be given even a simple snack. The way they are treated affects how they view themselves and others.

To them, the only person to be trusted is themselves as their primary caregiver. They are looking out for their own good, making sure they take care of themselves. Because of this, they have a hard time opening up and trusting anyone to care for them. They think they do a very good job at caring for themselves.

For many children living today, they feel let down by the very people they should trust. Their parents are too self-absorbed or lost in addictions and hurts to realize the damage they are doing to their children. For some parents, they never had anyone to show them what it means to be a parent. They have no idea how they should take care of their children. For others, they think, *as long as my child is not getting into trouble, they are doing alright.*

Such was not my story. Dad and Mom sacrificed greatly for each of their four children. They did all they could to care for us and teach us that we could trust them. They also taught us to trust the God in whom they placed their trust. I learned very quickly that Dad and Mom said what they meant and meant what they said. If they said, no, no is what they meant. If they said they were going to be somewhere, they did their best to be where they said they would be. They exemplified trustworthiness and taught us to do the same.

They taught us to put our trust in God for everything, no matter how big or small. I remember many trips starting with a prayer for safety. This prayer was not used as a good luck charm. It was made out of a realization that God was the one who held our very lives in His hands. We were dependent on Him to help us go anywhere or do anything.

My grandfather suffered a tragic death while taking a church youth group on a trip when my dad was in high school. The vehicle that they were traveling in experienced a tire blowout, which caused him to lose control. They knew first-hand what could happen on the road. To them, every mile driven in safety was because of God's hand upon them.

Even though they showed my brothers, sister, and I what trust in God looks like, I had to learn how to trust God through my own experiences. This book is not to show how I have achieved a great measure of trust in God. Rather, as I have written the many stories you will read, I have realized how much I still doubt God. I wish I could say, "I have arrived. I now know how to trust God with everything." While total trust is the goal, I am far from being there. My trust in the all-knowing, all-powerful, all-present God is still a work in process. God is growing my trust in Him.

Chapter 2

DUTY OR COMMITMENT

"I beseech you therefore, brethren, by the mercies of God, that ye present your bodies a living sacrifice, holy, acceptable unto God, which is your reasonable service." (Romans 12:1)

There are times in our lives when we must stop and ask ourselves the question, "Why am I doing what I am doing?" What gets me out of bed in the morning? Or, what keeps me going day after day? I am a driven individual whom some people may consider a workaholic. I wake up in the morning with a desire to get going and not waste any valuable hours of daylight. My parents felt it necessary for their children to work for what they got in life. They did not believe in free rides. More importantly, they taught their four children to seek the Lord's desire for their lives. They instilled in us the need to live our lives, not just for a paycheck, but to live dependent on and trusting in the Lord.

Dad was a Christian businessman who worked diligently to provide for his family. Being a general contractor meant long hours on the job all week. He was out the door before seven-thirty each morning and often did not get home until six-thirty each evening. He often spent at least half of Saturday going and looking at other jobs to keep the business going. Even with this much pressure, he and Mom still found time to serve in our local church, Windsor Bible Baptist. They served faithfully in many ministries. To them, church was not a spectator sport. They were never just pew warmers. The business may have paid the bills, but it never got in the way of God's work. They made sure the job never got in the way of their relationship with their Lord and Savior.

They lived out of a devotion to the Lord and a worship for what He did for them on the cross of Calvary. It was not a duty; it was their lives lived as Paul writes in Romans 12:1, "a living sacrifice to the Lord." This led them to take an active part in the church. They set the example for us on what it meant to be a follower of Christ.

They took us to church whenever the doors were open and even sometimes when they were not. This meant being at church twice on Sunday. We attended AWANA[1] on Monday evening and Bible study and prayer on Wednesday night. Then on Friday or Saturday night, we cleaned the church. Sometimes it seemed to be a duty to us as children. To Dad and Mom, attendance in church flowed out of a personal relationship with Jesus.

It was not enough to take us to AWANA on Monday nights. They left early so we could pick up other kids in the trailer parks and apartment complexes near the church. They served as leaders and helpers during AWANA. Later they took on the role of AWANA commanders.

They did not leave the work of the church for others but did what they could to help further the Kingdom of God. Dad helped to lead the church by being on the deacon board and later served as board chairman. Some moms dropped their kids off for Vacation Bible School (VBS) and left as fast as they could, enjoying a couple hours of free time. Not our mom, she was inside making sure there were quality crafts for the kids to work on.

---

[1] AWANA is a youth program focused on discipleship and Bible teaching. The acronym AWANA, Approved Workmen Are Not Ashamed, is taken from 2 Timothy 2:15 which says, "Study to shew thyself approved unto God, a workman that needeth not to be ashamed, rightly dividing the word of truth."

My parents- LeWayne and Sue Colwell

Today, we hear of kids who feel their parents are too busy with the church work to care about them. This leads some to run away from the church. Worse yet, they reject the Lord their parents are serving. Dad and Mom made sure we were part of the work. We knew our parents loved the Lord, loved others, *and* loved us as well. It was not an either or; it was *both*. Their love for others and for us was evident in what they did and how they lived their lives. They tried to instill this love, devotion, and sacrifice in the lives of all four of their children.

Many times, I went to one of them and asked for their help with a decision I struggled to make. They listened with great interest and gave helpful advice, but in the end the answer was always the same. They asked in love, "What do you think God wants?" Sure, they had deep, heart-felt desires for us. Dad loved it when we went to work with him. He, like many fathers, wanted his children to follow him in the business. But more than this was their desire for their children to grow to love the Lord. They wanted us to trust Him as Lord and Savior, and do whatever He gave us to do. Their joy was not based on whether we stayed close to home or not. Their joy came from seeing us developing our own relationship with Christ and following Him.

This was evident in the gifts they gave us. Many Christmases there were Bibles under the tree for each of us. If it was not a Bible, we got a devotional book or another book to encourage our walk with Christ. Inside the front cover of one Bible I received, Dad had written Proverbs 3:5-6. It said, "Trust in the Lord with all thine heart; and lean not unto thine own understanding. In all thy ways acknowledge Him, and he shall direct thy paths." They desired for us to live trusting the Lord and following wherever He led. Early in life, we were shown in actions and taught in words where our trust should be.

When we were old enough to read on our own, we received personal devotion books. With them came the encouragement to start having our own quiet time with God. They helped us to develop a personal, growing relationship with the Lord, whom they loved.

Every morning, when I got up early enough, I saw Dad sitting at his desk with his Bible open. He did not tell us to trust God and live another way. He lived it out. He showed it to us by his daily commitment to the Lord. Even if it meant getting up half to three-quarters of an hour earlier than he needed too, he made sure he gave the Lord the first part of his day.

Mom was no different. Each morning, she lay on her side, prayer journal in hand, telling God the deepest needs of her heart. As a stay-at-home mom, she had more than enough to keep her busy. With Dad working construction, there were many loads of filthy laundry to wash. With four kids, there were meals to cook, clothes to mend or make, and other household chores to fill her time. Yet, in all these tasks, she made sure she gave the Lord the time He deserved.

Dad saw the importance of being faithful to the Word of God. Mom saw the importance of being faithful to prayer. Both did not neglect the other, but practiced them on their own and as a couple. At night, they came together after a long day of work and chasing us kids to have devotions together. Exhaustion sometimes caused Dad's eyes to close before they finished. But they ended the day where it started, in the Word of God.

I knew their love for us came out of their love for the Lord and dependence upon Him. The older I get, the more I thank the Lord for the parents He gave to me. Dad and Mom were not perfect. They would be the first to admit their imperfections. But, they showed us what it meant to follow Jesus. Many of the lessons I have learned have come from the foundation they instilled in me early in life.

Even though Dad and Mom exemplified a total dependence on the Lord, this did not mean we automatically grew to be dependent on the Lord. At various stages of our lives, each of us determined how much we depended on Him.

I did not develop a deep trust in the Lord until I was in my early teens. My lack of trust showed through my early years. When I went water skiing, I feared putting my legs down below the surface. I worried about what might be down there. I went to bed each night, fearing the house catching on fire due to an electrical short somewhere. Ultimately, I was afraid of dying. I heard about hell and was afraid of going there. I still had to come to the point where I was willing to trust God enough to surrender to Him and His will in my life. I had all the knowledge I needed to cure my fears. The one thing I lacked was a personal relationship with Jesus Christ.

Chapter 3

FEAR OR PEACE

"These things have I written unto you that believe on the name of the Son of God; that ye may know that ye have eternal life, and that ye may believe on the name of the Son of God." (1 John 5:13)

We did not like the view around us. The people in the neighborhood we found ourselves in, did not like our presence either. We were not even sure how it happened, but we ended up driving through a sketchy neighborhood near Baltimore, Maryland. The houses stood condemned. The windows on many of them were broken or boarded up. People looked at us like we were from Mars. They wondered why we were driving through their neighborhood. We wondered how we could get out of there – soon! One of my parents said, "Lock the doors," while we all tried to figure out where we needed to go to get back to the interstate.

Each spring, our family took a long trip somewhere. We looked forward to our times together. These trips were both educational and fun. Sometimes we visited friends, like the time we traveled to Kansas to visit a family we had met at summer Bible camp. Other trips took us to national parks and monuments like the Natural Bridge in Virginia and the nation's capital.

Many memories centered around these trips and others like it. Most are sweet, except for the times we did not know where we were going. Dad and Mom got lost on their honeymoon due to a large New England snow storm. I guess that set the stage for the rest of their married life. Never fail, at some time during each of our trips, we found ourselves somewhere we did not want to be. This led to tense moments as we tried to figure out where we were, and more importantly, how we were going to get back to where we were heading.

My parents may have had trouble navigating through the highways of America, but one area where they did not seem to have trouble was helping us kids know where we were going when we died. They dedicated their time to showing us how to trust Christ as our Savior. Their desire was for each of us to grow and develop a personal relationship with Him. This desire was not something they were passive about. They did all they could to help teach and mold us into who God wanted us to be.

This teaching came through a variety of ways. As stated earlier, they took us to Sunday School each week at our home church, Windsor Bible Baptist. They took us to AWANA where we learned God's Word and the importance of hiding it in our hearts. Many of the verses quoted throughout this book came from my time in AWANA. On Saturday morning, we could watch cartoons, but not between ten and eleven. They "made" us listen to Children's Bible Hour and Ranger Bill. We grew to love the singing and adventures of both programs.

When we traveled, the radio was very rarely on anything other than the local Christian radio station. We grew up listening to radio preachers like Chuck Swindoll, J. Vernon McGee, and Oliver B. Green. If the radio was not on, there was always a Christian 8 Track or cassette. (Some of you are wondering what I am talking about. Go and ask your parents or grandparents.)

To them, if we were to live as Christ wanted us to live, they needed to give God many opportunities to influence us. These opportunities came either from our time at church or encouragement from them. As a young boy, they gave me four one-month devotionals which, if I shared with my siblings, would give us one year of devotionals. They wanted us to delve into the Word of God and make it a part of our daily lives, in the same way they were doing.

With all the Scriptural teaching in my life, you might think I was an angel. My brothers and sister picked on me saying that I was the angel of the family, but this was a fallacy. If I was an angel, I surely had horns. All joking aside, we learned at a very early age what it meant to trust God as our Savior.

At the young age of four years old, I asked Mom what it meant to accept Christ as my Savior. With great joy, she prayed with me as I trusted Christ as my Savior. I wrote the date of my salvation, April 24, 1976, in one of my early Bibles.

Even though I received Christ as my Savior at this early age, I did not commit my life to the Lord. I also lacked any assurance of my salvation until later on in life. Until this later commitment, I lived in constant fear and anxiety about death. I was afraid of getting sick and dying. I was afraid of a tragedy hitting our family. I feared my eternal destiny. I knew all the right answers, but did not know where I would go when I died. I do not doubt the fact that I trusted in Christ at the young age of four. But I did not have the assurance of a child of God until I was thirteen years old when I was at Bible camp with my parents.

My parents' desire to see us grow in our knowledge of the Lord led them to LeTourneau Christian Conference Center. Every summer we climbed into the old Ford Station wagon and headed out for a week of family Bible camp on Canandaigua Lake. Due to Dad's busy work schedule, this week was one of the only times when he allowed himself to break free of the business and enjoy life. We took the family boat and enjoyed water skiing, surf boarding, and moon lit rides on the lake. Those days on the lake gave us great times of fun and laughter as we unwound from the rat race of life. It was our family's paradise.

The time at the lake was only part of what Dad and Mom enjoyed so much. The strong Bible teaching we received during the week of camp kept them coming back. Each morning, we went our separate ways for a teaching time designed for our age group. Dad and Mom went with the adults, we children went off to various classes according to our ages.

At lunch, we all joined together for a scrumptious meal served family-style in the dining hall. We feasted on fresh corn on the cob, turkey, beef, and garden vegetables. Homemade desserts were never in short supply. (It was a good thing the cabins were up the hill as we ate like kings and queens.)

In the afternoon, we spent our free time with new and old friends. We went swimming at the lake, did loads of arts and crafts, enjoyed the boat, or played softball or shuffleboard. These times together made the camp a special place and something we all looked forward to year after year.

Each evening, we all gathered at the Tabernacle. Like Israel in the Old Testament, we gathered at the tabernacle to worship and hear from God, Himself. The Tabernacle looked like a barn and had sliding doors along both sides. This allowed us to feel the cool breezes from the lake and see the setting sun as it reflected off the lake. Built on the slant of the hill, all the wood benches faced downhill toward the stage.

After singing some Gospel songs like, "Victory in Jesus" and "Power in the Blood", a musical artist blessed us with a special number or two. The concerts we heard at camp kept us singing through the whole week. It was some of the best music we heard all year. Dad always loved the music at family camp. But the music was not the thing that kept my parents coming back every year.

The thing that kept Dad and Mom coming back each year was the evening chapel times. The Tabernacle where we met each evening served as a rustic sanctuary. People found rest for their weary souls as they gave their lives to the Lord. This happened many times over the course of each summer. For others like our family, it was a place to get rejuvenated for the rest of the year.

The sound Biblical teaching we received and the fellowship with other believers served as a tremendous blessing for each of us. Besides all this, they knew each of their children were being taught Biblically as well. We left each year after family camp with our spirits revived and our stomachs full.

The year that stands out in my mind the most was the summer when I was thirteen. I was never a bad teen. I never rebelled or questioned my parents' authority. I never snuck out of the house to see a girlfriend. I was a pretty good kid most of the time. Even still, I lived with constant fear and doubts about death and how my life might end.

That summer, my sister and I gathered with other teenagers in a small building near the Tabernacle. The building held various artifacts and memorabilia from R. G. LeTourneau, from whom the camp got its name. The air smelled stale and musty. Pictures of revival meetings that showcased a brief history of the camp hung on the walls. The environment of the building could not distract me from what I heard during that week of camp.

Each morning, Lyle Drake, the speaker for the week, poured his heart and soul into us teens. To be honest, I remember very little about his talks. There was something in him that I had seen in many of my Sunday School teachers and AWANA leaders over the years. He had a passion for the Lord and a deep love for each one of us who attended his sessions. He was not teaching because the camp could not find anyone else, or because he had to. He was teaching out of a genuine love for us and a desire to make sure our eternity was secure.

Friday morning began in the little hall, much like the rest of the week had. Armed with a message from the Lord, Lyle got up and gave the teaching for the day. When it came time for the closing prayer, he did something he had not done the rest of the week. In the middle of his prayer, he stopped. Lyle knew this could be the last time he would see each of us. He did not want us to leave without an opportunity to express our faith in Christ. He wanted each of us to leave knowing where we would spend eternity.

As he prayed, he thanked the Lord for the week and for the time he had with us. He thanked the Lord for His gift of salvation, then he stopped and asked us a question that caused me to stop and think. He asked, "Is there anyone here who does not know for sure that if they were to die today, they would be in Heaven?"

Here I was, having sat through hundreds if not thousands of Bible lessons and memorized more Bible verses than I could count. I could have been teaching the class helping others come to salvation. But, I did not know at that point, if I was to die, whether I would enter heaven's gates or enter the fires of hell.

His question hit me like a freight train. I did not know if anyone else in our little group had the same feeling I had, but the Holy Spirit convicted me of my lack of trust. I timidly raised my hand in response to his question. I did not have the assurance Lyle talked about. I knew what I needed to do. I did not need to talk to Lyle. I did not even need to talk to my parents. I needed to talk to Jesus and make things right.

Immediately after the prayer ended, I left the building and began to climb the hill toward the cabins. The Holy Spirit worked inside me, urging me to put my trust in Christ as my personal Lord and Savior. I needed to find a place to talk to the One who gave His life on the cross of Calvary to save the sinner I was. Halfway up the hill, I found a pine tree. There, looking out over the beautiful, blue waters of Canandaigua Lake, I bowed my head and confessed my sin. I thanked the Lord for dying on the cross and for saving my soul. I asked Him to live inside of me and help me to live the way He desired for me to live.

LeTourneau Christian Conference Center-
where I surrendered my life to Christ

The peace I immediately felt was undeniable. The doubt and unsettledness which had plagued me for years was gone. For years, I had been in bondage to fear. I knew God was a just God and I deserved punishment. *Now I knew!* God gave me His abundant life and forgave all my sins. I had a deep inner peace unlike anything I had ever felt.

I do not think I ever thanked Lyle for the part he played in bringing me to a place of peace with God through my Lord Jesus Christ. He may have never known the impact he had in my life that day. God had urged him to ask the right questions and he responded to what God laid on his heart. In turn, God worked mightily in my life.

Some time ago, I went back to the spot where I surrendered my life to the Lord and received His peace. The camp is not of significance, even though over the years, many others have surrendered their lives to the Lord here. The spot beside the pine tree above the tennis courts is not marked with a plaque or special marker. Both places hold a very special place in my heart, but the significance is not in the place. The significance is found in what happened long before the day I gave my life to Christ.

Christ willingly gave His life. He was wounded for my transgressions. He was bruised for my iniquity. He took my punishment. He did all that so I could have peace with God through Him. (Isaiah 53:5, Romans 5:1) I realized my life is not my own to do as I please. God created me to glorify Him. He desired for me to put my trust in what He did on the cross to pay the penalty for all my sin. This simple act of surrender made a lasting impact on how I have lived my life.

In God's Holy Word, the Bible, we read about the "peace which passes all understanding." (Philippians 4:7) In the Christmas story the angels promised "peace to all men" (Luke 2:14). Yet, there are so many people who go through life missing out on the peace God desires for all people everywhere.

You may be reading this book and be in the same place I was. You may be fearful of death. You may be anxious about what is happening around you. You may not know where you are heading in life. Things may be spiraling out of control. You may be struggling with a life-threatening illness, unsure if today will be your last on this earth. Your marriage may be in shambles. Your spouse may have told you they do not love you anymore. Your wife may have given up on you. Maybe you are at risk of losing your job; the company may be downsizing and you were the last one hired. You may be hiding the inner feelings of your heart.

The stories and lessons you will read in this book are not from someone who has it all together. There are times I hear the Lord saying to me,

"Oh, ye of little faith."

I share these stories hoping to encourage you and strengthen your walk with the Lord. It is my hope and prayer that as you read this book you, too, will develop a deep personal trust in the One True Living God. May the lessons I share save you from making the same mistakes I have made.

It says in Titus 3:5, "Not by works of righteousness which we have done, but according to his mercy he saved us, by the washing of regeneration, and renewing of the Holy Ghost." The work was done by Christ when He humbled Himself and became obedient to death; even to death on a cross. There is nothing I can do to make my own peace with God. God did the work Himself when He sent Christ to the earth.

I am not writing with the assumption that everyone who is reading this has put their faith in trust in the Lord as their Savior. The stories I share come out of my personal walk with the Him. My first act of total dependence on God was when I sat beside that pine tree in Central New York and made the ultimate decision of faith and trust. Without that foundation, there are no grounds to trust God for anything else.

Maybe you have realized you have no peace about the future. Maybe you need to take the first step of trust and say, "Jesus, I believe you are The Way, and the Truth, and the Life." Why not make today your day of salvation, peace, and assurance? The next chapter will help explain these truths to you.

Chapter 4

GOD'S PLAN FOR PEACE AND LIFE WITHOUT FEAR

"For he Himself is our peace, who has made us both one and has broken down in his flesh the dividing wall of hostility by abolishing the law of commandments expressed in ordinances, that he might create in Himself one new man in place of the two, so making peace, and might reconcile us both to God in one body through the cross, thereby killing the hostility. And he came and preached peace to you who were far off and peace to those who were near. For through Him we both have access in one Spirit to the Father." (Ephesians 2:14-18 ESV)

Before I go any further in this book, I want to tell you how you can live your life in peace with God and without fear of what may come. We live in a world that is full of conflict, sickness, diseases, and many other things that can steal our peace and give us fear. Without the hope of Christ, there is no peace; only uncertainty. This is not the way God created us.

In the beginning, God created the heavens and the earth and it was very good. (Genesis 1) He created the first man and woman, Adam and Eve, to have perfect fellowship with Him, and they tended and kept the Garden of Eden. (Genesis 2) God told them to be fruitful and multiply and fill the earth. Along with this, He gave one command, "Do not eat of the tree of knowledge of good and evil." (Genesis 2:17)

Satan, the evil one (Matthew 5:37), the deceiver (Revelation 12:9), the one who prowls around like a roaring lion, "seeking whom he can devour" (1 Peter 5:8), deceived the woman into eating the forbidden fruit and then giving it to her husband. (Genesis 3:6) Because of this act of disobedience, they and all mankind suffer from the curse of sin and death. Their act of disobedience took away the peace they had with God and destined mankind for God's judgment and wrath. (Romans 5:12-21)

Romans 6:23 says, "The wages of sin is death, but the gift of God is eternal life through Jesus Christ our Lord." The penalty for any and all sin is death. But, through the work of Christ on the cross, the debt has been paid in full. God offers a gift of eternal life to all who come to Him in faith, believing.

God sent His son Jesus to give us peace. John 3:16 says, "For God so loved the world, that He gave His only begotten son, that whosoever believeth in Him, should not perish, but have everlasting life." My peace does not come from what I get in life. It is not dependent upon my successes or failures. My peace comes from trusting in what God did by sending Christ to die on the cross.

John continues to write in verse seventeen. He says, "God sent His son into the world not to condemn the world, but that the world through Him might be saved." Christ came to pay the penalty of our sin, not to condemn us in our sins. His desire for all mankind is for them to put their total trust and dependence on Him. This is the only way to have total peace.

God gave us the Bible so we do not have to doubt. We do not have to live in fear. In 1 John 5:13 it says, "These things have I written unto you that believe on the name of the Son of God; that ye may *KNOW* that ye have eternal life, and that ye may believe on the name of the Son of God" (emphasis mine). God gives us His Word so we can know without any doubt whether or not we have a place waiting for us in His heaven.

Romans 10:9-10 says, "That if thou shalt confess with thy mouth the Lord Jesus, and shalt believe in thine heart that God hath raised him from the dead, thou shalt be saved. For with the heart man believeth unto righteousness; and with the mouth confession is made unto salvation." Salvation only comes from trusting in what Christ did for us on the cross.

This gift of peace is available to all who believe. Each of us must make our own decision. For me, it did not matter what my Dad and Mom believed. I could not ride their shirt-tails into heaven. I could not be saved because of whose son I was. The only way I could have peace with God was through believing in the Lord Jesus Christ.

The same is true for you. You may know all there is to know about the Lord. You could have read every book of the Bible, more than once. But if you do not put your faith and trust in Christ as your Lord and Savior, you are still headed to hell. Today is the day of salvation. Christ says, "Behold, I stand at the door, and knock: if any man hears my voice, and open the door, I will come in to him…" (Revelation 3:20)

Part II

TRUSTING GOD EVERYDAY

"For whosoever will save his life shall lose it: and whosoever will lose his life for my sake shall find it." (Matthew 16:25)

"He that loveth his life shall lose it; and he that hateth his life in this world shall keep it unto life eternal." (John 12:25)

"He is no fool who gives what he cannot keep to gain what he cannot lose." (Jim Elliot, Missionary Martyr)

Chapter 5

TRUSTING GOD FOR PROVISION

"And Abraham lifted up his eyes, and looked, and behold behind him a ram caught in a thicket by his horns: and Abraham went and took the ram, and offered him up for a burnt offering in the stead of his son. And Abraham called the name of that place Jehovah Jireh: as it is said to this day, In the mount of the Lord it shall be seen." (Genesis 22:13-14)

I t is one thing to see an example of trust and dependence on God; it is yet another thing to put that trust and dependence into practice. As I grew up, it did not seem like there were many ways in which my faith was stretched. I remember hearing stories of faith from others in the family, but I did not feel I had to stretch *my* faith muscles.

One such story stands out in my mind. One of my relatives left their house to visit their parents who lived several hours away from where they lived. They forgot their wallet and they did not realize it until they had traveled a great distance. They were too far from home to turn around and did not have enough gas to make it to their destination. Or so they thought. They prayed, trusting God to get them from Vermont to New York even as the gas tank read empty. They believed God performed a miracle as they trusted Him to help them in their impossible situation.

I know Dad and Mom had struggles and needs they prayed for. What I do not remember is any earth-shattering stories of how "God came through." There were times I knew money was tight, but we always had clothes on our back and food on the table. We never went hungry. They never made a big deal about not having enough. They trusted God to give them what they needed and were content with what He gave them.

Since Dad had the business, I never looked for a job. Anytime I wanted to work, he and my uncle gave me all the work I wanted. If I was not working for them, I helped my uncles with farm chores or a neighbor who needed a hand. I never knew what it was like to be desperate and have to look for a job. I always had work to do and money in my wallet.

Now do not get me wrong, we were not wealthy. There were times when Dad and Mom said we could not afford something we thought for sure we needed. With four hungry kids to feed and keep clothed, they did not have everything they wanted. In fact, Dad and Mom made great sacrifices to provide for our well-being.

From first grade through eighth grade, I attended Central Baptist Christian Academy. After I finished the eighth grade, my parents pulled us out of school to do homeschooling. One of the big reasons was the cost of education. My parents could not afford to have all four of us in the Christian school. In their opinion, public school was not an option.

Though my parents trusted the Lord to provide for their needs, it seemed to us kids that we always had what we needed. We did not see the hours they spent wondering and praying about how they were going to make ends meet. I never saw the tears they shed as they wondered how things would work out. Because they did not want us to worry about anything, they never made it a big deal to us. They took all their needs to the Lord, trusting Him to supply. I never had to flex my faith muscles. This lack of stretching of my faith muscles affected my outlook on life and God when I went off to Bible School. But I am getting ahead of myself.

When we got to high school age, Dad and Mom challenged us to consider doing one year of intense Bible study at Practical Bible Training School. They both attended there and knew it offered an excellent Biblical education. They told us, "It does not matter what you do in life, the year of Bible education is not going to hurt you."

They knew the Bible had to be the firm foundation on which we built everything else. Our education, our lives, our careers, and our families had to be built upon the principles of God's Word. They said, if God and His Word were the basis, God would take care of everything else. He would provide for our careers, our families, and every area of our lives.

Upon graduating from high school, I enrolled for my "one year of Bible school." I had no idea where I was going or what I wanted to do. Being the oldest child, I had a desire to please my parents. The Lord had other plans. He used this one year to give me a greater desire to please Him and to serve Him wherever He led me.

As I met people at Practical, I began to hear more faith stories. I heard awesome stories about how God worked in peoples' hearts. There was one person who had been a drug addict on the streets. The Lord reached down and, like the apostle Paul, called him from darkness into light. There was another student who was hardly keeping on top of his school bill. There was more than once when he lacked the funds to pay for school. He was close to dismissal when miraculously, at the last minute, God came through. The money showed up and he stayed and completed his education.

I began to get this feeling of, *what has God done for me?* In my soul, I longed to see the power of Christ working in me. I knew God was in me, but I never felt like I had seen God do a huge work in my own life. I knew He had given me peace in the midst of great fear, but I was never a horrible kid. I never did drugs or lived in immorality. God did not snatch me out of a desperate situation or save me from some gross sin. He saved me, but in my mind, that was it. I did not see how He was daily providing for me or helping me.

One night, during devotions with guys from the dorm, the Lord changed my perspective. As I talked to the fellow whom the Lord saved off the street, I shared with him how wonderful my home was. I told him that, as I listened to his testimony, I began to be envious, thinking, *What has God done for me?* With the wisdom of Solomon, he looked at me and said, "It is not what God saved you out of, it is what God kept you from." The Lord used those simple words to give me a new perspective.

My parents trusted God to protect their children and to keep them from danger. God honored their prayer of faith. God had not snatched me from the world; He in His infinite grace had kept me *from* the world. Sure, I was born in sin and all my righteousness was as filthy rags. (Isaiah 64:6, Romans 10:3) I still needed the Savior. God kept me from having to make heart-wrenching decisions. He made sure I did not get trapped in the world's way of thinking.

Who saved the man off the street? Who kept me from sin? The answer to each question was the same. *God.* It was all God. He works with each person to change them and draw them close to Himself. Sometimes He works behind the scenes where the difference is not as noticeable. At other times, He works in the open where people can recognize the change immediately. In either case, God is at work in people. Even though I had not recognized it, God had been working in me all along.

This was only one of many lessons the Lord taught me during my time at Practical Bible Training School. It was during that suggested "one year of Bible School" when the Lord impressed upon me His desire for my future. He was asking me to have more than a one-year commitment to Him. He wanted me to make a life-long commitment to Him. Again, just like I felt at the age of thirteen, the Lord was asking me to give Him more of my trust and a greater allegiance to Him.

During my classes, I sat and listened about how God provided a lamb for Abraham. God showed me that He was, Jehovah-Jireh, "the God who provides." God built on the foundation He had allowed my parents to instill in me. He taught me and trained me to trust Him to a greater degree.

The Lord used a missionary's preaching on the Great Commission to get me to where He wanted me to be. During the Mission Emphasis Week, I sat glued to my seat. The speaker spoke to my heart as he told about the great need for more workers for Christ's harvest. He said, "The fields are white unto harvest." (John 4:35) The Lord opened my eyes to what he saw. He gave me a desire to trust Him enough to go wherever He led me.

The guest speaker invited us to consider our part in the work. He challenged us to listen to whatever message the Holy Spirit spoke to us. He invited anyone who felt the Lord had been giving them a burden to serve Him to come forward.

The Holy Spirit did speak to me. He was asking if I was willing to surrender everything to the Lord. Would I be willing to serve the Lord *wherever* He called? I could not sit any longer. Did I trust God enough to go forward? Did I trust God to care enough for me to take care of me anywhere?

I went forward in surrender. Dad and Mom were not there telling me to go forward. My Sunday School teachers were not telling me that it was the right thing to do. My Bible School professors were there, but they did not offer me a better grade if I went forward. I did not go forward because of the missionary's persuasive words. I went forward out of a heart-felt commitment to the Lord, to honor Him.

I realized the Lord had saved me for a bigger purpose than just to avoid hell's punishment. He saved me not because of my goodness or upbringing. He saved me according to His mercy and was preparing me for His service. I could trust Him not only to provide for me, but also to give me the strength to serve Him wherever the field of service might be.

This service for Him was not to be a future event for which God was preparing me in Bible School. He gave me opportunities to serve Him right where I was. He opened my eyes to the needs on the streets of Binghamton and Johnson City, New York. Where I once saw homeless and drunk people, I now saw opportunities to speak of the Gospel and Christ's love for them.

I joined the weekly meetings of the Student Missionary Fellowship. I began to promote Christ's mission to the other students on campus. I met with a group of other students to pray for the Lord to reach people in North America. God wanted me to serve Him where I was. Service to Him was not a future event. I began to serve Him immediately.

We often look at God's call as some future event that we will do later in life. When God calls, He is asking us to serve Him *now, right where we are*. Sure, He calls us to future service, but if we are not willing to serve God here and now, how can we expect to be willing to serve Him in some other time and place?

I did see God do a miraculous work in my life. He took a timid, runt of a boy and gave him a voice to tell others about His love and grace. The Lord gave me a deep desire and passion to see His name preached without fear.

I could no longer just read passages like Romans 10:14, which says, "How shall they hear without a preacher?" Now I heard the verses speaking directly to me. How could the lost hear the Gospel if I had it and was not willing to share it? I began to see whole communities with no Gospel witness. I saw the whole of America as a mission field. I realized Christ had done a great work for me when He died for my sins. He desired for me to share His hope to the lost who otherwise had no way to hear or see His message.

I saw Him provide for me and keep me out of debt. Every semester, my bill remained completely paid off. Often, He provided the funds, not with a check in the mail, but by giving me jobs to do. He gave me a job in the campus maintenance department. He gave me odd jobs helping a couple of elderly ladies who lived near the school. And, He gave me work with my Dad's construction company.

In the end, God provided every penny of my Bible School training. God kept His promise to supply my every need. I had been looking to God to show Himself in extraordinary ways. In doing so, I forgot to look at the work He was already doing through the ordinary aspects of my life. Who supplied my dad and uncle with work so I could have a job? Who gave me peace when I was thirteen? Who kept me from drugs and other addictions? Who gave me a Godly home?

While I finished one phase of life, the training and learning were not finished. It has been nearly thirty years since I left the halls of Practical Bible Training School. God continues to train and prepare me for His work, teaching me what it means to trust Him completely in every area of my life.

Chapter 6

TRUSTING GOD FOR DIRECTION
IN ALASKA OR YUKON

*"Go ye therefore, and teach all nations, baptizing them in the name
of the Father, and of the Son, and of the Holy Ghost: Teaching them
to observe all things whatsoever I have commanded you: and,
lo, I am with you always, even unto the end of the world. Amen."
(Matthew 28:19-20)*

God asked me to surrender my life to Him at the Mission Emphasis Week at Practical Bible Training School. There, He gave me an unmistakable desire to see the Gospel of Jesus Christ preached in North America. The more I learned about the churches that were closing in the US, the greater my burden grew. I wanted to see people come to faith in Christ. Because of this burden, I started searching for opportunities to serve Him. I began to contact mission organizations who worked in the USA. My main focus was on the state of Alaska.

The draw to the Far North was due to my family's connection with long-term missionaries, Dwayne and Carolyn King. They served as missionary pilot/church planters in Alaska for decades. I met them when they traveled through our area when Dad and Mom invited them to our home so they could share the ministry with our family.

The stories Dwayne told about ministry captivated me. He could take a simple story and make it an exciting adventure. He told of hunting bears, flying planes, and airplane crashes he walked away from. He talked about leading people to the Savior. He saw the Lord do amazing and miraculous works across Alaska. He loved to tell anyone who listened. His passion to see the unsaved come to Jesus showed in his enthusiasm as he drew us into his stories.

As he told his stories, one community caught my interest. The community sat high in the north above the Arctic Circle and had no Gospel witness. There was no preacher, missionary, or Christian to my knowledge living in the community. The only way into the village was by airplane. God used these stories and others to cause me to consider having a part in the work. I wanted to go there and be able to share Jesus with the people there.

The more I heard from Dwayne, the stronger my desire grew to take the Gospel message to people who had no opportunity to hear it. There were people who had not grown up hearing of Jesus' love, grace, mercy, and forgiveness. They needed someone who would be willing to go to them.

I wrote to four mission organizations to find out if they worked in Alaska. Of the four, only two had active works in Alaska, SEND of Alaska and Baptist Mid-Missions. Baptist Mid- Mission's ministry focused on the use of aviation. Since I did not know anything about flying, I kept looking for other places where the Lord could use me.

SEND's work fit well with the burden God had instilled in me when He called me. The more I heard about how God was using them in the north, the more excited I became. They focus on small Aboriginal villages where there was no Gospel witness. SEND's purpose is to "Establish reproducing churches where they did not exist." They desire to help people grow in Christ.

Around the same time, I met Dick Camp, another SEND missionary to Canada's Yukon Territory. While on home service assignment, he stopped at Practical Bible Training School where I was a student. Dick's passion for the lost and his desire to see people come to Jesus was evident as he shared his experiences. He opened my eyes to yet another area of SEND's work in the north.

He talked about other villages in the Yukon that still did not have a Gospel witness. I knew very little about Canada at this point other than the fact it bordered the US to the north. I listened as he told me about ministering in the town of Faro, Yukon. My interest was still in Alaska because it was on American soil and that was where I knew God wanted me, or at least I thought so...

In different conversations, both Dwayne and Dick suggested I should be a part of SEND's Summer Missionary Program. SMP, as SEND missionaries often call it, had one purpose. The purpose was to show college age young people what it was like on the mission field. He said it would give me first-hand experience in ministering in a small community. There were various opportunities to serve depending on a person's interests and calling. They needed radio broadcasters, maintenance help, nurses, and village team members. The program ran for eleven weeks between June 1 and mid-August each year.

Dick thought since I was a missionary major, I should join the village teams. These teams traveled throughout the villages of Alaska and the Yukon, teaching Vacation Bible School. They also helped to lead Bible studies, and run Bible Camps. In many of these communities, the Summer Missionaries were the only Gospel witness the villagers saw each year. SEND quite often used the SMPers to get their "foot in the door" for a future full-time missionary.

To be on the village team meant doing one thing that petrified me. I would be teaching Bible stories to the children who came to Vacation Bible School (VBS). As a senior in high school, I tried to lead a sixth grade AWANA class and felt there were better qualified teachers. Sure, I had a heart to help them come to know Christ better, but I felt I was not cut out to instruct others. Again, the Lord asked me to step out in faith and trust Him to give me the ability to do what He asked.

During the last semester at Practical, I applied to the Summer Missionary Program. In those days, there were no digital applications. I filled out a hand-written application and mailed it through the United States Postal Service. It was weeks – which seemed like an eternity – before I heard back from the SEND office in Alaska.

SEND accepted me as a Summer Missionary to the villages of Alaska/Yukon. I looked at the brochure again. It said *Alaska/Yukon*. God was calling me to Alaska, right? He had not called me to Canada. Canada was a foreign country. He was not sending me there, or was He?

As I finished the last semester of Bible School, the cost of the summer program started to be on my mind. SEND always kept the price of the summer low so college students could afford it. The problem was, after three years of Bible School, the majority of my money had gone to pay off my school bill. How was I going to afford to pay for the summer while not working?

This did not catch God by surprise. He knew my needs even before SEND sent me my acceptance letter. He had already begun to work in the hearts of His people to provide *all* I needed. He used this experience to grow my faith.

As I prayed about the upcoming mission experience and communicated with friends and family members, the Lord began to supply the need. I watched as the Lord supplied for every aspect of the trip. He even supplied the cans of mosquito spray which kept the northern "Air Force" from eating me alive. What continues to impress me is the way God supplies *everything*. The Bible does not lie when it says, "My God shall supply all your (our) needs." (Philippians 4:19)

He *always* meets our needs, but His provision often comes from the most unlikely places. I have looked at people who had lots of money and resources. I have thought to myself, *surely, God will use them to help supply my needs*. I do this trying to make "a plan" for God.

The Lord does not usually supply in this way. Often, God meets our needs through people who have to live each day in faith, as we have, living one paycheck at a time. They are not living in great wealth, but in trust that God will supply their needs as well.

One such provision came from a couple whom I had known for many years. They heard about my mission trip and felt the Lord leading them to supply the airfare for the trip. I was speechless when I heard what they were going to do. What had I done to deserve such a generous gift? In reality, I had done nothing to deserve it. God chose to give them a burden and they listened to the voice of God speaking to them.

This has happened time and time again over the years. I am reminded of what the Bible says in Malachi 3. For years, Israel had been cheating the Lord and not bringing Him all He had required. Because of this, they were seeing the Lord's punishment on them. We read in verse 10, "Bring ye *all the tithes* into the storehouse, that there may be meat in mine house, and prove me now herewith, saith the LORD of hosts, if I will not open you the windows of heaven, and *pour* you *out a blessing,* that there shall not be room enough to receive it." (emphasis mine)

There are ministers who use this verse to preach a prosperity gospel. If a person is generous to God, their troubles will be over. These people promise abundant riches to those who give. There are many ministries which have swindled thousands of dollars from people with this promise.

This is not what the Lord is teaching through the rest of Scripture. God does promise blessings. He also promises trials. He promises to give us peace in the midst of these trials. These trials though, are what strengthen our faith and trust in His ability to care for us and to meet our needs. (James 1:3) He promises to meet our needs, but He does not promise riches to all who give to His Kingdom. When we expect God to give us wealth beyond all measure because we tithed to Him, we set ourselves up for disappointment when we are faced with trials of our faith.

The principle I believe God is teaching us here is, "You cannot out-give God." God does give some people riches when they give. As a young man, I read the story of R. G. LeTourneau. He believed he could not out-give God. Over the course of his life, he increased the amount of his tithe. He started giving ten percent, then twenty. At the end of his life, he was living on ten percent of his salary and giving the other ninety percent back to the Lord.[2]

Many times, we wait to tithe until the end of the month or at the end of the year to make sure "there is enough left over." God asks for the first-fruits of our labor. It is when we give to Him first that He strengthens our faith by stretching what we have left.

Seeing the Lord provide for my airfare to head out that summer was not the last time I saw God provide for my needs. God continues to meet our every need, even three decades later.

As the program started that first summer, the Lord caused me to depend on Him to a greater degree. He knew I needed this total dependence in the future as we served in Ross River. I had to trust Him not only for the finances, but in everything. I was to minister in His power, not in my gifts or abilities. My abilities were small, but as I trusted Him, He showed me, "I can do all things through Christ, who gives me strength." (Philippians 4:13)

Shortly after orientation began, the staff of the Summer Missionary

Program asked me to teach a Bible story to a group of kids. The kids were not just any kids, they were missionary kids who probably already knew the story by heart. How was I going to teach them?

For hours I studied the material and poured over the Bible story. With fear and trepidation, I stood to teach the story. I prayed and prayed for the Lord to give me courage and for me to be able to communicate the story in a clear way. God answered my prayer. He did more than that, He gave me a love for sharing His story with anyone who will listen.

After a week of orientation, the staff met to assign us to the teams we would be with for the rest of the summer. There were between fifteen to twenty of us who would be traveling into the villages. Another group about the same size stayed at the mission compound. Their jobs included helping to run the radio station, maintenance department, and Cross Road Medical Center.

We anxiously awaited to hear where we would travel. After hearing the missionaries talk about each of the villages, my heart was set on going with Dwayne King above the Arctic Circle. I "knew" God was calling me to take the message of Jesus to them.

Again, God's plan did not match my plan. We gathered in the chapel of Alaska Bible College to receive our team assignments. One by one, the staff wrote the names on the board. As I watched each name as it was written, I grew more anxious. The Alaska teams were listed on the board, first. There was no sign of my name. The leaders must have made a mistake. Did they not know God's desire for me? As they continued to assign us to the teams, I saw it! I had a spot on the Northern Yukon Team. Heartache and devastation overwhelmed me. The Yukon Territory was part of Canada. God had called me to serve in the USA. There had to be a mistake.

The staff did not make a mistake. They had spent hours in prayer and seeking the Lord's will and felt the Lord saying, "Send him to the Yukon." During this time in SEND's history, the Yukon presented a greater need. While there was still a work to be done in Alaska, SEND was focused on several Yukon villages where there was no one who preached the Gospel on a regular basis.

Had I made a mistake in thinking God was giving me a burden for the USA? Was I only interested in Alaska due to my family's connection with the Kings? Or, was God at work trying to do something bigger in my life as I stepped out in faith? God called me. He directed me. He provided for me.

Tears filled my eyes as I listened to the staff tell me their reasoning for putting me in the Yukon. I trusted the Lord to bring me to the north and He had. He had given me a burden to share the Gospel to the lost. Now I had to trust that the Lord knew what He was doing in sending me to the *Yukon Territory of Canada.*

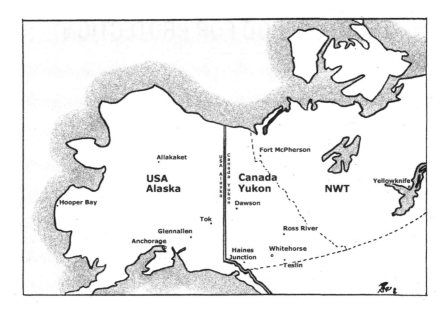

SEND North's ministry area. Image
drawn by Daniel Buehler.

Chapter 7

TRUSTING GOD FOR PROTECTION

"For we wrestle not against flesh and blood, but against principalities, against powers, against the rulers of the darkness of this world, against spiritual wickedness in high places." (Ephesians 6:12)

It did not take long before I saw why God sent me to the Yukon. As we conducted Bible Camp, the Lord showed me kids who needed to see the love of Christ. In our Vacation Bible School programs, we taught kids with limited to no knowledge of the Bible. Walking the streets, I met hurting people who struggled to find meaning in life. I found communities that lay in great spiritual darkness.

In many villages, there was no missionary. There was no pastor. There was not even a church. The kids we ministered to had no one to teach them who Jesus was. The youth had no one to tell them where to find the answers they were looking for. The adults had no one to tell them where to find freedom from their addictions. Worse than that was the fact that the devil had a strong foothold in many of these communities.

In Sunday School, I learned stories about people who were demon possessed and healed by Jesus. At Practical Bible Training School, my mission's professor had served as a missionary in the Philippines. Day after day he shared his real-life experiences with enthusiasm. He told stories of demon possessed individuals who lived in constant torment by the devil. I sat in amazement and disbelief. I had never met a person who was demon possessed. The stories grabbed my attention. Such events happened in the

Philippines or in the jungles of some far-away country, but did they happen in North America? I did not think I had anything to worry about.

This all changed the summer I traveled through the Yukon as a Summer Missionary. For the first few weeks of the summer we joined other Summer Missionaries (SMP) in Dawson City. We ran a VBS for the children at the local church, which SEND helped to start in the late sixties to early seventies. Dawson City, home of the Klondike Gold Rush of 1898, is much different than many of the other towns in the Yukon. It has a strong mining presence due to its Gold Rush history and it is a popular spot for tourists. We loved our days there.

Besides holding the daily VBS program, we used the time to prepare for the following week in which we served as camp counselors at Kamp Klondike Bible Camp, fifteen minutes outside of the city limits. The camp was rustic with only a few buildings. There were no cabins or electricity. The kitchen was a "shack" no bigger than some small bedrooms. The kids slept in tents. Most of the games and activities were simple, and they involved a ball on a brushy "field."

To help prepare and orient us to camp, we spent hours with the pastor, Lyle Anderson, and his wife Rita. They treated us like royalty as they helped us learn what ministry looked like in the Far North. They told us about the long winters and helped us see some of the Yukon by taking us up the Yukon River on their small fishing boat. But, most of all, they showed us their love for the people of their community. Lyle's excitement for the Lord's work and passion for souls were a great combination. His contagious smile and hardy laugh rubbed off on anyone who got too close to him.

Like many pastors in the North, Lyle worked to supplement the church salary. This did not stop him from serving in the ministries of the church or from showing us what ministry looked like. He worked hard all day with a construction company. Then, he stayed late into the evening, teaching the Bible to the campers. He loved to tell stories. God gave him a gift in being able to jump right into any Bible story. He would tell it with the type of enthusiasm that made us feel like he had been there when it happened. The kids (and we counselors) sat mesmerized by the campfire each night.

Sitting and listening to the Bible stories was one of the easiest parts of camp. The kids kept us running from sunrise until sunset. The mosquitoes swarmed around us like flies on a rotten piece of meat. They sought to devour our blood anytime we stopped moving. Our trust had to be in the strength of the Lord as our own strength failed us many times.

Like a flash of lightning in the sky, our time in Dawson came to an end. We said, "goodbye" to the lovely folks in Dawson City and headed down the highway to other villages. Looking back, I see how God was already working to lead me to return to the Yukon. During one of our times with Pastor Anderson, he said, "Look for a house, you will be back." We both laughed, but little did I know the truth of those words.

The SMP staff filled our schedule with one to two weeks in each of the following villages; Mayo, Faro, Pelly Crossing, and Ross River. With joy and enthusiasm, we entered each community, ready to conduct a Vacation Bible School. Even though VBS was our main ministry, we also held adult Bible studies, evening youth outreaches and did whatever we could do to spread the Word of God.

In each community, SEND had a contact person who showed us and helped us know where to have VBS. We held VBS in curling clubs, hockey arenas, youth centers, and even at a picnic pavilion. We never knew where we were going to meet. Each community had its own adventures and unknowns. As we committed each village to the Lord, He orchestrated the details completely.

In most of the communities, we were on our own. In the town of Faro, though, we worked alongside Ted and Sally Baker. After being on our own for much of the summer, it was a breath of fresh air when Ted gave us the community tour. He, like many other SEND missionaries, shared the work he saw God doing in their community with excitement. Sally's oven-baked chicken and sweet tea were extra blessings after having to fend for ourselves for several weeks.

In one community, I got the privilege of leading a young child to the Lord. After the Bible story, she came and started to ask questions. She asked how she could be saved. With great joy and angels rejoicing in heaven, I was able to help her pray and show her what it meant to trust the Lord as her personal Savior. The words she prayed were so simple and genuine. I wanted to hear more. I wanted to see more people come to Christ.

It did not matter which community we went to; the message was the same. Our Bible stories helped those who listened to know how they could have a personal relationship with the Lord. As we taught, we watched as children responded to the truth of the Bible. Some of the children were like dry sponges, soaking in the truth they had never heard before. In others, we built on the foundation laid by Summer Missionaries from previous years. We hoped and prayed we could disciple them into strong, committed Christians.

One Sunday morning, we hopped into the old, blue, Chevy truck and wound our way down the Yukon's twisty highways. We completed a week of VBS in Mayo and headed to Ross River for ten days. The sun reflected beautifully off Little Salmon Lake as we bounced along the gravel of the Robert Campbell Highway. The brilliant stalks of pink Fireweed lined the road like fence posts around a field.

Halfway around the thirty-mile-long lake, a tractor trailer hauling ore from the Faro mine came barreling around one of the road's sharp corners. He was taking his half from the center of the highway. On one side of the road stood a high rock cliff, on the other side, a sharp drop-off into the lake. The road looked too narrow for the two of us to pass each other. With the protection of God's guiding hand, we passed the ore truck. Our hearts were pounding as we continued down the road. We praised the Lord for His protection.

The sun shone brightly as we rounded the last bend in the dirt road leading into Ross River. Even though it was late evening, the sun would still be up for several hours. (In the months of June and July it never gets fully dark in the Yukon.) Below us, in the distance, we could see the Pelly River. On the opposite side of the River, rising steeply, stood what locals call Ross River Hill. The "hill" rises sharply from the river to a height of several thousand feet above sea level. It is a rolling hill with some clusters of spruce, aspen, and poplar, but is otherwise bare of anything but some small grasses and sage.

The town itself lies in a valley between the "hill" to the north and the St. Cyr Mountains to the south. Descending into the community, we saw only a handful of the close to three-hundred and fifty residents. A few people enjoyed an evening stroll. Some dogs wandered the streets looking for a free handout. Gophers darted away from the road as we disturbed their evening sun tanning session. It looked like a quaint little community. Little did we know the battle that lay in front of us.

Following the directions we had received from the SMP staff, we made our way to the center of town. In the middle of town, we turned left onto Ross River Ave. It did not take us long to find what we were looking for. A log church three blocks from the center of town served as our "home" for the next ten days. Located across from the school yard, it would be a great spot to set up and be close to where the kids would hang out. We ran evening activities for the teens and youth at the school. The inside of the church would be used to hold our VBS program.

In the 1960s, an Independent Baptist missionary felt led by the Lord to start a church in the community. The Lord blessed his efforts and he established the Ross River Baptist Church. It once stood as a beacon of hope to the residents of the community. Now it stood only as a reminder of past revivals. No full-time missionary had been in the community for several years.

The logs that formed the outside structure came from the local sawmill west of town. Two crosses stood on either side of the handmade wooden door, reminding residents of Christ's sacrifice. Three plastic "stained-glass" windows gave light to the sanctuary and broke up the thirty-eight-foot-long side wall. Dark wood paneling covered the bottom half of the interior walls, while a brilliant white paneling brightened the top half. Along the left side of the sanctuary were two small rooms. One served as a Sunday School room. The other housed miscellaneous junk accumulated from years of use. The simple layout worked great for our Vacation Bible School.

In a matter of minutes, we met the village contact, Ivan Bolton, or as he refers to himself, Ivan the Terrible. Decades before, he got tired of living the rat race of city life in Ontario and Alberta and moved north to the Yukon. He loved to live on the land using what the Lord provided from it. He was part trapper, mechanic, heavy equipment operator, and truck driver and one of the founding members of the Ross River Baptist Church.

He and his wife May came to know the Lord through the minister who came into the community in the late 1960s. They lived only a couple doors down from the church and served as the caretakers of the church.

Ivan visiting with Joe Greeson at the HOPE Centre.
Photo taken by Holly Greeson.

Ivan loved to talk and soon, we were listening to stories about Ross River. He did a great job at giving us a quick introduction to the community. He showed us where we could get power, water, and where to find the "bathroom." Our bathroom was an outhouse that looked like someone should have burned it to the ground.

The outhouse was the most run-down I had ever seen. A warped piece of weathered plywood served as a "door." It looked like it came from the last century. The hinges that held the door were in desperate need of oiling. Every time we used the door, they screeched so loud half the neighbors knew when we were using the facilities. A piece of Styrofoam insulation covered the plywood seat. Ivan told us the insulation provided "heat for those sitting at minus fifty." To say it was rustic would be an understatement. It was rough, but it worked in the absence of any indoor plumbing.

After educating us on the important details of the town and telling a few more stories, Ivan returned to his home. We began to set up the camper. At this point, it had been a long day and we were feeling quite hungry. As we started cooking supper, we began to hear the noise of something hitting the roof of the camper. The weather outside was clear, it was not raining, but what was causing the noise we heard? Looking out through the small window in the side of the camper, we saw a handful of kids throwing pebbles onto the roof. They were hoping we would come out and spent time with them.

We opened the door of the camper, stepping into the evening light. As we put our feet on the dusty ground, about half a dozen children surrounded us. We did not know who they were, but they knew exactly what we were doing in their community. In many of the communities of the Far North, there are few activities that keep the kids busy in the summer. They looked forward to SEND's SMPers coming, knowing they had our undivided attention. They knew we were there for them and had activities planned to keep them busy.

Bored kids were a normality in many of the communities of the north. They did not exactly like to attend school. Yet, the school gave them some routine and something to wake up for every morning. In the summer, there was no pool for swim lessons. There were no baseball leagues or summer schools. Bored kids wandered looking for something to do. They roamed together looking for anything to entertain them. Sometimes this meant a dip in the cold Pelly River, at other times, it might mean kicking a soccer ball around the fields.

When the Summer Missionaries arrived, they looked to them to provide activities. From just after breakfast until one or two-o-clock in the morning, they descended upon us. Sometimes we played games or colored pictures. Sometimes we played UNO or kicked a ball around. Most of all, we took time to teach them about God and what He did for us by sending Christ to die on the cross for our sins. It was the love of Christ, which they received from us, that kept them coming back year after year.

It did not take us long to introduce ourselves. We told them who we were and what we had planned for the week. As we went around the circle, each child told us his/her name. Toward the end of the introductions, we came to a young boy who looked to be no more than twelve years old. He wore a worn, faded blue t-shirt, blue jeans and the laces of his shoes dangled untied. The rest of the kids looked at him as we asked, "What is your name?"

With all seriousness he looked and said, "Hello, my name is Satan." I stood by the camper stunned. Had he said what I thought I heard? The rest of the kids laughed at what he said. I did not find it to be a laughing matter. In all my years of life, I never met someone who wanted to be called Satan. Satan was the evil one, no one wanted to bear his name.

For ten days, we endured the trouble caused by this young boy. I know he was not Satan. He had, however, given Satan control of his body to do his will. He did all he could do to destroy any opportunity he could for people of his community to hear the truth of Christ.

He came into the church one day while we were giving the Bible lesson and asked who wanted to go get ice cream with him. Of course, he distracted the kids as he and a couple others left and headed over to the store. Another time, he grabbed a three-foot piece of log that was laying on the ground and used it as a battering ram on the side of the camper. When he got into the camper, he ripped the screen out of the door. He did all he could do to distract us and others from the work the Lord was doing in Ross River.

Those days in Ross River were some of the toughest days I had to endure during that summer. I had never before faced such open opposition or persecution. No one had ever challenged me during a Bible story. The kids in my first AWANA class may have been energetic and had a hard time listening, but they were not rebellious and defiant. As a Bible School student, I faced drunks on the streets of Binghamton. I expected them to rebel against the truths of Scripture. I never expected to see a child so hardened by sin and possessed by the Devil.

This experience caused my dependence on and trust in the Lord to increase. Both the couple with whom I was traveling and I had nowhere else to turn. We were strangers in the community, and other than Ivan and May, we knew very few others. We could not run to friends or family every time the boy came around. We *had to depend on God,* there was nowhere else to go.

We should be depending on God at all times, but we often forget this truth when things are going well. This was one of the first times in my life when I had to trust the Lord in the midst of a difficult situation.

To help us through those difficult days, we wrote verses out on little sticky notes and plastered the cupboards and doors of the camper with them. We spent a copious amount of time in prayer asking God to work in the boy's heart. We asked God to protect us and use us for His glory.

We trusted the Lord and He came through. No, the boy did not stop his shenanigans. In fact, twice, he chased us to the edge of town by throwing gravel at us from the edge of the road. He still caused distractions when he could, but during this time, God used the Holy Spirit to work in my heart.

Mixed feelings flooded over me as we completed our assignment. I was relieved to be done, but sadness filled my heart. The days in Ross River had been physically and emotionally draining. I felt like I had been in a battle. In reality, I had been.

In Ephesians 6:12 we read, "For we wrestle not against flesh and blood, but against principalities, against powers, against the rulers of the darkness of this world, against spiritual wickedness in high places." Jesus was offering life, freedom, and peace to the people of the community through us as His servants. At the same time, the evil one did all he could to keep the people in bondage. The battle was real and we were in the midst of it.

I realized we only had ten days in the community. What happened the other three-hundred and fifty-five days of the year? The need of the people to hear the truth did not change. Who was going to be in Ross River to let their light shine for the Lord? Who was going to take the Gospel message to these people Satan was luring to destruction?

God began to open my eyes to the job He had for me. There, in the back seat of the old truck, the Lord gave me a burden for the people of Ross River. The Lord changed my heart and helped me to see the plan He had for me in the Yukon Territory. In the chapel at Practical Bible Training School, He had asked me to give my life to serve Him as a missionary. Now He was showing me where He wanted me to be that missionary.

He opened my eyes to the intensity of the battle for souls within the hearts of even the youth. It would still be several years before I returned to Ross River as a full-time missionary. First, the Lord had to supply a helper for me; one who could compliment me in ministry.

Again, He asked me if I trusted Him enough to give my life to serve Him. It was not on American soil where I thought God had called me. It was still His mission field and the fields were white unto harvest. Could I trust God enough to leave my home in New York and travel across the continent? Could I move into another country I knew very little about?

Would I be willing to move into another culture? Would I be willing to trust God with my life and my future?

This was nearly thirty years ago but, God continues to ask me the same questions today. Am I willing to trust God with my career even when it is tough? Am I willing to trust God with our kids? Can I trust God with my finances? It is scary to step out in faith and think about heading into the unknown in order to do what God asks us to do.

I am reminded of God's call to Abram, whom He later named Abraham. In Genesis 12:1, God said to him, "Go from your country and your kindred and your father's house to the land that I will show you." (ESV) When God called him, Abraham did not even know where he was to go. God said, "Go to a land I will show you." He had to step out in faith, leave his home and country, and trust God to have his best interests in mind.

It takes great courage and boldness to be willing to step out in trust and answer God's call. God is faithful. There are many verses in Scripture where God promises to never leave us or forsake us. Paul writes, "Faithful is he that calleth you, who also will do it." 1 Thessalonians 5:24. God never calls us and then leaves us on our own. He calls and He continues the work in us to bring it to completion. All He asks is for us to trust Him enough to step out in faith.

Chapter 8

TRUSTING GOD FOR CONTENTMENT

"And the Lord God said, 'It is not good that the man should be alone; I will make him an help meet for him. Therefore shall a man leave his father and his mother, and shall cleave unto his wife: and they shall be one flesh.' And they were both naked, the man and his wife, and were not ashamed." (Genesis 2:18, 24-25)

In elementary school, I had a "girlfriend." She and I were an item from our early elementary years up through my pre-teens. We held a fake wedding on the bus as we headed to school one day. That sealed the deal. We were the couple to play Joseph and Mary in church Christmas programs. If there was ever a pair the church thought would be together for the rest of their lives, it was us.

Then something happened; she moved away. We wrote letters, but things began to change. It was not the same. The physical distance caused us to have emotional separation. In junior high, she gave me the "talk" no young man wants to hear. She said, "I'm breaking things off." My eighth-grade mind was a wreck. How could this be happening to us? We were going to be together forever. I thought we would get married and live in joyous bliss until death separated us.

During this emotional time, I remember standing outside on the porch with my dad and mom. In tears, I spilled my guts. How could she end things? What was I going to do? As an early teen this hit me hard. They felt my pain, but as they did so often, they turned my eyes to God. They said, "God has someone else in mind for you. Trust Him to work things out." They encouraged me to pray about a wife and let God lead me to the right one. I knew they were right. I knew God had a plan. I committed the matter to prayer, asking for the Lord to provide the right wife for me.

All through high school and on into Bible school, I spent a considerable amount of time looking for a wife as I continued to pray. It was my dream to have a wife and two kids someday. I figured Bible school was a great place to find a wife who followed Jesus.

I dated a few girls, but never found anyone I felt God was telling me I should commit my life to. Either they wanted to rush into marriage or I was rushing and they were pushing on the brakes. None of the relationships worked out.

As I traveled north, I kept my eyes open, looking for the one I had prayed for. Could God have a wife for me among the other Summer Missionaries? Could there be an eligible young lady in one of the churches I connected with in the Yukon?

No matter how hard I looked or tried to encourage relationships with the eligible ladies, nothing ever worked out. As I read through the Bible, I began to notice what Paul had written about being content in the state where he was. (Philippians 4:11) It was not wrong of me to be looking for a wife, but it was wrong for me to let it hinder my ability to be content. In His time, He would provide. I had to continue to trust in His perfect time.

After my first summer with the Summer Missionary Program, SEND asked if I was interested in serving as an intern with the church in Dawson City. I enjoyed working with the people there, and since my first summer in the Yukon, I longed to return. The internship would have me working under the Pastor, Lyle Anderson. I could gain valuable ministry experience while working under an experienced pastor. I could lead Bible studies and preach on occasion and fill in for Lyle when he went on vacation. I would be able to connect with kids who had come to the Bible Camp the summer before.

This opportunity excited me, except for one thing, I had to live alone in a community I knew little about. If that was not bad enough, I would be there through the darkest and coldest months of the winter. Because of its position between two ridges, Dawson only gets a few hours of daylight during the month of January. The temperatures plummet to minus sixty-five degrees Fahrenheit (-54 Celsius). Could I handle such isolation? Could

I handle the cold? I got cold in New York when it got down to zero Fahrenheit (-20 Celsius).

I knew I could trust the Lord to help me handle all this and more. He could provide the strength I needed to endure the darkness, cold and isolation. After much prayer, I decided to trust God and agreed to do the internship. By mid-January 1993, I was back in the Yukon.

I loved the work when I was out and about visiting the people from the church and some of the kids I had seen at camp. During this time, some of the people from the church introduced me to the sport of curling, one of Canada's favorite past times. As an American, we look at curling as a very boring sport, but let me tell you, games can be pretty intense. We enjoyed our times together.

I was quite lonely during the evenings when I came home to the empty house. I did not even have a dog to take for a walk or a cat whose fur I could stroke. It was quite different from my home. I grew up in a close-knit family and was rarely alone. There was always something going on. My longing was to have someone to share my days' experiences with.

As I trusted the Lord, He did bring people into my life. There were generous people from the church who took me under their wing. Sometimes Betty or Sally, my neighbors, knocked on the door to drop off fresh home-made bread and had me over to their house for supper. At other times, John or Chuck and Bonnie invited me to spend the evening with them. Sometimes, I got to spend time at Lyle and Rita's home. I was eating somewhere other than my house at least once a week. This helped to fill the quietness of the evenings. Besides that, I did not have to cook for myself, which was never a strong talent of mine. The loneliness which I felt in the evenings grew intense.

On those nights when I sat alone in my cabin, I learned how to "be still and know" the Lord during these times of quietness. The Lord drew me to Himself as I studied and poured over His Word. It was during these times of quiet where I solidified my personal beliefs about who God was to me.

For two decades, Dad and Mom had taught me what to believe and had demonstrated how to trust the Lord. I had to decide for myself what I was going to believe. Did I trust God enough or did I need something or someone else to fill the void I was feeling?

I struggled with 1 Corinthians 7, where Paul wrote, "Let every man have his own wife," and "if a man cannot contain himself let him marry." God knew how I felt inside. He had given me the desires I was struggling to control. I did not want to be alone. Did I want a wife so much it was hindering my relationship with the Lord? Was my desire to find a wife keeping me from trusting God to be all I needed?

Now don't get me wrong, I don't feel it is wrong to desire marriage; especially to a Godly woman. The desire to have a life-long partner was why God gave Eve to Adam in the Garden of Eden. He said, "It was not good for man to be alone." (Genesis 2:18) It is why God said, "A man should leave his father and mother and cleave to his wife." (Genesis 1:24)

It was during these long, lonely winter nights the Lord helped me to see that He was worthy of my trust. He never said to me, "Tim you do not need to marry" or "You will be a single missionary." He did challenge me by asking, "Am I enough for you?"

This question is one that still lingers in my mind even years after this six-month internship in the Yukon. God continues to impress upon me the fact that, *He is enough.* We do not need anything else. He is and will always be enough.

He gives us a help-mate because He knows our inner needs and desires. He created us with a need for companionship. He made it so we would be better together than apart. (Ecclesiastes 4:9-12) He created us with sexual desires as a part of His plan for filling the earth and growing His Kingdom. (Proverbs 5:18) Nothing, though, is to take a higher place in our lives than the place He deserves.

When the Lord finally got that point across to me, I had peace. He led me to take a different approach. I did not stop looking for a young lady who was willing to go where the Lord led us. Instead, I decided the Lord was worthy of my trust and He was going to get the glory. If He was asking me to serve Him as a single missionary in the north, then I would accept His will and go forward. Nothing was going to keep me from following the goal He had given me to serve Him in Canada's Far North.

I applied to be a career missionary with SEND International. My intention was to return to the Yukon as a church-planting missionary. During the application process, I spent time in New York working with my dad and uncle in their construction business. As the Lord provided, I found opportunities to serve in my local church.

Several months after applying, my brother started to build his house within sight of our childhood home. He had met a wonderful Christian girl from our church and they were getting ready to begin their life together. Since I knew a bit about wiring, they had asked me if I could help them wire the house. In the evenings, we spent a few hours trying to finish building their home before their wedding date.

Less than a week before the wedding, we were installing the last of the light fixtures when one of my brother's fiancée's friends stopped by to get her dress for the wedding. I was working in the kitchen when she walked in. She was the most beautiful woman I had ever laid eyes on. Her Italian heritage showed in her dark complexion. She had dark brown, shoulder-length hair and lovely brown eyes, which caught my gaze. Her smile was enough to make me almost fall off the ladder I was standing on.

Several days later, we found ourselves at the wedding together – well, not together yet. During the reception, she got up and left with another man's coat. I did not realize it at the time, but as she sat down her dress caught on the metal chair and ripped. I have to admit, there was a feeling of jealousy. Even as it came over me, I wondered where those strange feelings had come from. I knew little more than her name, but Gwendy had caught my attention in a big way. Little did we know what God had in store for us.

A week after the wedding, my brother and my now sister-in-law called and asked if I wanted to go on a triple date with them. They invited Gwendy and another young dating couple from our church. I agreed to dinner and miniature golf later in the week. I wanted to spend time getting to know her, but I wanted nothing serious at this point. I had a ticket booked to head back to the Yukon for another summer of ministry. The flight was in less than two weeks.

Gwendy and I immediately made a connection. We were both interested in each other, but neither of us wanted to commit to anything that might distract us from our life goals. She was going into a nursing program and wanted nothing to distract her. I was going north for another summer of village outreach and wanted nothing to get in my way.

We enjoyed our time around the table laughing together. After supper, we found ourselves doing the dishes together. Since family was important to both of us, the conversation centered around them most of the time. She told me about her three brothers and how often there were dishes left in the sink. As the only girl, she often had to finish the dishes. I found out she hated to have dishes left in the sink. Without much thought, I said, "If you cook, I'll do the dishes." She still holds me to this promise over twenty-five years later. I have the better end of the deal. I get her delicious homemade meals every day and she gets to enjoy a clean kitchen (most of the time).

After another date a week later, we knew we wanted to spend more time together. On the second date, I asked her an important question which was a key in our relationship going any further. I said, "If the Lord called you to be a missionary, what would you say?" She said, "I would be willing." Those simple words were all I needed to hear.

To say the rest is history would be to miss how the Lord worked in our love story to bring both of us to the point where we were ready to say, "I do." Two days after that important conversation, I was on a plane headed back to the villages of the Yukon. I had only spent a few short times with her, but she was all I could think about.

This summer was different from the two previous ones. Whenever there was a break between ministries, I wanted to be on the phone. We spent hours talking together about everything. Her studies, my ministry, our families. We learned a great deal about each other during that summer apart. We wrote lengthy letters. (There were no cell phones and email had not yet become popular.) We looked forward to the fall when we could spend time together face-to-face.

I prayed for the Lord to give me a young lady who loved Him and was willing to serve on the mission field. Gwendy had recently met the Lord. Her mom had been sick with cancer and a friend invited her to Lester Baptist Church. It was there she found the love of Christ and trusted Him as her Savior. As the Lord had done with me, He was working to prepare her for what He had planned for her.

As we got back together in the fall, our love for each other grew. We spent hours together. We walked through nearby parks, took drives around the country roads, exploring areas we had never been to before. We loved to enjoy the sunsets together and going to church with each other.

We did almost everything together. It felt good to share the highs and lows of life with her. As we prayed and read the Bible together, the Lord drew us closer to each other.

Somewhere along the line, I realized I had fallen in love with her. She was no longer someone just to hang out with. She was the one I wanted to spend the rest of my life with. There were nagging questions still in the back of my mind: was she cut out for the Yukon wilderness? Could we be happy working side-by-side, day after day? More importantly, was God calling her to be in the Yukon where He had called me? Only the Lord could answer this question. While man looks on the outward appearance, "God looks on the heart." (1 Samuel 16:7)

In late January 1995, I returned to the Yukon to work with a missionary couple in Teslin. I spent four months with them learning what ministry was like in another Yukon community. Half way through my time in Teslin, Gwendy came north to visit. I spent two weeks introducing her to the people I ministered to. It was there, on the playground, where the Lord broke her heart for the people of the Yukon.

We had gone to the park with the missionary kids when some of the community kids came around. The kids were playing around when one of them grabbed a handful of sand and threw it toward one of the other kids. They immediately went to Gwendy for help. It was there, as she looked into the eyes of a hurting child, the Lord said, "I can use you here, for my glory." She returned home, a changed individual. She knew God had a place for her in the Yukon. She could use her gift of caring for people in the far reaches of North America.

When I returned to New York in June, I was on a mission. We had been apart long enough. She needed to become my wife. I knew I could not live without her, nor did I want to. I prepared a steak dinner for her. I dropped to one knee and popped the question. To my delight, she agreed.

Looking back after finding out how good of a cook she is, I wonder if she said yes because she felt sorry for me. In reality, as I trusted God, He gave me much more than I could ever have dreamed or asked. She is everything I am not. I was sheltered from the world. She grew up in the world. Her home life was full of hardships. When we married, she had already lost both parents and with her older brother, had been left to care for their two younger brothers. My home was full of wonderful happy memories. She had suffered such loss. God brought two opposites together to form a team to honor Him.

I trusted God to do what He deemed right. A wife was on my prayer list for most of my teen years. God knew all along what kind of person we each needed to survive the rigors of ministry. He gave me a wonderful, Godly wife, who has served faithfully by my side for twenty-five years. Her heart for hurting children, her love for serving, and her unshakable drive helped us as we have served the Lord together.

I agree with what Solomon wrote in Proverbs 18:22. This verse says, "He who finds a wife finds a good thing and obtains favor from the Lord." (ESV) I asked the Lord to provide the right woman who would complement the ministry He called me to. God provided much more than I could ever have asked for. I am blessed beyond measure.

Two hearts united as one- December 30, 1995

Chapter 9

TRUSTING GOD FOR THE OWNERS MANUAL

"All scripture is given by inspiration of God, and is profitable for doctrine, for reproof, for correction, for instruction in righteousness: That the man of God may be perfect, thoroughly furnished unto all good works." (2 Timothy 3:16-17)

Gwendy and I celebrated our marriage, surrounded by around two hundred and fifty friends and family on December 30, 1995. The wedding was simple yet beautiful as we took full advantage of the Christmas decorations. The only bad thing about the day was the smell of Limburger cheese, which some mischievous members of my family put on the door handles and exhaust system of our getaway car. As it warmed, the smell permeated the whole vehicle, making it an unenjoyable ride. It could not hamper the joy we felt to be beginning our life together.

After a gorgeous honeymoon in northern Pennsylvania, we began to set up our home together. Our first home was a trailer, which a neighbor had traded in for a newer model. We did not mind the classic seventies model equipped with a pink toilet and tub. While it did not look great on the outside, it did not matter, we knew we would not be in it for long. Gwendy did a great job of making it feel comfortable.

We got married knowing our time in New York was only temporary. Soon, we would move to the Yukon. Since we only planned to live in it until the move and then get rid of it, we got permission from my dad and uncle to park it on their property, saving us the expense of buying land.

Life was busy. I was working construction fifty or more hours a week. We served in our home church by helping to teach kindergarten – second grade in the AWANA program. In the evenings and on weekends, we enjoyed our times working together in ministry.

Life was simple. During the first year of marriage we decided not to have any television. We loved to go to garage sales and antique stores looking for various "treasures." We painted the old paneling and gave the old trailer some new life. We built wood projects together as our house began to become our home. We loved our time together, laughing, playing games, and talking.

We love adventures and spontaneity. I came home some Friday evenings and Gwendy would say, "Let's take a trip to Lancaster." Soon, we were in the car making the four-hour trip to the Amish Country. The sight of farmers working their fields and the sound of the clip clap of horse's hooves was something we never tired of hearing. Of course, no trip was complete without purchasing a wet bottom shoofly pie.

Each spring, we planted a garden and spent many evenings in the summer growing vegetables and canning. Gwendy made homemade salsa and a variety of jams and jellies. She loved to feed me as much as I loved her cooking.

One night I came home from work and asked what we were having for supper. She looked at me and said, "Chicken fingers and fries." With a smile on her face she said, "I made them." Inside, I thought to myself, *yes, I know you cooked them*, but I doubted she made them from scratch. It was not until later that I realized she had made the meal from scratch. I had both many times before, but most of the time they had come in a box. I am forever amazed at how much God blessed me when He gave Gwendy to me. He knew I needed someone to feed me as my cooking abilities could qualify me for Worst Cooks in America.

It did not take long before we realized our family was going to be growing. The two of us had somehow become three. We were going to have a baby shortly after our first anniversary. We were going to be parents. I was not too sure how I felt about being a dad. I had committed to being the kind of husband God asked me to be; who would cleave to his wife and "forsake all others as long as we both shall live." Now, I had someone else to love and care for. Could I do it? Was I able to take care of both of them?

We excitedly picked out colors for the spare room and began to gather furniture. We got a changing table, a crib, a dresser, etc. Each piece of furniture came with a manual telling how to put the pieces together. However, following directions has never been one of my strong suits.

As a freshman at Practical Bible Training School, the maintenance supervisor gave me the job of wrecking a big upright piano in the guy's dorm. I heard the directions to break the piano in pieces so we could take it out of the building. What I had failed to hear was one important direction – the one that told me the location of the piano. Instead of going downstairs where the derelict piano was, I took the sledgehammer and went upstairs. All the while wondering why I was wrecking such a good piano. I gained the title of "piano wrecker" after this incident.

With wonder and anticipation, we watched our baby on the ultrasound. Who does not feel a twinge of pride and amazement seeing the little baby inside of her mother's womb? I am reminded of Psalm 139:14, which says, "I will praise thee; for I am fearfully and wonderfully made: marvelous are thy works; and that my soul knoweth right well." Growing inside of my wife was something God had brought together through us. God had taken care of every detail.

We counted the weeks and followed the baby's progress with each new stage. Soon, the day came for us to have our first child. Gwendy had been in labor all night. She did not want to disturb my night's rest so she let me sleep. In the morning when I woke up, she told me she thought we should be going to the hospital instead of heading off to work. The delivery did not come that easy. She was in labor for over twenty-four hours. Finally, the baby decided to make her entrance into this world. After waiting nine months, we were holding *our* baby.

The first night, as Gwendy lay in bed, I stood holding Jocelyn in my arms. I looked at her tiny fingers and toes. She weighed only seven pounds and several ounces, but she was all there. With fear, I held her in my arms, afraid I might drop her. She looked so tiny and fragile.

The doctor had told us how "simple" it is to care for a baby. "If they cry, they need to eat, burp, sleep, or have a diaper change." How was I going to be able to follow those instructions? Could I do this job God had given to me?

There was no instruction manual tied to her foot or packaging list taped to her back. She came into this world without any user manual. Now it was up to us to nurture her and take care of her.

Our family begins

As I pondered this, I realized she did have an *Instruction Manual*. It had not come attached to her foot, but we already had it. God gave us His instructions in the Bible long before Jocelyn had been born. He had written advice to new parents and older parents alike. He said in His word, "Train up a child in the way they should go." (Proverbs 22:6) He did not just tell us to train them, He told us how to go about doing it; all I needed to do was follow His teachings. His Word continues to instruct and teach me in the way I need to go and how I should live.

As our family has grown from one child to five and as we have added kids through taking in needy children, one thing holds true. As people come to me and ask for advice about a problem they are facing, there is a place I can take them. As our children get older and begin to go out on their own, they can take the Manual with them.

God's Word provides us with all the instruction we need for raising our children. (Proverbs 13:24, 22:6, 23:13-14, Ephesians 6:4, Colossians 3:21) His Word gives us all the instructions we need for life and Godliness. (2 Peter 1:3, Hebrews 4:12, 2 Timothy 3:16) God's Word gives us direction in life. Isaiah 40:8 says, "The grass withereth, the flower fadeth: but the word of our God shall stand forever."

While ideas, stories, fads, stores, and people come and go, God's Word remains constant through all of life's adventures. We have learned to search the Bible for the answers to life's questions, because it always speaks the truth to any topic.

Chapter 10

TRUSTING GOD FOR ANSWERED PRAYER

"...ye have not, because ye ask not. Ye ask, and receive not, because ye ask amiss, that ye may consume it upon your lusts."
(James 4:2-3)

Shortly after Gwendy and I began our life together, we joined SEND International. Our plan was to serve the Lord in the community of Ross River in Canada's Yukon Territory, where I had served as Summer Missionary in the early 90s.

When we got married we both had small cars. Gwendy had a Ford Escort and I had a Ford Tempo. The first vehicle we purchased together was a Ford Taurus. You could say we were Ford fans. In reality, all the cars were small for our growing family. They were neither comfortable or reliable to drive across the country, nor could either pull the moving trailer we needed to move our belongings to the north. They served us for a time, but needed to be replaced.

We started looking for a four-wheel drive vehicle. Experienced missionaries told us this was important for life in Alaska and the Yukon due to the harsh driving conditions. Winters can be cold and long with roads covered in snow close to six months of the year. In the summer, the many miles of gravel roads get slippery with the summer rains.

For months we looked for a vehicle. Several people suggested that we buy a Suburban. It had nine seats, which made it good for transporting a growing family and taking kids to camp. It had a large cargo space that could haul the groceries of a large shopping trip. Many people in the Far

North do not shop like we used to when we lived in New York. With the supermarket a couple hundred miles away, they stock up on food once every four to six weeks at a time. The community where we would live was two hundred and fifty miles from the city center.

During this time, SEND asked us to attend the three-month Missionary Development Program (MDP) in Nipawin, Saskatchewan. The purpose of the program was preparing young missionaries for remote living and helping them to be more effective in their ministries. Students received training in topics such as, language acquisition, cultural awareness, and how to teach one-point sermons and received mentoring from experienced missionaries. Gwendy and I enrolled in the program for the spring of 1999. With the trip to Saskatchewan in focus, we felt the pressure to locate a vehicle soon.

In the Broome County area of New York, where we were living, there were many dealerships. Every time we had a chance, we drove around the lots looking for the right vehicle at the right price. We were young and had two children, so money was a big issue. We did not want to burden ourselves with debt by taking out a loan, as this could hinder us on the mission field. This limited our options. We had spent hours looking, but could not find anything that fit our budget.

Finally, one evening, about three weeks before we were to leave for Saskatchewan, we were lying in bed talking about our limited options. We were not sure what we should be doing. I asked Gwendy, "What are we looking for?" We discussed the vehicle we wanted, but never prayed specifically about what we wanted. This time we even talked about the color we wanted. After hearing this, we committed the need to the Lord and asked Him to supply. This was not the first time either of us had prayed for the Lord to provide. However, this was the first time we prayed together and committed it to the Lord for His timing and provision.

In Matthew 18:19-20, we read, "I tell you truly that if two of you on the earth agree about anything you ask for, it will be done for you by My Father in heaven. For where two or three gather together in My name, there am I with them." Together we stepped out in faith asking God to meet the need He already knew we had.

The next day, I went off to work. Gwendy and the kids had to go to Binghamton/Vestal for some groceries. Gwendy decided to take a drive through one of the dealerships we had visited before. On the way through the lot, she saw it; the vehicle we had prayed about! There sat a 1994 navy blue Suburban. As soon as she saw it, she fell in love with it. She could hardly contain herself until I got home from work that evening. She excitedly told me about her find. As soon as we could, we went back for a closer inspection.

We stepped into the dealership to ask about the vehicle that had caught her eye. To our surprise, the salesman who greeted us was the pastor at one of the local churches. We met him several months earlier when we shared about our future ministry at his church. We chatted a bit before leaving to take the vehicle of our dreams and prayers for a test drive.

It was beautiful, inside and out. The royal blue paint glistened in the sun. The cloth seats were comfortable. While it seated nine people with no trouble, the back two bench seats folded down leaving a large cargo area. The area was big enough to hold a pile of four-by-eight-foot sheets of plywood or several boxes of groceries. The half-ton frame was equipped with 4x4 and a generous thirty-nine-gallon gas tank. It was five years old, but showed little signs of anything but normal wear. There were no oil leaks. It was in great shape. The three-fifty Chevrolet engine purred like a kitten as we drove around the area near the dealership.

We fell in love with it and knew we wanted it. We felt we had found God's answer to our prayers. The only trouble was that it was over our budget. How were we going to afford it?

On the way back toward the dealership, we talked about the price. We knew how much we had set aside to buy a vehicle. This beautiful vehicle was several thousand more than we had saved. We agreed, no matter how much we loved it, we would offer them what we had and leave the rest to the Lord.

As we walked into the dealership, we did not have to say anything. The salesman could tell by the look on our faces, the Suburban was what we were looking for. We shared our enthusiasm as we stepped into his cubicle to talk about the price.

We told him our dilemma of loving the vehicle, but not having the cash to pay the price listed on the windshield. As a bi-vocational pastor, who knew what it was to stretch every dollar, he understood our desire not to go into debt. We made an offer that was several thousand dollars below the asking price. He grinned knowing his boss would never accept the price.

As he left the office to seek approval from the sales manager, we sat wondering what the outcome would be. We were confident that God knew the need. He also knew what was in our bank account. He had to work in the manager's heart if we were to have it at the price we named.

It did not take long for the salesman to return to his office. We already knew the answer. It was what we expected. His boss had given us a counter offer, which was still over our budget. We thanked him and said, "If the Lord does not have this one at the price we can afford, there will be something else." As much as we wanted the vehicle, we had to trust God to provide within our budget.

We left the dealership discouraged and beginning to think we were not going to find the vehicle we were looking and praying for. We had peace knowing God was in control. We kept thinking, though, *if only we could afford to spend a bit more or if only the manager lowered the price.* Was it wrong to spend a bit more than we had and go into debt? We agreed, we would trust God and see what happened.

Two weeks went by. We continued to pray for the Lord's provision, but again, found nothing new. Less than a week before it was time to leave to go to the Missionary Development Program, we received a phone call. It was from the dealership. They had not sold the Suburban and would accept our offer if we were still interested.

Joy flooded over us. God had answered our prayer. With three days left, God had come through. He was not late. He was on time, *His time.* I do not know how the vehicle even stayed on the road for the half-hour trip home. We were so elated.

Three days later we headed to Saskatchewan for our training. This was the first of many trips with that Suburban. It helped us move north a year later in 2000. It took the first group of kids with us to Kamp Klondike in Dawson City in 2001. In 2004, it took us across the United States and helped us safely return from our first term of service. It has seen many miles on rough Yukon roads. Oh, the stories it could tell if it could talk. While we no longer rely on it for long trips, we still use it for hunting. It continues to be a blessing from the Lord.

There are times when we pray and it seems like our prayers have fallen on deaf ears. It seems like our prayers go no higher than the ceiling. There are other times when everything seems to fall into place as God answers our prayers exactly how we prayed them. I do not think there is a secret code where if we pray a certain way, everything will fall into place. God is sovereign and knows the end from the beginning. He knows the intentions of our hearts. He knows what He is trying to accomplish in and through us. His desire is for us to trust Him, *always.*

This vehicle has done more to encourage my faith than many sermons I have heard. It sits in our driveway as an emblem of God's answer to one of our prayers. Every time we drive it down the South Canol for a fishing trip or out the Robert Campbell Highway for firewood, I am reminded of that night in 1999. Gwendy and I cried out to the Lord and He heard us. I am reminded of the joy we had in finding God's answer. He knew the need we had then and He knows every need we continue to have. He does hear and He does answer.

Our answer to prayer

PART III

TRUSTING GOD IN MINISTRY

"For the which cause I also suffer these things: nevertheless, I am not ashamed: for I know whom I have believed, and am persuaded that he is able to keep that which I have committed unto him against that day." (2 Timothy 1:12)

"Trusting God is not a thought or a feeling; it is something we do." (Pastor Alvin Bueckert)

Chapter 11

GOD GIVES THE REASON FOR MINISTRY

*"Now the God of hope fill you with all joy and peace in believing,
that ye may abound in hope, through the power of the Holy Ghost."
(Romans 15:13)*

As ministers for the Lord, many times people question why we do
what we do. What would make us uproot our children to live in
a foreign country, far from any loved ones? What would make
someone leave what we grew up with to move to where we needed to adjust
to a new culture? What would make someone keep ministering to a people
who do not seem to want to hear the Gospel?

It is easy to give a Sunday School answer and say, "God." Ultimately,
He is the one who called us to serve. He is the one who led us to the village
of Ross River. He is the one who has given us the passion and desire to
stay. This answer does not answer the curiosity of most people, nor should
it. Why do we stay in the Yukon, when life could be easier in some other
place?

Each summer, during the first ten years in the north, Gwendy and I
were part of SEND's Summer Missionary Program (SMP). I served as a
Summer Missionary in the early 1990s but when we moved north in 2000,
we joined Don and Millie Ressler, Ken and Karen Pregizer, and Michael
and Beth Johnson as leaders. Our job was to work alongside the other
couples and help mentor and train the teams as they traveled through the
Yukon.

SMP started with summer workers in the 1960s. Many of these

summer workers came to assist in work projects which needed to be accomplished in the short summers of the north. In 1969, Don and Millie Ressler came from Pennsylvania on a one-year, short-term assignment. With the encouragement from Leander Rempel, director of SEND North (then Central Alaska Mission), this year of service turned into a life-long commitment of seeing the Gospel of Jesus Christ spread across Alaska, Yukon, British Colombia, NWT, and even into Russia.

The purpose of SMP was to have a significant impact in the lives of young people and help them to grow spiritually and serve the Lord wherever He led them. When SMP started, SEND North used a variety of means to reach the people of Alaska. They had a hospital to help meet people's physical needs while they helped with their spiritual needs. They ran a radio station to get the Gospel into the bush where a lack of roads made it difficult. A Bible College started to train leaders who could go back into the communities as pastors, Sunday School teachers, and church leaders.

All these needed to be maintained, so the mission also had a maintenance department. In the winter, career missionaries kept these ministries going. In the summer, though, it was the Summer Missionaries who provided relief and help to the full-time missionaries. It was not unusual in the early days to have over forty summer missionaries.

SMP did not believe in throwing young want-to-be missionaries into the work and wishing them well. The thing that made this program successful over the years was the attention to training and mentoring these young missionaries. This helped the Summer Missionaries to grow more confident in what God called them to do and to be able to step out of their comfort zone.

The program ran for eleven weeks each summer and started with two weeks of intense preparation on the grounds of Alaska Bible College in Glennallen, Alaska. During this time, the SMPers received training in teaching Vacation Bible School, how to lead songs, lead a person to Christ, and be camp counselors. Much of the instruction they received focused on how to relate to the cultures present in the various people groups of the north and how to be sensitive toward the differences they faced in ministering to them. In every area of training, these Summer Missionaries received instruction on how to make the most of every opportunity to share Christ with whoever they met.

After receiving cultural education, they received training specific to their area of ministry. The radio personnel received training in announcing and in how to reach Alaskans with the Gospel message. The maintenance personnel learned where to find all the tools and tips to make sure their work stood the test of Alaskan winters. They learned to look at their time on maintenance not as a job, but as a service for the missionaries they were helping. The nurses received training on meeting the physical needs of their patients.

After the two weeks of preparation, each Summer Missionary was commissioned by the SEND North Missionaries. They then began their summer of ministry. The day everyone separated was always emotional. Individuals who had only met less than two weeks prior were bound in a unity of purpose, to see the north reached with the Gospel of Jesus Christ. Tears flowed as the village teams departed Glennallen for other communities along the road system or accessible only by air.

For the next eight weeks, the various teams served as the Lord opened doors of opportunity. Sometimes in a bush camp in the northern Yukon. Other times it was to help teach kids at a village Sunday School. There were special times when teams participated in cultural events. These allowed the Summer Missionaries to experience and get a taste of life through the eyes of the people to whom they ministered.

Each SMPer had many God-given opportunities to see what the full-time career missionaries faced every day. They would no doubt, sometime during the two months, experience the highs and lows of ministry. They would leave at the end of the eleven weeks having a full view of ministry, both the things of joy and some of the hardships.

The beauty of SMP was the time when everyone gathered back together at the end of the summer. With smiles on their faces and joy in their hearts, they shared how the Lord used them. Those who worked in Glennallen on the radio, maintenance, and medical center told stories of their work in local churches and how they helped with Native Bible Conference. The village teams told stories of how God opened doors of ministry in Bible Camps and Vacation Bible School programs. There were stories of changed lives in the villages and communities as well as in the Summer Missionaries themselves.

The sharing and excitement continued as the SMP loaded onto the bus and were treated to a spectacular trip in Denali National Park to see Mount McKinley. It was a time as Millie Ressler said, "to unpack your mind," from the experiences of the summer. Each SMP left Alaska/Canada as a changed individual, having seen what God could do through lives committed to Him. The bonds between the SMP continued for years to come as they wrote, called, visited, and sometimes even came back.

One of our SMP teams getting ready to enter Yukon.

The Resslers took this ministry seriously and stayed for many years. Their time in Alaska ended in October of 2020. Because of their hard work and dedication along with the team that worked with them, many of these SMP'ers dedicated their lives to the Lord and to His service. At one point, about seventy-five percent of the full-time missionaries with SEND North had gone through the Summer Missionary Program. While this is no longer true, the people who were changed by SMP continue to minister in many places around the world, even today.

It was this program that gave us a multi-national team in the mid-2000s. The team members came from Germany, USA, and Canada, each with a story of how the Lord had directed them to serve in Alaska/Yukon. Each one of them was seeking the Lord' direction in future ministry and what it might look like. They engaged us with many questions about what it was like to live in the north. How did we seek to reach out to the people of our community?

How did we endure the highs and lows of ministry? They listened as we told them some of the same stories you are reading in this book.

I do not know if we were dwelling on the negative of life during this time or if we were just being real in sharing everything. But one of the team members asked, "Why do you continue to do what you do in the midst of such adversity and such hard circumstances?" They were asking, "What keeps you going day after day, set-back after set-back?" "Why don't you leave and find a more fruitful ministry?"

The question, "Why do you do what you do?" is one we have answered many times over the course of our ministry. We have not continued because of the great results we have seen over the years. The harvest has been slow. We are not in ministry because it is easy. There are times it feels like we are banging our heads against the wall. There are times we have shed tears for individuals who seem to be making right choices and then fall into sin. We ask ourselves why we have not seen more fruit. We are not in ministry because we love the Yukon. We do love the Yukon and the people God has allowed us to minister to. But that love is not why we have stayed in the same place for twenty years.

The answer is simple. We remain where we are because God gave us a clear call and has not told us to leave. We continue to minister day after day, year after year, because God is faithful. In 1 Thessalonians 5:24 we read, "Faithful is he that calleth you, who also will do it."

God is the One who, in His great mercy, saved us. He is the One who called us to fulfill His great commission. He is the One who prepared us for His service. He is the One who promised never to leave us or forsake us. (Hebrews 13:5)

Gwendy and I began our ministry with the belief that the God of hope could change the lives of those who trusted in Him. The only way the people could hear the message is if we went and told them the truth. God called us to be His light to the people of the Far North. He never promised there would be hundreds who came to Him. He never promised an easy life. He never promised a life without discouragement. He never promised we would see the end results.

He promised to meet all our needs, "my God shall supply all your needs according to His riches in glory by Christ Jesus." (Philippians 4:19) He promised a harvest in due time, "let us not be weary in well doing: for in due season we shall reap, if we faint not." (Galatians 6:9) He promised all these blessings not only to us, but to all who are willing to put their complete trust in Him.

Our faith is not in men, what they do or do not do. It is not in how they respond or do not respond. Our faith is not in the number of people who repent from their sins and turn to Jesus Christ as their Lord and Savior. Our faith is not in the number of people who attend our fellowship on Sunday. Our faith is in one person, Jesus Christ. In Hebrews 12:2, we read, "Looking unto Jesus the author and finisher of our faith; who for the joy that was set before Him endured the cross, despising the shame, and is set down at the right hand of the throne of God."

Yes, there are times of discouragement. There are times when we look around and wonder, "what have we accomplished for all our toil and trouble?" There are times when we do not have joy in ministry. There are times Kid's Bible Club is a mess. There are times when we look at some who have trusted Christ and wonder why they are not walking closer to Him.

We cannot let those things determine our trust in the Lord or our faithfulness to Him. Our eyes are not to be on the world around us. Our eyes are not to be on what is going bad or even what is going right. Our eyes are to be fixed on one Person, on the One who willingly endured the cross, despised its shame, and sat down in the glory of the Father.

Tim and Robert meeting in the old church.

Christ endured the pain of the cross for sinners of whom Jeremiah 17:9 says, "The heart is deceitful above all things, and desperately wicked: who can know it?" Jesus endured the cross for people whose "righteousness is as filthy rags." (Isaiah 64:6) Christ did it for the drunks on the street. Christ did it for the sinners in the pew. Christ did it for the teen who never rebels. Christ did it for the wayward prodigal son or daughter. Christ did it for me. Christ endured the cross for you.

Our hope is in Christ. 1 Peter 1:3 says, "Blessed be the God and Father of our Lord Jesus Christ, which according to his abundant mercy hath begotten us again unto a lively hope by the resurrection of Jesus Christ from the dead." Our HOPE is alive; it is not dead. Our HOPE has power over the wind and the waves. (Mark 4:39) Our HOPE has power over the lame. (John 5:8-9) Our HOPE can make the vilest sinner clean. (1 John 1:9) Our HOPE can give sight to the blind. (Mark 10:46-52) Our HOPE is the One who is with us through the "Valley of the shadow of death." (Psalm 23:4)

What awakens you and fills you with vigor and enthusiasm for the days ahead? What drives you when the going gets tough? What gives you a passion for life? What makes you keep working when the boss is not around? Why do you do the things you do????

Chapter 12

GOD GIVES THE PASSION FOR MINISTRY

"But my God shall supply all your needs according to his riches in glory by Christ Jesus." (Philippians 4:19)

One of the hardest things for me to do as a missionary is to trust other people to provide for our needs. In trusting others for our monthly support, we are actually having to trust God on a regular basis. This trust is something many of us have a hard time doing. We plan ahead for retirement. We try to have a bit of a reserve in case something tragic happens. We buy health insurance and life insurance. We buy extended warranties on cars, washing machines, computers. All this can cause us to trust what we have instead of trusting the One who promised to meet all our needs.

Growing up, we were always taught that a man should work for his food. If a man does not work he should not eat, and a man is worthy of his hire. (2 Thessalonians 3:2, 1 Timothy 5:18) All these are Scriptural principles about what God expects of us. We are not to be freeloading off the government or anyone else.

After going to missionary training, we realized that part of being a missionary meant going out and raising support from churches. To me, it felt like I was begging for money. It felt like I was not meeting my family's needs. I was relying on others to do the work. We did not want to be begging for money. We did not want to be writing letters every couple of months stating we were in financial distress and needed more money. I needed to reconcile the fact that we were doing the Lord's work and He was using others to provide for His work. We were not going for a free ride. We were laborers in His Kingdom.

One day as I was contemplating all these mixed-up thoughts, I was talking to Mom. Mom was a great prayer warrior. She had already been talking to the Lord about what we had been going through. I told her, "I do not want to be begging for money." She said, "Share your heart. Let people see your passion. The Lord will take care of the rest." Those words have echoed in my mind many times over the years. She was telling me what I already knew. We needed to trust God. *We were not asking people to give. We were asking the Lord to supply our needs.*

I knew she was right. God had already been working to provide for our needs. Didn't He already supply a vehicle for us? Didn't He provide my first airplane ticket to go north? There were many other times when I could say, "God provided." Every time I had gone to do a short-term mission trip or an internship, the Lord had always provided for what I needed.

With those words in mind, we contacted churches in our local area. God had laid it on our hearts to contact churches no more than two hours away. Our purpose was to be able to stay in the local area each time we came back from the mission field. In this way, we would be able to focus on those churches instead of traveling halfway around the country.

It was a hard and daunting task trying to get churches to give us an opportunity to share our passion with them. For every four to six churches we contacted, we were able to share in one. Many pastors let us know they were not looking to support any new missionaries. To this we replied, "That is fine. Can we come and raise up prayer partners?" Some agreed and others said, "No."

One church we contacted was without a pastor. The person on the phone explained the situation. They were a small church and without a shepherd, they were in no position to support us. I gave the usual response except I added, "I could fill the pulpit for a Sunday if you would like."

In our training on support raising, we received the advice not to go to a church without a pastor. The pastor is usually the one who champions the missionary. Like I said earlier, I sometimes find it hard to follow directions. The contact at the church took us up on my offer.

There was a problem; the church was outside our travel range. We had trusted God to provide within two hours of home and this was three and a half hours. If we went to this church, was it showing we were not trusting God? We felt the Lord telling us we should speak at the church.

The day came for us to go. I have to admit, we were less than spiritual about it. We were going because we felt we had to, not because we wanted to. The trip was long for our two-year-old and a newborn. They had to get used to traveling; we were going to be doing a lot of it on the trip north.

When we got to the church, there were few people there. The sanctuary could seat between seventy-five and one hundred, but today, only around twenty people gathered. We did not care if there were twenty people or two hundred and twenty. We introduced ourselves and shared, with enthusiasm, about the church planting work in the Yukon that God had called us to do. We preached a message from Exodus 4 about God using what was in Moses' hand to help him be willing to give God's message to others. We enjoyed our time with those wonderful folks. On the way home though, we said we would never see anything from that church. They were a struggling church who needed a shepherd.

Again, God had other plans. Several members from the church committed to praying for us on that day and have been praying faithfully ever since. Some of the ladies committed to supporting us for a small amount every month. That small church with only a few people has been a part of the Lord's work in the north since the very beginning. It all started by us being willing to go where God led.

There were many times during the course of our two and a half years of deputation (raising funds) when God sent us to small congregations. He was preparing us for the work of church planting in the Yukon where we rejoice if we have twenty people. In my home church we had around seventy-five kids for a night of AWANA. In the ministry God was calling us to, we would be doing well if we got one-third as many kids.

One small country church was having a five-day VBS and asked if we would be willing to come and share with their kids about life in the Yukon. *The church was one and a half hours away!* I was still working construction, which meant taking time off. It also meant an extra expense in gas to cover the three hours on the road each day.

Close friends said we were crazy to even consider driving that far every day. Why drive all the distance every evening to teach VBS? It was not going to get us any more support. We prayed about it and felt the Lord telling us to go in faith.

We had a marvelous time, not only with the kids, but also with the adults. Our friends were right, it did not result in extra financial support for the ministry. God used the time to prepare us for the countless hours of travel we would have when we moved north. To take kids to camp in Dawson City, we drive seven hours each way. To get to our mission headquarters in Alaska, we have to drive eighteen hours. Getting groceries is even a long trip in many people's eyes. It takes us close to five hours to get there.

To this day though, the church and its members have a close connection with the work because of the many hours we spent with them. Trusting God as a missionary is more than raising money; it is serving others in such a way to bring them closer to Him.

There are times we find it hard to share God's message with others. It may not be convenient. We may have other things we think are more important. We may fear sharing the truth because of what others may think. In 2 Timothy 1:7-9, Paul writes to Timothy and says,

...God hath not given us the spirit of fear; but of power, and of love, and of a sound mind. Be not thou therefore ashamed of the testimony of our Lord...Who hath saved us, and called us with a holy calling, not according to our works, but according to his own purpose and grace, which was given us in Christ Jesus before the world began.

The work God did in us – first at salvation and then in calling us to serve in the north – is not something He expects us to keep to ourselves. The Lord desires for us to stand without fear and share His message with others. When we trust Him enough to be willing to go where He wants us to go and to do what He wants us to do, He accomplishes great things through us.

Chapter 13

GOD GIVES WHAT WE NEED FOR MINISTRY

"The heart of man plans his way, but the Lord establishes his steps." (Proverbs 16:9)

Yes, nine months is how long it takes to wait for a baby to develop inside the womb. We know this for sure as the Lord has blessed us with five wonderful children. But this chapter is about learning to wait for the Lord's time.

From my first visit to the wilds of the Yukon, I could not wait until the next time I could set my feet on Canadian soil again. In the early 90s, I was there for at least three months every year. I had been there for two six-month internships. During the first one, I served in Dawson City with Pastor Lyle Anderson. During the second one, I went to Teslin and worked with SEND Missionaries, Dieter and Kristiana Borchmann.

Both gave me different experiences. But God used each of them to give me a greater desire to live and minister in the Yukon. Every time I left, I could not wait until I could return. I knew God was preparing the way by giving Gwendy to me as a helper. I knew His timing was perfect, but I was anxious to settle into our home in Canada's Yukon.

We got married in December of 1995. Our goal was to move to Ross River as soon as God allowed. With that in mind, we attended the Candidate Orientation Program. COP is SEND's orientation program where we were officially accepted as SEND members and could begin raising the support we needed. In July 1996, SEND appointed us as Church-Planting Missionaries headed to the Yukon.

By March of 1997, we were contacting churches and scheduling meetings. For two and a half years we traveled almost every weekend to various churches in the Southern Tier of New York and the Northern Tier of Pennsylvania.

We traveled north above Syracuse, New York. To the south, we went down almost to Williamsport, PA. Our travels took us into the Delaware Water Gap, the Finger Lakes region, and even to Staten Island. We saw New York in the spring, summer, fall, and winter. We travelled in snow, sleet, hail, freezing rain, and sunshine. We travelled through areas dense with deer and occasional accidents, but the Lord kept us safe during the many miles of travel.

Our travels took us to small country churches with only a few people and large churches with a couple hundred people. We taught Sunday School and Vacation Bible School classes. We spoke at AWANA Clubs. We were in churches on Sunday mornings, Sunday nights, and Wednesday evenings.

Every time we went to a new church, we trusted God to meet our needs. Back then, SEND required us to raise forty-eight hundred dollars a month for our salary, housing, insurance, and mission costs. In each church, we introduced ourselves, telling who we were, what we were going to be doing, who we were doing it with, and what was needed to get us back to the Yukon.

I enjoyed going to each church and meeting other believers. It was a different story for Gwendy and our children. It was hard on them to be in a different, unfamiliar church each Sunday. Gwendy did a great job at making sure that wherever we were, the kids felt safe and cared for. Each of them carried a hand-made blanket. No matter where we traveled, they had their piece of home with them.

As I wrote in an earlier chapter in 1999, we had enough support for SEND to agree for us to do a three-month training program in Saskatchewan. This time served as a nice break from the support raising trail. Sitting under experienced missionaries telling us about their ministries in remote Canada made us more eager to get settled and begin ministry in the Yukon.

We returning to New York with a new fire in us. We not only knew where we would be serving, but we also had the training we needed.

As we trusted the Lord, He continued to provide. Little by little, the remaining support came in. Sometimes it came as a five dollar-per-month faith promise; at other times it came via a one hundred dollar-per-month faith promise. It did not matter the size of the gift, we thanked God for each dollar as He supplied it.

Toward the end of 1999, we began the twelve to eighteen-month process of applying for Landed Immigrant Status in Canada, which would allow us to live and work in Canada. After mountains of paperwork and a thorough medical examination, our application was in the mail. We had to wait for the Canadian Consulate to review everything and call us in for an interview.

We did not think much about the application but trusted the Lord to work everything out in the proper time. We spent our time raising the rest of our support. The longer we were raising support, the further away from our home we had to go. Sometimes, this meant we did not get home until close to midnight some Sunday evenings. The nights were short and I had to be up early Monday morning to work construction. God kept providing. He gave me work during the week and meetings each weekend.

It was beginning to wear on us toward the end. We looked forward to the day when SEND could give us permission to leave for the field. That day finally came in April of 2000. The Lord supplied every single penny of our support and we were heading north.

When we got married, we knew we would only be in New York for a short time. That short time ended five years later. We bought a tilt-deck trailer like landscapers use to transport their mowing equipment. To this, we fastened plywood to make a box to pack everything into. We also rented a small U-Haul to help us lighten the load between my parents' and our vehicles, as they would be helping us transition to the north.

Soon, we were busy packing all the things we needed to move. Everything got inventoried and place into boxes. Every box had a number and every item in the box got listed on a master list. This list would need to be presented to the Immigration Officer when we arrived at the border to move into Canada. They would have to review our list to make sure we were not importing anything illegal.

We spent weeks packing and sorting. Dishes were bubble wrapped to protect them on the forty-two-hundred-mile trip across the country.

Pieces of furniture were wrapped in blankets to protect their surfaces from all the highway dust on the final leg of the journey. The kids' toys sat in boxes labeled for quick access when we got to our new home. Today, many preachers and missionaries can have a whole reference library on the hard drive of their computer. Back then, I had volumes of study books covering several large shelves, all of which were placed in boxes and labeled.

It did not take long for both trailers to become full. We worked well into the wee hours of the final morning in Windsor. The last-minute cleaning, mopping, and all those final odds and ends left us exhausted. But, everything had been packed. We were ready to embark upon our cross-continent move. Everything had a place and every place had a thing.

We said good-bye to our families and headed up Route 79 toward Windsor. I was pulling the twelve-foot U-Haul; Dad and Mom were pulling the tilt-deck trailer. We only traveled five miles when Dad stopped and said, "I cannot pull this trailer all the way to Alaska." When we had packed everything, we had tried to pack it heavy toward the front of the trailer. Because it was a tilt-deck, there was still too much weight on the rear of the trailer. Every time he went over forty-five mph, the trailer swerved like a snake down the road. There was no way we were going to be able to use it to move.

What were we going to do? We did not want to repack everything. We wanted to be on the road. Where were we going to find another trailer so we could get on our way? We headed back to my parents' house and prayed. God knew the need and we committed it to Him.

God had everything planned out. He knew where we could get a trailer that would help us move and continue to be an asset to us once we settled. Within a couple hours, Dad and I had found an eight-foot wide by sixteen-foot-long tandem axle trailer with a pull-down door in the rear. Besides being exactly what we needed, we could buy it for a very good price. Within five hours we had the trailer at home and everything repacked. We lost a day, but gained a much better and safer way to move. God, once again, supplied our needs.

Dad and Mom had never been across the continent before. Jocelyn and Jessie (our second-born daughter) loved those special days with their grandparents. Together, we made our way across the US, going through New York, Pennsylvania, Indiana, Illinois, Minnesota, Wisconsin, and

North Dakota. After that, our journey took us north into Canada, as we crossed the Canadian Prairies, going through the provinces of Manitoba, Saskatchewan, Alberta, and BC.

We saw grizzly bears, sheep, moose, majestic mountains, fast moving rivers and snow-capped peaks. The beauty of God's creation lay spread as a painter's canvas. The time we had "together" was such a blessing. Even though we could not ride together, the CB radios we had installed made it easy to communicate and "enjoy" the trip together.

After about two weeks on the road, we finally arrived at SEND headquarters in Glennallen, Alaska on Mother's Day. Our temporary home – another mobile home – looked like it was built around the same time as our New York trailer home. This one however, boasted the olive-green tub and shower and it had a green exterior. The kids called it the Green Bean. We did not mind what it looked like or the shape it was in. We were one step (and many miles) closer to moving into the Yukon. Now we continued to wait for the Canadian Government to give us permission to make our home in the Yukon.

The days ticked by with no word from the Immigration Department. We were anxious to hear that everything was in order to be able to go to our final destination. We were advised by SEND staff to get settled in Glennallen and make it our home in the meantime. I did not want to do this. Glennallen did not need another missionary. They already had many living there who worked with Alaska Bible College, Cross Road Medical Center, and the radio station, KCAM. I wanted to be in the Yukon where there were people who had no opportunity to hear the Gospel. God had called us to serve in Ross River, not to live in a Christian community. Despite our desire not to unpack in Alaska, we unpacked the bare essentials of our home. The rest we left in storage for the final move.

Soon after we settled into our home, the Summer Missionary Program started. Even though we could not live in the Yukon, there was nothing to keep us from ministering there. We joined the Yukon team and traveled throughout the summer. It felt good to be back in the villages sharing the Gospel. Our children loved the Summer Missionaries and they, in turn, enjoyed having the kids as part of the team. It even made for an easier time getting established in the communities to hold VBS. When other parents saw our children, they often joined us.

Half-way through the summer, we flew back to New York City for an hour interview with the Canadian Consulate. At the end of the interview, the officer said everything looked to be in order except for one letter. We needed a letter from someone in Canada who would be helping to get us settled there. Finally, after months of waiting, it looked like we would soon be able to settle and set up our home.

We returned to Alaska and sent the needed letter within days of our return. The letter was postmarked the first week of August. For weeks we waited for an answer, but got no word. The weeks turned into months and we wondered why we had not heard. We phoned the office, but only got a recorded message. We waited and waited some more.

I have never been very good at waiting. I wanted to make the final move and begin the work in Ross River. The Lord knew what we needed. I left the construction field working over fifty hours per week. Now I was a village missionary with no time clock and no boss standing over my head. The only thing getting me out of bed in the morning was the desire to do what my Father in Heaven had in store for me that day.

We also needed to learn about how things work in the north. Water tends to freeze when it gets minus forty. We learned how to install circulators on the water lines and the importance of making sure everything kept running. It took our water line freezing once before this lesson stuck.

We learned a great deal about ministry in these nine months. We had great mentors in Don and Millie Ressler. They had served as missionaries with SEND for nearly thirty years at the time we arrived. They took us under their wing and taught us how to live with and reach the people of the north. The lessons they taught us were not things you find in a textbook. They showed us by living a consistent life wherever they were.

Don served in the maintenance department at SEND's Glennallen compound. He was called to fix anything that broke and keep things going through the extremes of summer and winter. It did not matter what the task was, he faced it with a willing attitude and worked at it until completion. If there was someone who needed to talk, he was right there to listen. It did not matter if the work was left undone for a while – people were most important.

Millie served as a nurse at the Cross Road Medical Center. For years, she had seen people at their worst. She cared for them, bandaging their wounds and showing the sincere love of Christ. The same was true for her. It did not matter if the waiting room was full of people. If someone had a spiritual need and needed to talk with her, she took whatever time was necessary.

Don and Millie with our children

Together, they ministered in two communities up the road from Glennallen. They took students from Alaska Bible College to one of these villages during the mid-week to conduct what they called Kid's Church. Kid's Church was much like a Vacation Bible School or Kid's Bible Club. The time we spent with them in these villages was invaluable in helping us begin our ministry.

The cottonwoods and aspen trees turned brilliant yellow and vibrant red. Fall came to the Copper River Valley. Days turned into weeks. Weeks turned into months. The seasons changed, and we still heard nothing from immigration.

The harsh winter of interior Alaska began to settle in. Several times we went into our cargo trailer to find winter clothes, boots, and other things we thought we would not need until we were finally settled. The time ticked by and still no word.

At the end of November, we faced a dilemma: if our immigration letter came, would we go before Christmas? We decided to spend Christmas in Glennallen no matter what. Our first Christmas on the mission field was not much. Most of our decorations were still in storage. We bought an artificial tree and only used the top section. Gwendy and the girls made little ornaments to hang on it and a felt angel for the top of the tree. We did not need much, we were happy to have each other. There was an uneasiness inside of me. I wanted to be home, not in New York, but in the Yukon. Gwendy kept encouraging me to stay in the present. She was right. God had everything under His control. Why did I have such a hard time trusting Him?

For months, I had been trying to reach the immigration office to make sure they had received our letter. I could never get in touch with a real person – only a recorded message. Finally, after the first of the year, I was able to talk to someone. They told me they were still waiting to receive the letter we had mailed in August. I could not believe it. All this waiting. We were waiting for them to respond to our letter. They were waiting for us to send the letter we had already sent.

It is never easy to wait for something that we have set in our minds. I have no doubt that God "lost" the letter so His purpose would be done. We read,

"To everything there is a season, and a time to every purpose under the heaven: A time to be born, and a time to die; a time to plant, and a time to pluck up that which is planted; A time to kill, and a time to heal; a time to break down, and a time to build up; A time to weep, and a time to laugh; a time to mourn, and a time to dance; A time to cast away stones, and a time to gather stones together; a time to embrace, and a time to refrain from embracing; A time to get, and a time to lose; a time to keep, and a time to cast away; He hath made everything beautiful in his time: also he hath set the world in their heart, so that no man can find out the work that God maketh from the beginning to the end." (Ecclesiastes 3:1-6, 11)

God was working the timing of everything; if only I would depend on Him.

Once we learned about the missing letter, I resent it. Within a week we had permission to move into the Yukon. We headed away from Glennallen during the coldest, darkest time of the winter, but we were on our way.

On February 6, 2001, we officially "landed" in Canada. With great joy, we crossed the border at Beaver Creek, Yukon and became residents of the Yukon Territory of Canada. It was not that we disliked Glennallen or the people there. We were so happy to finally be HOME. We concluded our time of waiting, planning, and preparing. We finally made it to the Yukon in *God's perfect time.*

Looking back on the time in Glennallen, I can see how God was making everything beautiful in His time. I had planned out my course. I had decided when I wanted to move, but I could not compete with what God had planned in *His time.* God knew the time of adjusting we needed. He knew the mentoring we needed. He knew the friendships we needed to establish to help us through the tough times of life and ministry. God knew it all. He was not caught off guard with a lost letter. He knew it all along. I just needed to trust His timing and not push for my own.

Chapter 14

GOD GIVES DIRECTION FOR MINISTRY

"Not forsaking the assembling of ourselves together, as the manner of some is; but exhorting one another: and so much the more, as ye see the day approaching." (Hebrews 10:25)

Descending into Ross River on February 7, 2001, was such an exhilarating feeling. The day was clear. The temperature hung around minus thirty Fahrenheit (-34 Celsius). The snow decorated the spruce trees. It looked like someone had covered them with powdered sugar. A few clouds dotted the sky, trying to block out the sun's brightness.

There was no welcoming committee; no people lined the street and only a few dogs came out to welcome us to our new home. Over twelve inches of fine, granular snow covered the one hundred feet of driveway. We had to shovel it off before we could get the moving truck close to the house.

Previous to our taking ownership, the property had been home to a hunting outfitter. He used the property to keep his horses and crew before heading out to the mountains to hunt. A four-foot-high board fence surrounded the seventy-five by three-hundred-foot lot. The boards blackened from years of weathering. A few of the posts had rotted off at the ground causing the fence to look like a snake going through the grass in the summer.

A large, twenty-four-by-forty-foot, garage sat at the southwest corner of the lot. Two big barn doors allowed access for us to park our suburban. It also had plenty of room for storage while we unpacked and organized the house. One end of the garage was closed off and insulated to provide a miniature apartment. It later served as my office.

Next to the garage stood what looked like a small shed. It actually housed the well that provided drinking water for the house. Dried blood on the plywood floor showed it had been used as a meat cooling shed by one of the previous owners.

The log-sided house occupied the center of the lot. A large picture window gave generous portions of light during the short days of winter. Behind the house lay a beautiful lawn, covered with fine snow in which the kids enjoyed playing.

At the back of the lot, someone had built a ten-by-sixteen-foot greenhouse. The plastic, which covered half the walls, flapped in the breeze, showing signs of years of use. It did not look like much, but worked to grow some fresh produce under the heat of the Yukon's summer sun.

For years, we prayed, planned, and trusted God to bring us to this point. Now we stood in "our house" in Ross River. Before we began to unpack, we sat in the empty house and prayed. We committed the home and ourselves to the Lord for the work He had brought us here to do. It was *God who had brought us here*. God would have to help us do His will.

The house was small for our ever-growing family, but we did not mind. We were *home*. We had two kids. One was four years old and the other two, and we had another one on the way. We entered the house through a ten-by-ten arctic entry, which we used as a pantry and mudroom. The door into the main part of the house led into a medium sized kitchen.

On one side of the kitchen stood a wall of cabinets that was eight feet long. On the opposite wall stood the stove and sink with a few feet of countertop between the two. The refrigerator was against the wall away from the entrance. The spacious layout gave us enough room to bake cookies, make pizza, and host birthday parties. Gwendy used it to feed many people over the years. She fed community members, Summer Missionaries, interns, volunteer teams, and many others.

The living room was the right size for our family and big enough to hold Bible studies. It was the full width of the house and was about twelve feet wide. At one end sat a beautiful cast iron wood stove. The stove served us well when the thermometer dropped to minus fifty Fahrenheit (-46 Celsius).

HOME Sweet HOME

Off the living room were two bedrooms; neither were very big. One was seven and a half feet wide-by-ten feet long. The other was ten feet square. Gwendy and I took the smaller room and built a loft for the girls in the larger room. The girls loved having their own space. They did not care where they were as long as we were with them. It was home.

We needed to do a great deal of work. The carpets smelled of cigarette smoke and needed to be replaced. The water line to the house had frozen in December and would have to be thawed. We were thankful for Jim and Milt, two maintenance guys from SEND, who had come to help us unpack and get settled in. Both were jacks of all trades and had many years of experience in northern living.

As an expert carpet layer, Milt went right to work laying the new carpet in the living room and two bedrooms. Jim grabbed the welder he had brought with him. He hooked it to the copper water line hoping the current from the power and ground leads would thaw out the pipe. As they worked, we got busy trying to sort and unpack what had been in boxes for nine months.

At one point in the afternoon, Jim came and said, "I do not know if we are going to be able to get the water going." He had the welder on the pipe for quite a while at that point. How were we going to survive without water? The kids needed baths. We needed water to drink and cook.

I have noticed many times in my life, I have waited to bring my needs to God as a last resort. I try to handle situations and difficulties on my own until I cannot do it anymore, then I turn them over to the Lord. In reality, I should be taking them to God at the beginning. As we committed the water and pipes over to the Lord in prayer, an amazing thing happened. The water started to trickle a wee little bit. It started slowly and soon it was running a full stream of water. We had water to the house.

It did not take us long to make that house a home. After three days of hard work, Jim and Milt were on their way back to Alaska. We stood alone in our house, ready to start introducing people to Christ.

Gwendy and I were active in our own churches before we got married. Once we got married, we served together in Windsor Bible Baptist Church. We loved working with the SPARKS age in the AWANA program. Once we moved to Alaska, we were active in Chistochina Chapel with the Resslers. Much of our social life revolved around our churches. This was one of the biggest adjustments we had when we first came into the Yukon. Our community did not have a church. They needed one and this was the reason we had moved to the north.

Starting ministry in a small community can be a tough task. There were people in our mission who felt it was not a good idea for us to go right into Ross River. They felt we should spend our first term in another community getting acclimated to the north. They thought, *"they are going to be too isolated to survive."* Our nearest town was an hour drive away. Our field office was in Glennallen, Alaska, over seven hundred and fifty miles away.

Our community was off the beaten path. It had many social issues. (What community does not?) We were living far from the people who supervised us. Our closest help were the Bakers, who were missionaries with SEND in Faro, forty-five miles away. We got together with them almost every week for most of our first year in the Yukon. Those times of prayer, sharing, and getting our questions answered were a great help in getting us settled. In many ways, we were alone. Well, not really, we had God, who promised to "never leave us or forsake us," Hebrews 13:5.

Many felt it best for us to start somewhere else and after a year or two, make the transition into Ross River. We had a strong leading from God, which said we should move right into the community and start the work.

God had promised to be with us wherever we went. We knew He was with us as much in that small community as He was when we were living in New York. He had been with us every step of the way to get us into the Yukon and He would continue to lead and direct us as we settled.

All the education we had received proved to be valuable those first few years of ministry. The time at Bible School, Missionary Development Program, various summers with the Summer Missionary Program, and internships had helped to bring us to this point. We had no one standing over us every day telling us what to do. We had to go where the Lord led us each day. There was no clock to punch in at the beginning of the day or to punch out at the end of the day. The beginning of the day was never a problem for me.

My problem was in knowing when it was time to stop. In the construction business I could see results at the end of each day. As a church planting missionary, I knew the goal we were shooting for. We came to Ross River to see a church established. Our goal was to train people to follow Jesus in all they did. At times, it was hard to see the results of our labors. We could go weeks or months without seeing tangible results as we trusted the Lord to soften hearts.

How does a missionary go from having no church to having a vibrant, growing church where its members are reaching out to others in their community? It takes a great deal of faith and trusting God to work in the hearts of the people He has chosen. This means following the leading of God and knowing when He is working and where He is not working.

In 1 Samuel 16:7 we read, "But the Lord said unto Samuel, 'Look not on his countenance, or on the height of his stature; because I have refused him: for the Lord seeth not as man seeth; for man looketh on the outward appearance, but the Lord looketh on the heart.'" I could look at people and try to figure out who was the most spiritual. I failed because I did not see the heart of man like God does. We needed to follow God and have Him lead us to the people with whom He was working.

Sometimes, as I walked down my driveway and headed into town, I prayed a short prayer; "Lord, lead me to where you want me to go." I headed up the road and the Lord led me. The still small voice of the Holy Spirit would speak and tell me where to go. He was specific, when I listened.

There were times I argued with the Lord. I said things like, "But, Lord, they drink a lot" or "They are hard to talk to." I would walk right on by and head to another house only to find them not home. Then I started to listen to the Lord and go where He wanted. I like to say I am never like Jonah, but the truth is, Jonah and I are very similar. In the Bible, we read how the Lord told Jonah to go and preach God's coming judgment on the people of Nineveh. (Jonah 1:1-17) He decided, instead, to go the opposite direction and disobey God. He thought he had been able to get away with his disobedience until the Lord sent a huge storm to get his attention. You can read more of his story in the book that bears his name in the Bible. I have learned over the years, God sometimes uses drastic measures to get our attention.

As I trusted God, He led me to the right people. As I listened to the Lord, we began to meet people the Lord was bringing closer to His Kingdom. I remember one lady Gwendy was talking to. She knew we were Christians, but wanted nothing to do with the Lord. She and Gwendy went for a walk one day. At the start of the walk, the lady laid out some ground rules. She said, "I do not want to hear anything about God. You do not need to preach to me." Gwendy listened and continued on the walk. By the end of the walk, the lady was asking Gwendy what she believed. She soon became one of the ones to attend the Bible study in our home.

We had a desire to see the children come to know Christ and pursued being able to hold a weekly Bible Club in the school. The Lord had already been preparing the heart of the principal. He not only agreed to our holding it there; he also gave us the key to the school and said, "Do whatever you want." He invited us to take part in the annual Christmas program, even having us read the Christmas story from Luke 2.

It did not happen overnight, but in His time, the Lord was bringing people into a right relationship with Him. There was a fellow I visited whom I had heard was a believer. He had quite a testimony about how the Lord had saved him from a life of alcohol. There was no doubt the Lord was working in his life. Yet, whenever we invited him to attend one of our Bible studies or events he never came.

One day, I felt the Lord asking me to stop by his house in the middle of the day. I stopped what I was doing and went right to his home. As I walked in, I prayed for him. Little did I realize what that simple prayer had done in his life. Before I had arrived, he had taken a puff on a marijuana joint. He said he felt the darkness closing in on him. As I prayed, he had confessed his sin to the Lord and surrendered to His control. The Lord continued to work in his heart as we prayed for him. In time, he became a dedicated follower of Christ.

While we had a church building fully equipped for us to use, we hesitated in starting to hold church services for several years. We did not want to be playing church. We wanted to hold services because the people of the community knew they needed to have fellowship with each other. We held special services on Easter and Christmas. We spent the majority of our time holding Bible studies, visiting homes, teaching Kids Bible Club and working with people one on one.

The church is more than a building- It is God's people.

As we kept working with individuals, we prayed for the Lord to lead us to the proper time to start official services. It was hard not to have church when church is something we were both so accustomed to. Over the course of five years, we had a group of faithful believers who were growing in their faith. As they grew in their walk with the Lord, they started asking when we were going to start having church.

In 2005, the Lord brought two Christian government workers to our community. They had a strong faith in the Lord and a deep desire for fellowship. They pushed us to start holding regular weekly services. After considerable prayer we went ahead and started having services.

The first few years of services were ones of considerable ups and downs. We knew there would be at least the five of us there. Beyond that, we could have two or as many as ten others, depending on the Sunday. It was good to be in the house of the Lord each week. It was even greater to see people coming and developing a stronger relationship with the Lord.

The one thing I often struggle as a missionary/pastor is this – how do we instill the desire to do more than just come to church in the hearts of people? How do we inspire them to be active for the Lord? How do we get them to want to be a part of what is happening instead of watching what we do?

To many around the world, and even in our community, church seems like a spectator sport. The thinking is *I come and sing, but it is the missionary/pastor's responsibility to lead the singing, preach the message, and tell us what to do.* I praise the Lord for the people to whom He has given a heart to serve Him and take part with His work. Without them, there would be no church.

It seemed to us that the people were hesitant to get involved in the church. Much of their hesitation came from the fact that they thought we would live in Ross River for only a short time. They figured we would leave after a few years and move to another place of ministry. The first minister who had come in the 1960s had done a great work in leading people to the Lord through evangelism. Soon after the work was going well, God led him to go somewhere else. The people who were a part of the church, at that point, felt betrayed. They did not want to become involved with church again only to have the pastor/missionary leave.

It took our living in Ross River for eight years and two trips to and from New York before things changed. It was only after this time that people began to realize, we were not planning on going anywhere unless God led us. They needed to see us keep coming back before they were going to pour their lives into the ministry.

We kept trusting God to work in the hearts of the people He wanted in His ministry. It was His work and He accomplished His purpose, His way. We had to be like Abraham and go as the Lord showed us the path.

When God first called Abraham in Genesis 12:1, God told him to go to a land that, "I will show you." He called Abraham to follow Him, but He did not tell him where he was to go. He asked Abraham to step out in faith. As he trusted the Lord and followed Him, God made the path clearer to him. As we trusted the Lord enough to follow Him, He continued to work and change people for His glory. We love to see Him molding people into His image, as the potter does with the clay.

The old log church

Chapter 15

GOD GIVES FRUIT IN MINISTRY

"Broad is the way that leads to destruction, narrow is the way that leads to eternal life and few there be that find it." (Matthew 7:13-14)

O ne ministry that has affected many people in Ross River is Kamp Klondike. Each summer we crammed as many kids as we could into our vehicle and drove three hundred and fifty miles to Bible Camp on the outskirts of Dawson City. As a Summer Missionary in the 1990s, I served as a counselor at Kamp Klondike and gained a great appreciation for its purpose. Since the 1970s, SEND missionaries and the folks at Dawson City Community Gospel Chapel have had the same vision; to give the children of Dawson City and other communities of the Yukon a deeper understanding of who Jesus Christ is.

The camp started as little more than a couple wall tents and a small cook's kitchen with a screened-in eating area. Screens were a necessity because of the countless bloodthirsty mosquitoes, which loved the mossy area around the camp. The screens did one of two things. They either kept the mosquitoes outside or they helped to trap them inside. This depended on how long the campers left the door open. The "cabins" were ten-by-twelve-foot wall tents draped over wood platforms. Each summer, ten to fifteen kids descended on the camp for a week of canoeing, archery, stilts, and crafts.

Since the very beginning, the activities of camp were secondary to the real purpose of the it. Kamp Klondike existed and still exists to make sure the children who attend the camp know how to come to a true faith in

Jesus Christ. The fun for the kids was important, but even more important was seeing the children come to grips with who Jesus Christ is and what He had done for them. No camper could ever leave Kamp Klondike and say they had not heard about what Jesus did for them on the cross.

As I shared earlier, during my upbringing we had spent many hours at LeTourneau Christian Conference Center on Canandaigua Lake. It was there I had recommitted my life to the Lord. I fell in love with camp at LeTourneau, but it was at Kamp Klondike where I saw first-hand how effective and necessary camp was in the life of children.

When we moved into Ross River, we looked forward to being able to take the kids from our community to Kamp Klondike. For many of the young people we took to camp, it was their only exposure to the outside world. Many of the children who came to camp lived in isolated communities. The time they spend at camp allows them to make friends with kids from other communities.

The love they get to experience and the teachings they receive are invaluable. For many who come, they get to spend one week not having to worry about a relative coming home under the influence of drugs or alcohol. They do not have to worry about someone pushing them out of bed and disturbing their sleep. They get to experience the love and peace of Christ. This is something few get to experience in their everyday lives. They can enjoy the week of fun activities, good food, lots of Bible teaching, new friends, and much more.

Kids by the canoe pond at Kamp Klondike

The first summer, we piled our family – at the time only four of us – into our Chevy Suburban with four kids from Ross River. The following summer, we doubled and took eight. Each summer, the number grew.

One such summer, we had more kids than we could fit in the Suburban, so we drove the car along as well. The sun shone brightly as we pulled out of Ross River. The twelve kids were blurry-eyed from waking up before nine in the morning; especially since some had gone to bed only a few hours earlier.

I must say, until this point, ministry had been wonderful. We were getting used to living in a small community. We loved the fact that we could work with various age groups. Our ministry did not focus just on the children, although in the summer it did take the majority of our time. We also held a weekly Kids Bible Club in the school during the winter. Our desire was to take what the kids learned at camp and build off that through the winter and vice versa. Each ministry complimenting the other. Usually the children were well behaved, respected the rules, and enjoyed being with us.

The trip from Ross River to Kamp Klondike takes around seven to eight hours, depending on how many stops we made. One stop we often take is in the town of Carmacks. It has a nice campground where we can let the kids run for a while as we get their lunch together. Lunch is usually Gwendy's delicious homemade bread, slathered with homemade peach, raspberry, or strawberry jelly and peanut butter. Rice crispy treats or homemade chocolate chip cookies and a juice box make the lunch complete.

As we were getting lunch together, we noticed two of the children were not staying with the group. They wanted to do their own thing. When we asked them if they could listen to the rules they responded negatively and showed no respect for us. At this point, Gwendy and I talked about whether we should take them home. The rest could fit in the suburban and one of us could take the other two back. We did not want to see them miss out on an opportunity to hear the Gospel, but we worried about the trouble they were going to make for us and the others at the camp if they continued on with us.

We never had to face this before and our hearts have always been to see the children reached with the Gospel and learn what it means to follow

Him. After talking it over, we decided to continue on with the whole group. Things did not get any better during the rest of the trip or when we got to camp for supper time.

It did not take us long to see those two kids had no intention of respecting us or the rules of the camp. They asked to use the outhouse to go smoke. They made disruptions during chapel and left as many times as they could. It was hard to see such young kids hardened by what they desired. No matter how hard we tried to be nice and show them love, they responded with disobedience and disrespect.

It was evident to all the staff and counselors these two were not there to learn or to obey the camp rules. They were there to run their own lives. They wanted no one to tell them what to do or what not to do. The Devil was not only keeping them from listening, he was using them to keep the remaining approximately thirty-four kids from hearing the truth.

Never before had we not been able to reason with kids. Never before had we seen such hardened attitudes. Never before had we seen the Devil so hard at work to destroy not only these two lives, but also all those who were there for the week of camp. We knew Jesus' words, "The thief cometh not, but to *steal*, and to *kill*, and to *destroy*" (John 10:10), but to see it happening right in front of us in such vivid color was hard to take. Did these children not see what was happening? Did they not see how much we loved them? How could they be choosing to leave a place of safety, fun, and love?

Nothing seemed to get through to them. From Sunday evening through Tuesday evening, we worked with these two, trying to see some type of breakthrough. On Tuesday evening, the director came to us and said, "Those two have to go." They were ruining the whole mood at camp. We knew the director was right, but what would this do for our ministry? What would their parents say when they found out? How were they going to respond?

Gwendy and I decided I would leave camp first thing in the morning. I could drive them home and be able to make it back by late evening to continue on with the rest of camp. I guess two out of twelve were not bad odds. We still had ten others who had come. They could enjoy the rest of the week. We prayed for them to find the life Jesus talked about in John

10:10, "I am come that they might have life, and that they might have it more abundantly." Oh, how we prayed for their souls.

The next morning, after breakfast, the disciplined campers loaded their belongings into the Suburban. Along with them, six others from Ross River brought their belongings too. While they did not have to leave, they were making a choice to follow those two and leave the camp. The impact of this blow hit us hard. How could these kids leave a loving, peaceful, kind, God-honoring environment?

It was a picture of the Garden of Eden all over again. God had made Adam and Eve perfect. He gave them everything they needed or desired. They walked in daily communion with God, Himself. They knew no shame, no pain, no loss, or sorrow and yet they chose to disobey God.

Did these children not see the hope we had in Christ? Did they not care where they were going? As I was loading the luggage into the Suburban, another one of our campers came over and said, "Tim, do you think I should stay?" Of course, I wanted him to stay. Camp was where he could hear the truth. Camp was where he could learn what it means to be set free from a life bound by the slavery of sin. I knew what I wanted him to do, but I wanted him to do it for the right reasons. Looking at him and not wanting to push him to a decision, I said, "It is up to you. I think you should stay, but you have to choose."

I left him to think about it and finished getting the vehicle ready for the long trip down the highway. I said a quick prayer for him. My prayer was, "Lord, let him see his need to stay." But, as I often do when I pray, I doubted whether he would. Discouragement flooded over me.

If I was going to make it back before midnight, I was going to have to leave soon. With less than a minute left he looked at me and said, "I think I am going to stay." I was overjoyed. God had answered my cry. God had snatched one of his children from the claws of the evil one.

As I have thought over this story in the years which have gone by, I am reminded of these words, "Broad is the way that leads to destruction, narrow is the way that leads to eternal life..." (Matthew 7:13-14). In life and ministry, it should not surprise us when many people choose to make decisions against God's desire for them. Jesus went on later in this verse to say, "there are few who find the path" which leads to eternal life.

My friend who almost left did more than stay for the rest of the week.

He listened intently to the Bible lessons each morning. With fervor, he heard the evening chapel messages. God worked in his heart. Later on, he chose to follow the narrow path which leads to eternal life. He found what it means to have abundant life. *We may have lost eight during the week of camp, but the angels were rejoicing over the one sinner who repented.*

To this day, Kamp Klondike Bible Camp continues to impact the lives of children and counselors alike. Instead of ten to fifteen campers from Dawson City for one week, the camp runs for three weeks. During those three weeks, between seventy and ninety kids hear the Gospel each summer. Instead of only being for the children of Dawson City, kids from Ross River, Yukon, and Ft. McPherson, Northwest Territory (NWT) also have the chance to attend. The camp only allows kids from communities where a missionary or pastor is present. Their desire is to see kids not only come to know Jesus as their Savior, they also want them to become part of the local church wherever they live.

In 2000, a beautiful, insulated dining hall replaced the screened in lean-too dining hall. The new dining hall can serve up to forty-five kids plus staff each week. Eight cabins replaced the two wall tents. Bunk beds replaced the bed rolls on the hard floor. The campfire pit where kids used to sit and become mosquito bait each evening for chapel time has been replaced with a screened in chapel with an all-weather game floor.

Cabins at Kamp Klondike

While the facilities have changed over the years to accommodate more children, the mission and vision of the camp has remained the same. The main staff of the camp come from the Dawson City Community Chapel. Many of them have been working at the camp each summer since the first summer in the 70s. Their passion and love for the Lord is evident as they start each week of camp. To them, it is a matter of life and death. They want to make sure each child has the opportunity to receive Christ as their Lord and Savior. Without them, countless young people would not have come to know Christ in a personal way.

Chapter 16

GOD GIVES LOVE FOR MINISTRY

*"Lo, children are a heritage of the LORD: and the fruit of the womb
is his reward, As arrows are in the hand of a mighty man; so are
children of the youth." (Psalm 127:3)*

In today's narcissistic culture, it is easy to get stuck thinking children
are a bother. Taking care of them can be seen as one more task added
to our already full "to-do" list. Even I, a product of good parents who
showed immense love, can forget the children around me who do not come
from good homes. I can get so caught up in the ministry and become
like Jesus' disciples in Matthew 19. The people brought children to see
Jesus, but His disciples tried to send them away. They felt Jesus had more
important things to do.

I have been thankful over the years for Gwendy's perspective on
children. While I grew up in a secure home with a dad and mom present
most of the time, Gwendy grew up in a home where her mom was left to
care for her and her brothers. Her dad worked out of town and only came
home on the weekends. While he loved his children, his own personal
struggles sometimes caused Gwendy to long for a more stable and secure
home life.

My dad worked hard to provide for his family. We could not wait for
him to get home each evening and spend time with us. Sometimes we
wrestled on the floor of the living room, other evenings we played hide
and seek in the big old farm house. He gave much of the time when he
was not working to show us his love and how important we were to him.

He showed us the importance of hard work and a job done well. More importantly, he showed us the love and affection we desired and needed.

Our moms held similar roles as they held the families together while our dads worked. Gwendy's mother did all she could do to protect and care for her four kids. Her time on earth was cut short when she lost her battle with cancer just days after Gwendy turned sixteen.

My mom sacrificed much to raise us. She homeschooled all four of us. She started teaching me in ninth grade and gave us all a great education. She continued to be a powerful force in my life through her prayers and encouragement, even into my adult life.

Our upbringing has a great deal to do with how we live our lives. When we started in ministry, I trusted everyone. The evil that happens behind closed doors never crossed my mind. My home had been safe and secure. My ignorance and lack of exposure kept me blinded to the evil around us. For Gwendy, the things she had endured had opened her eyes to the atrocities that can happen when people choose not to follow God in their lives. Trust was something a person had to earn, it was not something to throw at those who did not deserve it.

When it came to raising our children, protecting them from harm was always at the top of her list of priorities. She wanted to keep our children from facing the same things she had to face. Her passion to protect children made her aware of those who might need a safe place to go. For this reason, our home has often been a safe haven.

Many of the children in our community have spent a night or two or more in our home. It is not uncommon for a child or two to come and ask us if they can sleep over on a Friday night. Usually it is not because they want the joy of spending a night with our kids. They often ask because they do not feel safe going to their own home. On occasion kids will say, "Dad or Mom is drinking...Can I stay with you?" Many times, they try to hide the real reason for desiring to come to our home.

There is never a dull moment at our home.

We have also opened our home as foster parents. Parents sometimes need a break from the rigors of raising their children. They will give us the privilege of caring for them. The kids may be with us for a weekend or even two weeks. At other times, there are issues in the home and mom or dad need to get personal help. Children have come live with us for longer periods of time. This may be one month or as long as six months.

It seems like we have a revolving door and never know who is going to be at our extra-large oak table. Our regular visitors have a toothbrush with their name on it in the bathroom. Some even have a pair of pajamas in the dresser. Everyone receives a smile and is shown the love of Christ.

Over the years, our children have developed a great love for the children we have taken in. Some have become like brothers and sisters to them. When someone asks how many kids we have, it is easy to say, "we have five to whom we gave birth." After that, the numbers get a bit fuzzy.

We have an "adopted" daughter, Janelle, who served as a Summer Missionary. She and our kids fell in love with each other. At the end of the summer, we threw her a surprise party for her twenty-first birthday. It was the first party she ever had. During the party, we gave her a "Certificate of Adoption to the Colwell Family." Little did we know how that simple act of kindness would affect her. She had a very challenging upbringing and the love we showed to her encouraged her greatly. She spent a couple Christmases with us before beginning her own family. She and her wonderful husband have made us proud grandparents of three gorgeous children in Alaska. There are many more whom the Lord has allowed us to have a significant impact on their lives.

We are the proud parents of a master's degree student. With pride and joy we have seen many of our "children" learn to drive and receive their driver's license. These come after rough stops, nail biting moments, and scary trips around town. We have waited anxiously for the birth of several of our "grandchildren" as former foster children become parents. Some have invited us to be part of the birth. It is such a joy to be a part of welcoming their child into this world. All this and more comes from a willingness to take care of children other than the ones we gave birth to.

Jocelyn, Janelle, and Jessie

A couple years ago we attended a graduation ceremony for one of our "children." With joy, we accepted the invitation as we thought back to the time we had with this individual. The memories we have are not always joyful. There have been rough and tough times when we felt like giving up. Through it all, the Lord has brought strength and peace as we trust Him to help us care for His little ones.

Our home has always been very structured. Routine is a big part of our everyday life. Like clockwork, I woke the school-aged kids each morning and helped them get ready for school. By eight-fifty-five they were in the community school to spend the morning learning with their friends and neighbors. Since there was no cafeteria at the school, all the kids went home for lunch. They got one hour. Then it was back to school. In the afternoons, we often had community kids join our children. They loved to play inside our home during the winter when it was minus forty. In the spring and summer, they played in our spacious backyard. In the evening, we had family time or Bible studies, depending on which day of the week it was. The kids did not have time to get bored. Our home thrived on doing things together.

One day we got a call from the social worker. One of the parents in our community was struggling to take care of their four children. The oldest was in their teens and the youngest was still a toddler. He asked if we would be willing to take the children for a two-week trial. After talking it over and praying about it, Gwendy and I decided to take the kids for two weeks. After that time, we let the social worker know if we could do it long-term.

We had three kids of our own who kept us busy. The oldest was around ten years old and the youngest was around six. They lived a structured life. The kids we welcomed into our home had lived a life of freedom. Much of the time, they could go where they wanted, when they wanted, how they wanted. The struggle that took place the first week was extremely hard. We did try to keep all four in the beginning, but the oldest wanted no one to tell her where to go or what to do. We spent a couple of days looking for her after school. She did not want to be a part of our home. After a week, the social worker relieved us of the responsibility of caring for her.

The next oldest wanted to follow in her sibling's path. She asked to go out after school. When asked why she said something like, "just to wander with friends." We encouraged her to come and play with our kids. They always had fun in the afternoon. They built forts, played games, kicked a ball around the yard, and whatever else they could find to do. The first three days were a battle every afternoon. Why did she have to be different from everyone else? We were ready to pull our hair out with frustration. There was no way we could do this long-term. It was not going to work. Our kids were struggling with the lack of structure, the others with too much structure. The tension was killing us. We were about to call the social worker and say, "This is not going to work."

As we committed the matter to the Lord in prayer and asked for wisdom, He began to work. He gave us wisdom and direction. Amazing things started to happen. As we were firm but loving, the kids started to notice, the rules were not bad. There was safety in the rules. Instead of wandering the streets, they filled their time playing in the grassy yard. The structure they thought they hated was giving them the stability they needed. The confines of the backyard gave them the peace that had been absent from their lives. They enjoyed the three-square meals each day and eating their vegetables. (Well, most did. One tried to hide green beans in his clothes so he did not have to eat them.)

The two weeks turned into a month. The month turned into two months. Before we knew it, the three kids had spent six months with us. We never did make the phone call asking for the social worker to find another home. The children never asked to leave. God blended us all together as one big, happy family. In time, the kids were able to reunite with their mom.

Of course, the time was not without its challenges. Anytime there are seven kids under thirteen years old living under one roof, there are bound to be difficulties. At times, there were wars for attention. But all in all, our kids enjoyed having the extended family. Our children started to see the others as their brothers and sisters. Things calmed down. In fact, to this day they see them as their brothers and sisters.

What was even greater than this change was the change that took place within the hearts of the children. Our children learned what it means to show love to the "orphans and widows" of the world. They learned what it was like to have to share their possessions and space with others.

The children who came to live with us learned about Jesus. From our day-to-day teaching and talking about the Lord to how He helped to take care of us, we shared Christ openly with them. They learned more by going to church and Kid's Bible Club. They saw our example as we prayed at meal times. They heard the Bible as we read devotions before bed. They listened and the truths of the Scriptures began to take root in them.

After a few months, one of the children came to Gwendy. She started asking questions about Jesus and what it meant to have a relationship with Him. Gwendy was able to lead the child into a personal walk with the Lord as Savior of her life. In the years that have followed, these three have not doubled our trouble. They have doubled our blessing.

Trusting God in the midst of a difficult situation is never easy; especially if we like to be in control. When the house is in chaos it is easy to want to give up or throw in the towel. In James 1:3-4, we read, "Knowing this, that the trying of your faith worketh patience. But let patience have her perfect work, that ye may be perfect and entire, wanting nothing." If we had not chosen to endure those first two weeks of absolute madness, we would have missed what God had in store for us. As we trusted God to lead us and direct us, He not only gave us the help we needed, He also changed hearts. We received another blessing of an extended, growing family.

"Unless the LORD builds the house, those who build it labor in vain. Unless the LORD watches over the city, the watchman stays awake in vain. It is in vain that you rise up early and go late to rest, eating the bread of anxious toil; for he gives to his beloved sleep. Behold, children are a heritage from the LORD, the fruit of the womb a reward. Like arrows in the hand of a warrior are the children of one's youth. Blessed is the man who fills his quiver with them!" (Psalm 127:1-5 ESV)

Whether it is foster kids, Summer Missionaries, or Interns, there is always lots of love to go around. Michelle, Jessica, and Sarah (SMP and Interns) with our children.

109

Chapter 17

GOD GIVES FAITH FOR MINSTRY

"If ye have faith as a grain of mustard seed, ye shall say unto this mountain, Remove hence to yonder place; and it shall remove; and nothing shall be impossible unto you." (Matthew 17:20)

We have all heard sermons speaking about mountain-moving faith. We have all heard stories of people who had enough faith to move a mountain. We have all listened with a touch of disbelief to stories told about how God came through miraculously during someone's time of need.

Growing up, I heard the story about a church who was having parking lot troubles. Their lot was way too small for the plethora of people who had been coming out to worship together. They needed to expand to allow for more cars to park. They had one problem, a mountain of sorts. They had a huge hill in the way of their progress.

The estimates from well-meaning, earth-moving companies began to trickle in, but the cost was much higher than the modest budget of the church. So, they did what we all should do. They prayed in faith believing God could move their "mountain." Shortly after they began committing their mountain to the Lord in faith, God moved the mountain. A highway project was going through their area and the contractor needed a large amount of fill. He came with his equipment and moved the mountain for free. The church had their parking lot and it cost them nothing to have the mountain moved. God provided what they needed when they needed it most.

As we listen to stories like this, we say, "I wish I had faith that large." I know in my own life, my faith in what God can do is much smaller than I wish it was. I know what it is to trust God for things. We never had a lot when I was growing up, but we knew what we had was from God's bountiful hand. Was He not the one who "owns the cattle on a thousand hills?" I felt like even though I trusted the Lord to a certain extent, I did not have mountain-moving faith. I still doubted God in many ways. He always met our needs according to His riches in glory, through Christ Jesus my Lord. (Philippians 4:13)

One night, while reading through the Gospels, I came to the passage that talked about having enough faith in God to be able to move mountains. During this devotion time, the Lord began to challenge me to trust Him to an even greater degree. In the quietness of my bedroom, I prayed, "Lord, increase my faith." Little did I know how those words would later affect my decisions the next day and what God would show me. I learned the hard way, He is worthy of *all* my trust, for everything.

The next morning, I had to leave home and drive five hours into Whitehorse to pick up a student who needed to come home. I had to make a round trip on this day as we had Wednesday evening Bible Study at seven. The clock in the car told me it was just after seven when I left. If I did not have any troubles, I would have plenty of time to get into Whitehorse and return for Bible Study.

As I pulled out of the driveway, I looked at the gas gauge and my heart sank. I only had about three-eighths of a tank of gas. Our gas station in town did not open until nine, and if I waited, there was no way to get back for Bible Study. I knew if I was to make the ten-hour round trip, I needed to get going. As I looked again at the gauge, I thought about what the Lord had challenged me with the night before. Was He asking me to step out in faith and trust Him? As I pulled out of town I repeated the prayer I prayed the night before, "Lord increase my faith."

Driving down the Robert Campbell highway toward Faro, I began to question my sanity. I doubted how far our fuel-efficient Chevy Cavalier would go. Part of me was wishing I had stopped at our friend's home on the way out of town while the other part of me was curious to see what the Lord would do. As I continued on my way I kept praying.

Halfway through the hour drive to Faro, I looked at the gauge and said to myself, "If I am still at the quarter-tank mark at the turnoff I am going to continue going toward Whitehorse." My eyes focused on the fuel gauge. The fuel needle seemed to be glued in its place until a quarter mile from the junction of the road leading into Faro. Almost on cue, as I got to the corner, the gauge dropped. I had under a quarter of a tank of gas. I was faced with the dilemma that we often face. If I went in and got gas, I would never know what God could do. If I did not get gas, I may end up stranded along the side of the road for a while. What should I do?

I should mention here, I am in no way saying you should pray for more gas when God has given you the knowledge and understanding of how far the car will go. On this day, I knew the Lord was telling me the same thing He had told the people of Israel. He challenged them in Malachi 3:10, about paying Him His portion of the tithe. He said, "Bring ye all the tithes into the storehouse, that there may be meat in mine house, and *prove me now* herewith, saith the Lord of hosts, if I will not open you the windows of heaven, and pour you out a blessing, that there shall not be room enough to receive it." (emphasis added)

Like never before in my life, I felt God challenging me to be willing to step out into the impossible and test Him in ways I had never been willing to before. His desire for me was to be willing to get out of my comfort zone and to trust Him. I did know the car did not have enough gas. I did know where I could get gas. I also knew what God had placed on my heart the night before. Even as I drove, He was challenging me to trust him more.

I drove right past the turnoff and continued heading toward the next community, Carmacks, one and a half hours away. Part of me was saying, "you are so stupid," while the other part of me was praying, "Lord, increase my faith." My mind went to the story of Elijah and the widow's oil that never ran out until the time God brought rain on the earth (1 Kings 17:13-14).

Elijah and the people of Israel had been going through a difficult time. Famine had ravished the land. Elijah was hungry. As he enters the city of Zarephath, he met a widow who is picking up sticks to make her last meal. She was about to run out of food and was preparing to cook the last bit of bread for her and her son. Elijah told her to cook a meal for him first and then cook for her and her son. The widow did as Elijah asked and her oil and flour never ran out until the famine was over. My prayer was, "Lord let my gas be like the widow's oil. May it not run out until I get to Carmacks, even if I have to coast into the gas station.

As I drove down the spruce-lined highway mile by mile, a battle continued to rage in my mind and soul. Was this the smart thing to do? Should I have gone into Faro and gotten gas? The further I drove, the more I began to doubt, but still the prayer of my heart was, "Lord, increase my faith."

As I neared the halfway point to Carmacks, the faith I had diminished. My faith tank was as empty as my fuel tank. The needle of the gas gauge went down much faster than I had hoped and prayed. I knew I was in trouble if "I did not do something." So, I did what we often do when God asks us to step out in faith. I began to look for my own solution to fix the problem. Along the side of the road in a gravel pull-out, a diesel truck sat idling. Inside, a construction worker lay in his bed enjoying the last few moments of shut-eye before his day started. The smell of the diesel fumes filled my nose as I knocked on his door and asked if he had any gas. My hopes were dashed as he told me, "No." I was not surprised. Why would he? He was driving a diesel truck!

I had a desire to have faith the size of Elijah's when he called fire down from heaven. (1 Kings 18:20-40) In reality, the doubt of Thomas (John 20:25) filled my mind. I pulled back onto the road and continued my prayer of, "Lord, increase my faith," while wondering what I was going to do when I did not make it to the next town. I had already figured out the end of the story. God was going to let me down. I had trusted Him, but this misplaced trust was going to leave me stranded.

Even as I write this, I realize how much I doubt God on a regular basis. I have a desire to see God show me what He can do, but am unwilling to step out in faith and go through what is uncomfortable. I have made fun of Peter in Sunday School and church for almost drowning when he asked Jesus to tell him to come. But, would I have had enough nerve to step to the edge of the boat? I would have been like the rest of the disciples. I would sit in the comfort of the boat and wait for the Lord to join me. God is often asking us to get out of our comfort zones and trust Him. He wants to show us what He can do when we trust Him completely.

As I continued to plot out the end of the story, I had an idea. I knew exactly how I could fix "God's problem." On the left-hand side of the road, I saw a sign for a campground. I knew the campground very well. Gwendy and I had stopped in there on occasion. The campground was at the edge of a gorgeous lake where large trout loved to swim. Fishermen from all over the territory came to this spot to relax while seeing if they could catch some fish. There were always campers, boats and people in the campground. Few fishermen that I know leave home without gas to spare. Someone would have enough gas to get me out of my predicament.

The car bumped down the one and a quarter mile gravel road leading to the campground by the pristine water's edge. The fog was rolling off the lake as I made my way through site after site. Each one was like my gas tank, empty. Not one person was fishing, not one camper sat parked in the midst of twenty-thirty sites. Not one tourist was enjoying the sound of the water lapping against the shore. I had never seen it so empty; even to this day, there are always people there. On that day, there were no boats, people, campers, and definitely, no gas. I had made a wasted trip to fill my faith (gas) tank my way.

I made the one and a quarter mile back onto the dusty road and onto the highway, and still had to travel forty-five minutes before I reached Carmacks. Not long after pulling onto the highway, it happened. The bright orange low fuel light came on letting me know I should do what I already knew I should have done – get gas. Normally in our car, we have about twenty minutes of driving when the fuel light comes on. Yes, we had run out of gas before; not trying to grow our faith, but because we had not been aware of the amount of gas in the tank before we left for a trip.

Still I prayed, "Lord, let my gas be like the widow's oil. May it not run out until I can coast into the gas station at Carmacks." I did not ask for a lot. I only wanted enough to coast into Carmacks. The battle was still raging in my mind between trust and doubt. I knew the reality of the situation, but wanted to experience the unknown blessing of a steadfast faith.

Yes, it happened, before I got into Carmacks; the fuel pump sucked every last drop out of the tank. I coasted to a stop within sight of Carmacks. Just down the road from where the car stopped sat a campground and restaurant nestled in the tall, black spruce trees. Dejected, I trudged along the road until I found the owner who offered me a jerry can so I could get the gas I needed. I lost an hour between the time it took me to walk to the campground, get the gas jug, go to the gas station and then get back to the car and drive back into Carmacks.

After I got on my way again, I clocked how far it was from where I coasted to a stop to where the gas station was. The car had stopped the exact distance I had taken on my side trip into the campground to fix things my way. The wasted two and a half miles to fix things my way had cost me an hour of time and helped me learn a valuable lesson – trust God and do not doubt.

I'd like to say I learned my lesson. I like to think of myself as a superhero of faith like those written about in Hebrews 11 in the Biblical Hall of Faith. God did teach me through this incident to trust Him in an even greater way. He taught me He is worthy to be trusted for everything, every day, and in every way. There are still times when we have fallen prey to the doubts of a double-minded man. We are like the man in the Bible to whom Jesus said, "Do you believe?" and he responded, "Lord, I believe, help my unbelief." (Mark 9:23-24)

Lord, we believe, please help our unbelief.

Chapter 18

GOD GIVES FORGIVENESS IN MINISTRY

"'For the invisible things of Him from the creation of the world are clearly seen, being understood by the things that are made, even his eternal power and Godhead; so that they are without excuse: Because that, when they knew God, they glorified Him not as God, neither were thankful; but became vain in their imaginations, and their foolish heart was darkened." (Romans 1:20-21)

One of the things our family has enjoyed on a regular basis while living in the Yukon is the vast wilderness. A drive of ten minutes out of town in any direction gives us the feeling we are in the middle of nowhere. The beauty of God's creation surrounds us in brilliant splendor everywhere we turn.

To the south, we can travel the South Canol Road into the St. Cyr mountain range. This mountain range is an extension of the Canadian Rockies and has snow on the highest peaks most of the year. About fifty miles from Ross River are the beautiful blue green waters of Lapie Lakes, one of our favorite spots to go. These lakes sit nestled in the mountains. Even in the heat of the summer, the air coming off the lakes is cool and refreshing.

To the east/west we have the Robert Campbell Hwy. To the eest, one can travel through two hundred and forty-five miles of untouched wilderness. The only buildings along this road are cabins built by local people who like to get out of town. To the west, our nearest town is Faro, which is forty-five miles away.

To the north across the Pelly River, we have the North Canol Road.

The road leads two hundred and seventy-nine miles from Ross River to the Northwest Territories (NWT) border and is one of the most diversified roads around. In Ross River, the road starts along the Pelly and Ross Rivers. After a couple hours of dense spruce forest and wide expanses of willows, the beauty of the Itzi and Sheldon Mountains rise near the road. These spectacular snowcapped mountains stand tall against the background of the bright blue Yukon sky. Past the mountains, the road continues to wind almost aimlessly along the Macmillan River.

The road itself follows the trail blazed by the US Army in 1943. Toward the end of World War II, it was thought that oil reserves would be needed. The US ran a pipeline from oil wells from Norman Wells in NWT all the way to Whitehorse to get oil to the refinery. The road helped maintain the pipeline for its short lifespan. Due to the ending of the war, oil needs diminished. If history is true, the machines that helped lay the pipeline used more oil than ever flowed through the pipe.

Although the pipeline shut down in 1945, the road has continued to be one of the most beautiful drives in the Yukon. Every summer/fall people from all over the world come through Ross River to drive the legendary Canol Road. The far end of the road in NWT has become the Canol Heritage Trail. There are International tourists from Germany and Sweden who have hiked and biked the whole length of the old Canol Pipeline. It is a wonderful trip for people who like isolation and battling mosquitoes.

The tourists are not the only ones who love to drive the Canol Road. Many of the locals love to travel the road in hopes of finding a moose crossing in the early morning or late evening hours. The north end of the road is a favorite hunting spot for caribou. It is a spectacular sight to see a herd of caribou crossing the tundra and know your family will have meat to live on for the winter.

From the first time I came into the Yukon to now, I have been awestruck with the beauty of this land we call home. Many times, I have looked at a magnificent sunset or a jagged mountain and wondered how people can look at such majestic scenery and say, "This simply evolved." God's fingerprints are all around us. The Psalmist was right when he wrote Psalms 113:3, "From the rising of the sun unto the going down of the same the Lord's name is to be praised." God shows Himself in the creation around us.

I am reminded of Romans 1:20. In this verse we read, "For His invisible attributes, namely, His eternal power and divine nature, have been clearly perceived, ever since the creation of the world, in the things that have been made. So, they are without excuse." No one can see the beauty around us and not see the hand of an Almighty Creator.

One of the many times I got to enjoy the beauty around us was in the fall when I got to go hunting with Rod (not his real name), one of the Native men from our community. For weeks, he had been after me to go on a caribou hunting trip with him up the North Canol. He and his family had a "tent frame" at the NWT border. (A tent frame is usually built using two-by-fours as the frame and plywood for the floor. Most of the time, the walls are made out of plywood or plastic, depending on how warm a person wants them to be. The frames were made for people to stretch a canvas tent over. Nowadays, people from the Yukon often stretch a tarp over the wood frame as a simple shelter from the elements.)

We left Ross River shortly after noon and began the eight-hour drive toward the NWT border. The distance to the tent frame was two hundred and fifty miles. The extremely rough road conditions only allowed us to travel between thirty to forty mph at top speed. The journey took most of a day.

The road may be long, but the views are like none other. The snowcapped mountains, blue-green lakes, vast stands of willows and spruce, and winding river valleys made the trip well worth the time. At spots, the road is not much wider than the width of one vehicle and the trees hang over it, making it look like a tunnel.

The temperatures for the trip could not have been better. In mid-August, it can freeze in the high country. During the trip, we had excellent weather. It was not too hot to spoil any meat we got, but was not too cold to make it uncomfortable when we were out on the land. Best of all, there was a slight breeze helping to keep the mosquitoes from overwhelming us.

By the time we made our way up the winding North Canol and reached the "tent frame," it was almost completely dark. It did not matter, we came equipped with flashlights and had the light of the truck to work under. We went to work and soon, we were ready to go to bed.

The "tent frame" stood at the far end of a gravel pull-off almost sitting on the border between NWT/Yukon. It was one of several similar structures in the area. This structure consisted of two-by-four walls covered with plywood. A thin blue tarp lay over the rafters to form the roof and was about twelve feet wide-by-sixteen feet long. There was no insulation in the walls, but a wood stove heated it with no problem. Even though the night temperatures only got down below freezing, we were glad to have the heat.

Simple, yet functional. The tent frame
makes a great home when hunting.

The stars shone in the night sky as we settled in for the night. I took a few moments to look out and enjoy the beauty around me. I am amazed by the brightness and sheer number of the stars. And to think, my heavenly Father knows each one of the stars by name.

I lay down in my thick, minus-thirty-nine-degree Fahrenheit sleeping bag and noticed the trickling of a small stream at the back of our camp. I loved this place and everything I had seen and done so far. This was going to be a great trip. I thanked the Lord for giving me the opportunity to enjoy such an experience. Almost before I could finish my prayer, the day caught up with me and I started to doze.

By morning, the fire in the wood stove had gone out and I was happy for the warmth of my sleeping bag. When my feet hit the floor, I realized how cold it was. They were freezing!! I started to shiver uncontrollably. The shivering was only short-lived as we started a fire blazing in the woodstove. Soon the heat from it filled the room.

Many of the elders will eat a big breakfast in the morning and then not eat again until they return from their day's adventures. I'm not usually much of a breakfast eater, but when it comes to being out on the land, I love a big breakfast. It always tastes better when you are breathing in the fresh mountain air. This morning's breakfast did not disappoint me. We may have been camping, but Rod served food that rivaled any restaurant. Thick sliced bacon, scrambled eggs, toast, and jelly filled us for the day ahead.

As we started our journey from camp, the thick fog that had descended upon us over night had begun to burn away in the "heat" of the morning sun. It took a while before we felt the heat as a thin layer of ice formed overnight on any standing water left on the road.

We crossed the NWT border and traveled the old road about fourteen miles to Dechenla, a lodge nestled right in the heart of the Mackenzie Mountains. The lodge looks out over a vast expanse of caribou moss and low brush. In the early years, visitors to the lodge could have looked out over the bowl-shaped meadow and seen hundreds, if not thousands of caribou making their fall migration.

Caribou continue to migrate through this area, but not in the herds numbering what they used to. Some people blame climate change; others blame over-hunting. Still others say the caribou have changed their migration route. Whatever the reason, it is still a wonderful spot to visit. My hunting friend hoped to find a caribou to help feed his hungry family for the winter.

About halfway into the lodge, we made a stop at a wildlife check-station run by NWT. The conservation officer greeted us with a smile and asked what we were doing in his area. Since Rod's ancestors had come from the area, it was not a problem for him to hunt on either side of the border. I was looking for meat for our freezer so I explored the possibility of getting some sort of non-resident tag for a couple days of hunting. The conservation officer told me the area was open only to traditional subsistence hunters from NWT or the Yukon. It was not possible for me to hunt on the NWT side, no matter what. I could go with my friend, but could not harvest any meat.

One of my favorite places to be- on the land with the elders

From the check-station, I could see and hear a river around the next corner of the road. The remains of an old bridge showed us where the crossing should have been. Built in the early 1950s, the bridge served only as a reminder of what used to be. Many, if not all, of the bridges on the NWT side have long since succumbed to the elements and are unstable, if they are present at all.

On this particular crossing, the waters of the rivers had eaten away the approaches to the bridge. The harsh winters had made the boards and beams rotten and unfit for crossing. Beside the former bridge, a "road" led us down to the water's edge. Rod took one look and proceeded to drive across the river. Coming up on the other side, I wondered if the two-wheel drive truck ever got stuck. We were going in places I never dreamed of going.

I did not have to wonder for very long. We came to a stretch of road that looked more like someone had dumped a load of boulders in the way. The boulders stuck out of the road's surface like waves on a wind tossed lake. After a stretch of about a quarter mile lay a creek appropriately named, Boulder Creek. There was no bridge on this creek; it was a "pick your path and hope for the best" kind of creek. The creek did not dampen our desire to get to the lodge.

We pressed ahead, bouncing over boulders until we got high centered. (High centered is when a vehicle runs over something which picks it up to a point that one or both of the driving wheels no longer contact the road surface and the vehicle is unable to move.) We were over two hundred and fifty miles from the nearest tow truck. No one else was around. Our vehicle was stuck. I sat wondering what we were going to do.

They call this the North Canol "Road."

Unfazed by what had just happened, Rod got out of his truck and went to the back. He took out the jack and went to work. He jacked one corner of the vehicle and placed rocks under the tires so we could get traction. As soon as the tires were able to move the truck, we went further down the road until we got high-centered again. We repeated the process. This happened three or four times. I began to wonder if we were actually going to make it to the lodge. We still had Boulder Creek ahead of us. If we did make it, how were we going to get back home? Were we going to have to repeat the same process on the way back? One last jacking of the truck and we made it to the water's edge.

The water crashed over the boulders making splashes of whitewater, which hid more rocks. *Are we really going through this creek?* I thought to myself. Everything I had been taught about driving went out the window – all those lessons about no driving when you cannot see what is under the water, and all the things I knew about hidden boulders. How were we going to make it through this? What happened if we got stuck in the middle of this raging creek? If we made it, were we going to be stuck on the other side of the creek? With the ease of a seasoned driver, we splashed through water up to the bottom of the doors.

I was overjoyed when we made it to the other side. After my excitement and nervousness calmed down, I saw what had made my friend so determined to get across. In front of me, spread out like a painter's canvas was one of the most beautiful places I had ever seen. The land lay open for miles in front of us. We were in a huge meadow surrounded by mountains. The brush on the ground was no more than knee high. There was not a sign of any modern development; only the raw beauty of God's creation. I had never seen anything like it before, and words cannot adequately describe how it looks. It was the biggest meadow I had ever seen and scattered throughout its low brush were a handful of caribou grazing on the plethora of caribou moss.

As we drove the rough dirt road, we saw what looked like a small camp scattered with five to eight log cabins surrounding the main building or what is called, the lodge. Built out of logs, the lodge towered two stories above the tundra. Spacious decks stretched off the second floor, offering visitors a three-hundred-sixty-degree view of the tundra, which surrounded the cabin. Perched on the deck, visitors could see caribou, arctic terns, ptarmigan, ground squirrels and many other creatures. The sun's rays shone through the clouds in long beams, which touched the mountains. God gave me a glimpse of the vastness of His glory sprawled out before me in snow covered mountain peaks and lush green valleys. The splendor of His creation lay before me in full color.

The beautiful grazing grounds near Dechenla'

The hosts of the lodge welcomed us with open arms. Each summer, they spend three months at the lodge welcoming scientists, biologists, nature lovers, and local hunters. Since there are not many who make the drive we just did, they love anyone who stops by for a visit. We were treated with northern hospitality as they gave us a piping hot cup of tea and some fresh made bannock. (Bannock is a traditional First Nation fry bread made with flour, water, and a bit of baking powder. It can be dipped in stew, smothered with jam, or just eaten by itself. It is a staple of wilderness living.)

As much as I enjoyed being out of the truck and was appreciating the beauty around me, I knew we needed to get going. We still had at least a two-hour drive ahead of us to get back to the camp. Even though it was only the middle of August, the days were getting noticeably shorter. It would not be safe to cross the creeks in the dark; especially Bolder Creek. I dreaded the trip back to camp. What if we got stuck and darkness closed in around us? As much as I was loving the beauty, I did not want to spend the night in the truck in the middle of the dark wilderness.

We crossed Boulder Creek without any problems. Not once did we have to stop and jack up the truck to get it over one of the huge boulders. The sun began to hide behind the mountains as we crossed the last creek.

Two wolves greeted us as we pulled away. They did not seem to mind our presence as they made their way through the willow. They were probably searching for caribou as a late evening snack.

We had spent the whole day traveling the countryside and not hunted even an hour. Did we not come to hunt caribou? I prayed for the Lord to give me a caribou so I could help feed a new missionary family in Teslin. Tomorrow would be different; we would hunt. As we finished making our way back to camp, we made plans for our next adventure. It had been a good day, but the trip was just beginning.

We arrived back at camp around eleven. We had made it a full day. By the time we ate our supper of roasted groundhog and got ready for bed, it was after midnight. Sunrise came earlier than we wanted it to the next day. The day had a different feel. We were hunting. We grabbed a quick bite and headed out on the four wheelers hoping to surprise some caribou.

We had not gone more than 1 mile when six caribou crossed the road in front of us. My heart started beating rapidly in my chest. I started to shake with excitement. I whispered to Rod, "Shall I shoot them?" He responded with, "No, it's ok." I thought we were hunting. Why had we not stopped and taken advantage of this blessing from the Lord?

We continued down the road as quietly as a four-wheeler can be. The fog still hung heavy over the land, making the air moist. We rounded the corner in the road and there stood the same caribou as before. They seemed to be offering themselves to us. They were going over land and we were traveling the road, but our paths met. This time I could not contain myself. I jumped off the four-wheeler and grabbed my gun. They were right there in front of us. Again, I said, "Shall I shoot them?" This time Rod only shrugged. I decided that was a yes to me and took off on foot.

I stalked the caribou for several hundred yards. Finally, I got a clear shot. The noise from my three hundred Winchester Mag echoed from the mountains around me. I could tell by the way the caribou moved I had hit him, but he was still moving slowly away from me.

I picked up my pace to trail him. I did not want him getting away. After several agonizing minutes I took another shot. Again, the sound echoed through the valley. This time the caribou stopped. Slowly I made my way over to him. I had heard stories of caribou, which were supposed to be dead, who jumped up just as a hunter got near them. I did not want any surprises.

After traveling another hundred yards of tundra, I saw my caribou. He was not a huge caribou, but would provide the meat our missionary friends needed. He looked to be two or three years old and weighed around two hundred and fifty pounds. He had a twenty-two-inch spread across the top of his antlers. With pride I stood beside him. I had shot my first caribou.

My caribou

As I made my way back toward the four-wheeler and Rod, I started to get a sick feeling in the pit of my stomach and my pulse quickened. I began to realize where we were in relation to the border. I had shot a caribou on the wrong side of the border.

Where we were camping, the road made a Y. The right side of the Y led straight into NWT. The left side wound its way back into the Yukon. When we left camp, we traveled across the border into NWT. We were intending to travel the road into the Yukon, but when we saw the caribou, we kept going straight into NWT. In all my excitement I had inadvertently forgotten which side of the border we were on. Instead of being in the Yukon I had gone one and a half miles into NWT.

What had I done? I am a missionary and try not to be a law breaker.

I did not intend to shoot the caribou illegally. I had let the excitement of the hunt cloud my vision of where I was. I knew the rules; everyone who hunts is responsible to know where he is. What should I do? I could not just waste the caribou. I decided to take it home and give it to my missionary friend like I had prayed about and confess to the conservation officer the next time I saw him. I would tell them where I had gotten it and accept whatever the consequences. Since I shot it in NWT, I had to report it to the conservation officer at the NWT checkpoint. I did not have to report it at the time, I just needed to make a report to him the next time we saw him.

In the meantime, I took the caribou back to Ross River and distributed it to the new missionary family who had recently moved into Teslin. We both praised the Lord for the provision of meat. I still had a sickening feeling as to the report I had to give when I saw the officer the next week.

For a week, I dreaded what I had to do. Fear gripped me. I had heard stories of people who disobeyed the law. I did not want to lose my license and ability to hunt. Worse yet, I did not want to go to jail. How was the conservation officer going to respond when I told him what I have done?

The following week my family and I drove north, during Labor Day weekend, for some much-needed rest and relaxation before the kids started school again. The weather had changed and the nights were cold as snow started to fall on the mountain peaks. This year, we decided to camp right at the NWT check-point, right next to the conservation officer. I would have to report my illegal act.

As we set up camp, the person I had been dreading came to us. The NWT conservation officer came over to greet us. I told him about the caribou and told him I had shot it on the NWT side. To my amazement he looked at me and said, "The caribou is probably gone, right?" I was shocked, he was not throwing me in jail. He was not taking my gun. I explained to him how I had given it to a family who needed meat. A sense of relief flooded over me. I no longer needed to carry the guilt of my wrong doing. I had been forgiven, or so I thought.

The story did not end there. When my missionary friend cut the caribou, the conservation officer in his town questioned him as to how he could have a caribou. He explained that I shot one and had given the meat to him. Everything would be good as I provided my caribou license number to the officer. No problem, a quick phone call and again, no more issue. Nothing more to worry about. Or was there?

The caribou kept coming back to haunt me. In March when the Conservation Officers of the Yukon were reconciling their numbers as to how many caribou were shot, they realized I had claimed a caribou on my license, but never reported it in Ross River. I got a phone call asking me to explain why I had never reported a caribou killed to Ross River. I explained the whole situation and that I had not reported it here was because I had reported it in NWT.

The whole matter started getting messy at this point. My conservation officer had to check with NWT to make sure I reported it. The NWT officer changed his mind. When I had talked to him in the fall, all seemed to be ok. Now things were different. He said I should appear in court in Yellowknife to face criminal charges for shooting an illegal caribou. The conservation officer from the Ross River district said she did not think it was necessary for me to appear in court. She trusted it was an honest mistake and I had learned my lesson.

After having to make a sworn statement accounting for everything that happened from the moment we started hunting to the moment I shot the caribou, I paid a fine and had the antlers confiscated. But finally, the whole ordeal was over. I *had* learned my lesson. Always be sure where you are when you shoot your gun.

This incident and all it entailed reminds me of the way many people go through life. The Bible says creation itself shows the hand of a Creator. Yet, many go through life paying no attention to their Creator. Ecclesiastes 12:1 says, "Remember now thy Creator in the days of thy youth, while the evil days come not, nor the years draw nigh, when thou shalt say, I have no pleasure in them."

I could have saved a whole lot of headaches and anxiety if I had paid more attention to where I was and listened more closely to Rod's direction. He had tried to warn me by telling me not to go after the caribou. Then in my persistence, he let me go. I feel this is the path my life takes many times in my relationship with the Lord. He tells me in the Bible and through the Holy Spirit what I need to do. In my persistence to do what I want, He lets me make choices He knows are not best for me.

As a loving Father, he welcomes me back when, like a sad puppy, I come whimpering home, asking forgiveness. First John 1:9 says, "If we confess our sins, He is faithful and just and will forgive us of our sins and cleanse us from all unrighteousness." I could save myself a whole lot of trouble if I followed His lead – *ALWAYS* and quit persisting on doing things my way. We can all be saved from a bunch of trouble if we follow the way of our Master, Jesus Christ. He knows the way and says "Follow me."

Chapter 19

GOD GIVES THE WORDS FOR MINISTRY

"But sanctify the Lord God in your hearts: and be ready always to give an answer to every man that asketh you a reason of the hope that is in you with meekness and fear." (1 Peter 3:15)

One of my favorite professors gave me a piece of advice that I have carried with me for thirty years of ministry. Dr. Barackman said, "Be ready always to preach, pray, or perish at any moment." Having been a minister for fifty years, he knew the importance of always having a message "in your back pocket." He learned this after having to give several sermons with short notice.

Over the years, I have tried to always be ready to preach, not only at a moment's notice, but also to make sure I have spent the time needed in preparation. Sometimes this is not always a possibility. Funerals come up. Churches have asked us to speak during a visit. I have been asked to fill in for another pastor who did not show.

This preparation comes in various forms. Sometimes it means getting up a couple of hours early on Sunday to make sure I have a completed outline and am comfortable with the morning's message. Sometimes preparation means spending time during the week going over Sunday's passage, making sure I have a firm grip on what the Lord wants me to bring forth. For me, this preparation always means I am spending time daily in personal devotions, giving God time to speak to me personally. I cannot expect God to speak to others if I have not been allowing Him to speak to me.

It is hard to give a message to others when I have not had enough time to prepare for the message myself. There have been times when life gets in my way and I get up to preach and I know very well I am not prepared to speak. Usually it is after these messages when Gwendy says something like, "You were all over today," or "I could not follow you." It is easy to get defensive; I know she is right because I did not take enough time to prepare for the important delivery of God's message.

I have often thought of Matthew 10:19. Jesus told His disciples, "But when they deliver you up, take no thought how or what ye shall speak: for it shall be given you in that same hour what ye shall speak." I could take this verse to mean, Jesus said I do not have to prepare, I just need to trust Him and the words will come. Jesus was not telling His disciples not to prepare. Instead, He let them know that their trust was not to be in the preparation. Their trust was to be in the promise that He was with them always and would work through them. Their trust was in Christ, Himself.

Jesus gave us the example of the importance of spending time in the stillness of the day with His heavenly Father. We read in the Gospels how Jesus withdrew from others to spend time in communion with the Father. (Mark 1:35, Luke 5:16) Jesus trusted the Father to give Him what He needed, but He saw the importance of taking time to prepare His heart.

All through Bible School and life, the Lord has impressed upon me the need to spend time with Him. There are times when my life is the epitome of what God desires. At other times, my priorities get out of balance. I find myself struggling to be ready to preach, pray or perish at any moment. There are times when I take hours to prepare for a message. Then there are times when I take only moments to prepare.

Even when my relationship with the Lord is at its best, there are times when I struggle to know where the Lord is directing me to preach. I sit in my office and read the Bible and the Word of God does not resonate inside of me or challenge me. I am left feeling like I have nothing to give the people of our fellowship. At such times, I get frustrated and wonder why it is such a battle. I know God's Word is "living and active." I know it is still changing lives even though its writings are thousands of years old. I am left feeling like I am at a wrong place with my heavenly Father.

Recently, a family in our community asked if I would do a funeral for their mother who passed away. I agreed and asked if they knew any verses which were special to their mom. They shared with me about a Bible she had and wanted me to use it to share thoughts. I love it when I am able to use a person's own Bible at their funeral. It lets the family see what was important to the one who died.

All week, my mind dwelled on the upcoming message. I even sat down at my desk a couple of times to write it out. Even though I have given more funeral messages than I can count, I take each one seriously. Each funeral message is a chance to share the Gospel with people who otherwise do not hear the message of God's grace and hope. It is a chance to remind them of the God they often ignore.

No matter how hard I tried, no matter how hard I thought about it, no matter how many passages of Scripture I read, I kept coming up empty. I prayed and asked the Lord to give me the message He wanted me to give. I prayed I could offer comfort to the family while giving the message of the Gospel to the many community members who would also be attending.

Only hours before the service, I told Gwendy I had to go back to the office and finish my message for the service. As I sat at my desk, I cried out to God. Tears streamed down my face as I pleaded with the Lord to give me His message. The tears that flowed down my cheeks were both from the desperation I felt and the pain I still felt inside due to my mom's passing earlier that year. The pain was intense. I knew I needed to prepare, yet my soul was empty. I needed God to work and fast. I only had two hours before the funeral.

As I prayed, the Lord reminded me of the words the family had told me, "We have a Bible verse for you to share." It is not uncommon to receive passages even minutes before the service. Usually, I just incorporate them into the message I prepared. Today, I had nothing prepared.

In my desperation, I made a phone call to the deceased sister's home and asked if she knew anything about the verse I was to share. She told me I needed to go to the deceased's home and talk to the daughter who had spent the night there. She might know what I was to share. I weighed my options. Should I stay and finish preparing or trying to prepare for the message, or should I take the time and go visit with the daughter? The choice was not easy. Yet, the Lord impressed on me the need to go and see the family before the service.

I arrived at the house and the door swung open wide. The house was quiet and no one seemed to be around. I made my way up the steps into the living room. Some of the family sat around the coffin of their beloved mother who suddenly left them. A few candles flicked on a small wood table at one side of the room. Pictures lined the walls reminding those who entered of happier times.

Upon entering, I hugged those present and offered my sympathy to them. We sat and talked of some of their memories. At times like these, I do not have to say much. The family usually likes to talk about what happened or of the things they remember. As much as I tried to keep my mind from wandering, my mind went to the sermon I needed to prepare.

After several minutes of listening, the granddaughter gave me a hardcover Bible. It looked like those found in bedside tables in hotel rooms. She opened it and showed me two passages the family had marked in the Gospel of John. Glancing at my watch showed me I had only an hour to put something together. The time crunch made me cringe, but did not catch God by surprise. He had everything all lined up. I rose to leave and headed back to my office.

I sat at my desk and read through the passages the family had marked out. The message God wanted me to share jumped off the pages of the Bible. In the passage, Jesus was comparing Himself to the good shepherd who cares for and knows his sheep. Excitement filled my heart as I meditated on the verses. The truth of Christ's words penetrated my weary heart and mind.

Immediately, God gave me a clear outline. I knew exactly what I was to share. God showed me how His love caused Him to have a great desire to know each of us on a personal basis. His love caused Him to seek us out. In His great love, He desired to give each of us the best life possible. And, most importantly, His love caused Him to be willing to lay down His life for us.

I spent days fretting because I had nothing prepared. Yet, God had the message He wanted me to give to the people. The time did not make a difference to Him. He felt no time crunch. He did not fret. He already knew what the family needed. I know in ministry, I must take the time to do the preparation, but I must continue to trust the Lord to provide the words to say at the right time. It is not my work/ministry. It is the Lord's. As I trust Him, He continues to provide not only the opportunities to preach and pray, but He also provides His words in His way.

PART IV

TRUSTING GOD WHILE OFFERING HOPE

"For in this hope we were saved. Now hope that is seen is not hope. For who hopes for what he sees? But if we hope for what we do not see, we wait for it with patience." (Romans 8:24-25 ESV)

"May the God of hope fill you with all joy and peace in believing, so that by the power of the Holy Spirit you may abound in hope." (Romans 15:13 ESV)

Chapter 20

HOPE IN DEATH

"And as it is appointed unto men once to die, but after this the judgment: So Christ was once offered to bear the sins of many; and unto them that look for Him shall he appear the second time without sin unto salvation." (Hebrews 9:27-28)

While growing up, I saw very few people die. The first death I remember was my great-grandmother. As a young boy, I stood in my room crying over her death, realizing I would never spend any more time with her.

Death hits people in different ways. Some people feel death like the stinging of a bee. Death hits these people hard, they cry over the loss, but soon they seem like they are back to normal. For others, death hits like a freight train. It knocks them down and the suffering, pain, and grief linger for years to come. Some never get over the grief of one death before another death hits them.

Since beginning ministry in the Far North, death is something we deal with more often than we like. Though our community is small, each year brings several deaths. Sometimes the deaths are elderly people who have lived their lives and we expect to die, but then sometimes we get hit with the shock of losing one from the younger generation. The hardest ones to deal with are the deaths that are a result of substance abuse and should not happen. Many times, the grief lingers with the family members who are left behind to pick up the pieces.

The constant string of deaths causes many to feel like they never get over one death before they have to deal with another one. This death after death makes them numb to the feelings they are experiencing. In others, the results get compounded and the person feels like they are living in a constant state of grief.

One summer, we got hit with a wave of many deaths. Every couple of weeks we were having another funeral. In August, we had four deaths within a week's time. The grief was almost more than any of us could bear.

Today, I am not afraid to die and I have come to appreciate the opportunities the Lord gives for us to encourage others during their times of grief. Do not get me wrong, I do not love to see people's lives cut short. Dealing with death is emotionally draining even when it is not a close family member. Seeing other people go through such pain and despair is hard.

I look forward to the promise made in Revelation 21:4. John writes "And God shall wipe away all tears from their eyes; and there shall be no more death, neither sorrow, nor crying, neither shall there be any more pain: for the former things are passed away." One day we will not have to deal with the sting of death. One day we will not have tears flooding our eyes over the death of a loved one. Sickness, pain, despair, and everything that goes along with the curse of sin will be forever gone. God will restore the broken relationship that started in the Garden of Eden.

With each death, the Lord brings about chances to make His love, grace, and Word known to those who grieve. This chapter is not so much one story, but it is a collection of various memories. Each story taught me a lesson about trusting God in the midst of death.

Suicide- One day, I drove through town to finish an important task. I do not remember where I needed to be, but I felt it was more important than what God wanted. I suppressed the still small voice whispering to me.

The Holy Spirit impressed on me the need to stop and talk to a young man I saw walking down the street. He stared at the ground as he slowly made his way across the main intersection. I knew who he was; I talked to him on occasion. He often drank and was under the influence of something other than the Holy Spirit. He struggled with depression and often wanted someone he could talk to. As I drove by, he looked as though he did not have a friend in the world. But I traveled somewhere, and I do not even remember where, but it was "more important."

As I drove by him, I may have even said a prayer asking the Lord to help him. At the same time, God asked me to be His hands and feet and reach out to this person in need. But I knew I needed to go somewhere, I just do not remember where.

A few days later I received a call from the Health Center. The nurse needed EMS (Emergency Medical Services) immediately. Someone's life was in trouble. Off we drove to the address given to us. When we arrived, the owner of the house led us to a room near the back of the house. On the floor lay the lifeless body of the man whom God had asked me to help one week earlier. I could have helped him a few days before. But now, it was too late for him. In his desperation, loneliness, and grief, He had taken his own life.

Now his eternal destination is sealed. I dare not be the judge, but I cannot help but wonder what might have happened if I had stopped. What if I shared the Word of God with him instead of heading somewhere I thought was more important? Would a simple word of love from God above have made the difference in this man's life? I could have helped if I had listened to the voice of God.

I learned a lesson that fateful day. When God places a burden in my heart to speak, I had best do it. The Lord knows better than we do what the people around us are going through. I need to trust Him enough to share His message when He gives it to me.

It seems we get caught up in OUR plans. These plans are "more important" to us than the message the Holy Spirit is laying on our hearts. As we trust God to give us opportunities to be a witness for Him, He opens the doors. It is our job to walk through the doors when the Lord opens them.

Drowning- She had been a camper at Kamp Klondike for several years as a child. The Lord had spoken to her heart during one of her visits and she received Christ with the genuineness and sincerity of someone twice her age. She knew what her decision meant and chose to follow Christ.

After the week of camp, we dropped her off at her home. We could feel the darkness and despair as we left her at the door. I wanted to shelter her from the evils I knew she was facing. Doesn't a good shepherd protect His sheep from the wolves and robbers that lurk about? I did not know what to do. So, I did the only thing I could do, I prayed for her protection.

Time went by and she became a young woman. She faced things no one should have to face. She started to mix with the wrong crowd. She started to make wrong choices. She started to drink and party. She fell away from the Lord, who loved her and gave Himself for her. The Evil One sought to destroy her and make her ineffective in her relationship with Jesus. Soon, her life choices would have an effect on the whole community.

We had driven home from Kamp Klondike the night before. Counseling kids, leading crafts, washing dishes, and caring for our young children had left us exhausted. It was one of the lazy days of summer, when a few extra moments in bed on a Saturday morning are of great value.

We decided we did not need alarms to wake up. The lawn could wait. The mountains of laundry would get done, but not now. The Rice Krispy treats for Sunday's drive back to camp could wait. We needed rest!!

In the early hours of the morning, we received a text. We did not like what we read. There were rumors of someone missing in the river. As much as we wanted to blame it on small town gossip, we knew there is always a bit of truth in every story. Soon the rumor became a reality. We were not ready to deal with the pain the news brought with it.

All through the night, this young lady and her friends had been having a "good time." They were living life to the fullest. At least they thought they were. Little did any of them realize where their choices were taking them.

In the wee hours of the summer morning these partying friends took a drive down a windy road that parallels the river. The road, an old trail to a woodlot, offers stunningly beautiful and majestic views as it winds in and out of tall poplar and spruce trees. This morning they did not notice the view. They were looking to have a good time. The end of this beautiful drive is a boat ramp leading right into the river. When these friends got to the end where they should have stopped, they drove right into the river.

In a panic, three of the four exited the vehicle and made it to safety. Our friend could not escape. She lost her life when she should have been enjoying it in its prime. In a time like this, we just want to roll over and go back to sleep. We did not want to face yet another senseless death. God expected us to rest, didn't He? The community was grieving. In one horrific event, our sleepy Saturday was turned upside down. Family members needed someone who could console them. A community needed to come to grips with what had happened.

This death hit the community like a freight train. People pointed fingers. They wanted to blame someone. Her life was snatched away from us. She was so young. She had her whole life in front of her and had so much to offer those around her.

It is easy to ask, "what if?" What if I had done more for this young lady? What if I had stopped the vehicle as it went screaming by in the early hours of morning? What if I had been able to teach them more about the Bible? The "what ifs" did not change the reality; she had died and there was nothing we could do.

In these times, the Lord asks us to be open to whatever He allows to happen. He wants us to look for opportunities to talk to a family member who struggles with the "what ifs." It might mean giving people a safe place to grieve, talk, and share their hurts. It may be offering a shoulder to cry on. It is being the hands and feet of our Savior in the midst of someone's valley of death.

These are times when we need to show others the same love Christ showed to the multitudes in Matthew 14 when He heard the news about John the Baptist's beheading by Herod. He withdrew to a solitary spot to be alone. When the crowds found out where He was, they gathered in a great multitude. The multitude consisted of more than a couple of people. There were even more than a couple hundred people. There were well over five thousand people. They were "needy people" who demanded His attention. Jesus and His disciples were dealing with their own grief and now, a throng of people surrounded them. In His time of personal grief and sadness, He spent the whole day ministering and healing people. He reached out with compassion when He should have been given compassion.

After spending the whole day with them, is it any wonder the disciples decided to help Jesus by trying to send the people away to get food? The people were hungry. The disciples were hungry. They may have even been "hangry." Yet Jesus, in love and compassion and in an act to glorify God His Father says, "You give them something to eat." Jesus had been ministering to people all day. He could have "punched the clock" and said, "I'm outta here." Instead, He took yet another opportunity to show how much He cared for others.

It is not always easy to show people the love of Christ; especially when the grief affects us to the core of our being. It is not always easy to be the one looked to for answers in times of trouble. It is in these times, though, that we see the power of Christ within us. It is not by our great abilities, our great strength, or our great passion for the lost. It is in His strength. "I can do all things through Christ…" (Philippians 4:13) It is in the moments when we are weak that we find He is the strength we need.

Most vile of all- Most of the deaths we deal with, the people are deeply loved by their families and their community. When they die, there is talk around the community about what the person did. People tell stories of their lives and the things they remember most about the person. Usually, the stories are positive and the person is praised for the life they lived. These times of sharing bring healing during the time of grief. Many times, it seems the community forgets the bad and the good of the person may even get exaggerated.

There is occasionally someone for whom the community gives a sigh of relief when they die due to the profound hurt they have caused. We dealt with one such person. When the person died, sadness gripped the family of the individual. As we listened to people talk around the community, the feelings were different. The people described him as being a bad person; in fact, they described him as a very wicked person. Of course, the Bible says, "there is none righteous no not one" (Romans 3:10-12), and the "heart is deceitful and desperately wicked" (Jeremiah 17:9).

But to them, this man was "really bad." People talked about the hideous things he had done and the pain he had caused to individuals in the community. He spent time in jail for crimes he had committed. There was no doubt, if a person fit the description of evil or vile, this would be the one.

As humans, we often classify people by how wicked we think they are. When God looks at every one of us, He sees sinners. For some, He sees redeemed sinners, saved and covered by the blood of Christ. When He sees others, He sees lost sinners, in need of the Savior. It does not matter if we sin three times a day, or three times a year. We are all sinners who need to trust Christ as our Savior.

Being a missionary/pastor in the community means we are to offer the love of Christ to anyone and everyone no matter their flaws, no matter the age or social status, and no matter the culture. Christ Himself said, "it is not those who are well who need a physician." (Matthew 9:12) Even if this man lived a vile and wicked life, even if he had not repented, he was still loved by his family. They were grieving as anyone else does who loses a loved one. They needed our support.

The man's family were friends of ours and while we had heard his name, we did not know very much about him. We prayed for the family during their time of grief. As we had the opportunity to, we shared words of hope and encouragement with the family.

The day arrived for the man's funeral. Unlike many of the funerals in town, I had not been asked to give the message at the service, but we went over to support the family. He chose to be buried in the community's old cemetery located across the river. The cemetery sits high on a bluff overlooking the Ross and Pelly Rivers. No granite headstones mark the graves here. Only wooden crosses, many of which have succumbed to the elements. Some of the crosses lay broken over the graves, while others lay lost in the tall grasses.

The heat of the summer sun beat upon a small group of us as we waited for the service to start. It was one of the hottest days of the summer. After dealing with the minus fifty degrees of winter, ninety degrees felt extremely hot to us.

As we waited, several family members gathered, talking amongst themselves. It did not seem to be the normal talk of a family gathered for a funeral. Something was wrong. Their puzzled looks showed they were trying to figure something out.

The family did have a problem. They had asked someone to say a few words about the man before they laid him to rest. The person they had asked had not arrived. The family then asked one of the elders from the community to say a prayer, but they had said no. It seemed no one wanted to have a part in laying this person to rest.

After some time, one of the family members came over to me. They explained the situation in which they had found themselves. They asked if I would be willing to say a few words in memory of the deceased. They had an even bigger problem, though, which was about to become my problem.

Before he had passed away, the deceased requested that no minister or priest have any part in his burial. If that was not enough to keep me from speaking, he also added that he wanted no words about God or Jesus to be spoken in the service. Early in life he experienced a great deal of hurt from a member of a religious institution. He lived with deep inner pain and turmoil for much of his life. Now he wanted nothing to do with anything bearing the name of Christ.

In ministry, I have often seen many whose hurts kept them from wanting to hear the truth of Jesus. They allowed the actions of church members to keep them away from the God who loves them. The family knew my position and my stance on God's Word, yet they felt they had no other option. They asked me to perform his service.

God had been preparing me for this moment. As you recall, in Bible School, my professors taught me to "be ready to preach, pray, or perish at any moment." During the previous days, God had spoken to me about things He wanted shared at the service. I was not sure I would have an opportunity to share, but God had given me a message. This would not be just any message. The family said, "Would you say something? The only stipulation is you must not say anything about God or Jesus."

How could I, in clear conscience, speak at a burial service and not say anything about God? He is the reason we speak. He is the reason we live where we do. He is the One we have chosen to give our lives for. I felt they were asking the impossible!

There are times when the Lord brings to mind the verse in Matthew 10:19. In this verse, He says, "But when they deliver you up, take no thought how or what ye shall speak: for it shall be given you in that same hour what ye shall speak." God, through His Word, gave me peace about getting up to speak. There was one thing I needed to do before I said my first words to those assembled. I gathered with a small group of Christians to pray for the Lord to work in these extraordinary circumstances.

I stood with shaking knees and a shaky voice. I told the small group gathered about the deceased wishes stating he had asked for no reference of God. I chose my words carefully, trying to honor the man's wishes the best I could. I started with the story of creation and how the Creator, in whom our community believes, had sent His Son to be a Great Teacher.

From there I moved to the story about the woman caught in the very act of adultery. The crowd brought her to this Great Teacher hoping He would punish her for her wickedness. Using Jesus' words, "He who is without sin cast the first stone," I was able to talk about how that Great Teacher had offered forgiveness even to a wicked woman.

With intensity, the people who gathered listened as I spoke. What the Lord used to speak to their hearts was my apology. Though I never knew the man and had never personally hurt him, I willingly accepted responsibility for the hurt and blame of this man. I apologized to the family for the pain "churches" had caused this man to feel. We were burying a man who had suffered hurt by the ones who were to show love. He was so hurt, he wanted nothing to do with the true message of love from Jesus Christ.

Going back to the story of the adulterous woman, I explained how the Great Teacher offered forgiveness and love to her. There was no doubt, the woman was evil. She was caught "red handed." She deserved to be punished. She was wrong. Instead of condemning the woman, the Great Teacher offered her forgiveness and love. He gave her a challenge to go and stop doing wrong.

I was able to share how the message He gave was a message of love and forgiveness to those whom society thought as the vilest of sinners. We all deserve punishment, yet we can experience forgiveness.

At the end of the message, I was able to change the wording from the Great Teacher to Jesus. This made it very clear to everyone Who was offering them forgiveness and love. It was not just some "Great Teacher," it was Jesus. He cared for this man. He cared for them. He did not come to hurt people and to punish them. He came to give His love. He came to forgive all our wickedness.

It took a willingness for me to go out of my comfort zone for this man's family to see the true comfort of the One who can restore broken relationships. It took my being willing to ask forgiveness, for wrongs I had never done, for this family to see Christ's forgiveness. In the end the family expressed their gratitude for the words of Christ which I shared. In the end, healing began to take place.

This whole incident made me think about how I live my life. Am I living in a way that makes the world want nothing to do with Jesus? Or, am I living in a way that makes the world long for and desire the life I have through Christ? When people look at me, who do they see? Do they see Jesus or do they see me?

We must build our lives on Christ, the sure foundation. This is the only way for others to see Him through us.

> "For other foundation can no man lay than that is laid, which is Jesus Christ. Now if any man build upon this foundation gold, silver, precious stones, wood, hay, stubble; Every man's work shall be made manifest: for the day shall declare it, because it shall be revealed by fire; and the fire shall try every man's work of what sort it is." (1 Corinthians 3:11-13)

Chapter 21

HOPE IN UNANSWERED PRAYER

"We are troubled on every side, yet not distressed; we are perplexed, but not in despair; Persecuted, but not forsaken; cast down, but not destroyed; Always bearing about in the body the dying of the Lord Jesus, that the life also of Jesus might be made manifest in our body." (2 Corinthians 4:8-10)

One of the highlights for us each year is when we join our co-workers with the SEND North family for Annual Conference. We travel to Anchorage from the far reaches of Alaska, Yukon, and Northwest Territories (NWT). The area is vast, covering from as far east as Yellowknife, NWT to as far west as Hooper Bay, Alaska. It stretches north above the Arctic Circle to as far south as the panhandle of Alaska.

The distance from the western point to the eastern point of the field is approximately the same distance as it is from New York City to Dallas, Texas. The distance from the southernmost part to the most northernmost point is approximately the same as it is from New York City to Charlotte, NC.

The land is as vast in area as it is in diversity. From the rain forests of Alaska's coast to the aridness of the interior Yukon. From sea level up to the highest peaks in North America, the region has it all. Some villages are accessible only by boat or airplane. Others are on the road system. Some are home to the Alaska Native. Other villages are home to the Canadian First Nation People. Some are home to the miners, settlers, and homesteaders. It does not matter which village the missionaries come from, the vision is the same. They are there to "make northern disciple-makers." They desire to see the people of this vast region come to a deep and growing faith in Jesus Christ and spread that faith to others in their community.

In some of the communities, missionary kids struggle to maintain deep friendships. They are neither a true part of the community culture nor are they a part of the culture where we, their parents, grew up. For these children, the time away is a time to meet with friends who have grown up in similar situations as they have. Even though they may see each other only once a year, there is a strong bond due to each understanding the other.

Evenings are often filled with laughter, tears and lots of stories about village life. Games such as President, Dutch Blitz, Skip-Bo and more bring families together for hours of enjoyment. It is not about the table talk as much as it is about being in a place where we can let our guard down and be ourselves. We do not have to make sure we say the right words or act the right way as is the case in many of the villages.

During the day, there are times to hear what God is doing in other communities in which SEND North has ongoing ministries. It is always encouraging to hear about what is going on in places we only dream of visiting. There are stories of changed lives from places like Hooper Bay, Kodiak Island, Yellowknife, Ft. McPherson, and Aniak. There are prayer requests from places like Faro, Pilot Point, Galena, and more.

During these meetings, we receive spiritual feeding as well as physical feeding. A plethora of fresh fruits and veggies go a long way to please our stomachs. For some of the missionaries who live where food is flown in, fresh produce is hard to get. The question during these meetings is not, *am I going to get enough food to eat;* the question is, *can I leave without making a huge change to my waistline?*

At our conference in the spring of 2013, we listened with excitement about one community that finished a time when they had committed to forty days of prayer. The missionaries spoke about people who had come to Christ for salvation. They proceeded to tell us about people who stepped into the waters of baptism. The ministry was going forward in leaps and bounds.

As we reflected on the story on the way home, we decided we should commit to forty days of prayer in our community. We desired more souls to be saved. We wanted more people to be baptized, and we wanted the ministry to go forward tremendously. We wanted people to see the power of God at work.

Baptism of Jessie, Robby, and Jocelyn

It was not as though there had not been fruit in our ministry. God continued to change the lives of people and we knew He was active. It was more out of a desire to see *big things* happen. We wanted big results.

We made big plans and promoted it amongst the people of our little fellowship. We looked forward to seeing what God would do in our community and ministry. We proceeded through the forty days of prayer.

To encourage our people, my messages centered on prayer and its importance in our lives. We printed calendars, assigning various prayer items for each day. We prayed for neighbors, our government, our community, and whomever the Lord placed on our hearts. We thought we had found the secret to a successful ministry, or so we thought. It was spending copious amounts of time in prayer.

We knew what we were looking for and what God was going to do. He was going to save more people. Our church was going to grow. People's dedication to Jesus was going to explode. Ross River was going to be different because we prayed. We had found the magic wand of God and all we had to do was wave it.

The time spent in prayer did have an effect. God did work. We saw people growing in their personal commitments to Jesus. We did not see huge results like we had desired, but we saw God move. Then it happened. God began to move in ways we never anticipated.

On May 15, we had almost come to day forty of our forty days of prayer. We were getting ready for spring to arrive. I awoke in the early morning hours with God speaking to me. He said in a still small voice, "Something is going to change."

I laid on my bed in fear. We were almost done our third term and were looking forward to home service. Would these be our final months in Ross River? Did God have another place for us to minister? We did not want to leave our home and the place God had us for the past thirteen years. We were content here, yet the message was clear, "Something is going to change."

As God always does, He kept His word. About four-thirty that afternoon things did change. The ice started to go down river with the melting snow. Instead of opening up and flowing down the river the way it should, it jammed near the back of our house. Within minutes the water was flowing into our home. It seeped through the back door of the house and poured through the front door.

Our home stood out in the water like an island in the middle of the sea. The water continued to rise as the ice further up the river continued to break loose. The mountain streams gushed with water, making the river overflow its banks. We rushed into the house and grabbed important documents and picked up what we could off the floor. To the kids' disapproval we even grabbed their homeschool books.

I stepped off the porch into waist-deep water on one of the last trips out of the house. The nearly freezing water stung my legs. I waded slowly to a high spot in the yard where we parked the van. The whole ordeal was surreal. It seemed like a bad dream.

In shock, we watched the house we had turned into a home become inundated with water. At approximately five-fifteen in the evening we left our home as we knew it. For twelve years we had built it into our haven. We raised our kids. We hosted birthday parties. We held Bible studies and visited with friends. Our refuge from life's difficulties was now swamped with muddy, stinky, river water.

In desperation, I made one last call before leaving the home. We needed prayer and I knew who I should call. My mom in New York answered the phone. The request was simple. "We need prayer. Our house is flooding." With that, we left the house.

Almost as quickly as it had risen, the waters went down. Three hours from when we were escorted away from the house by the RCMP, we were able to return. Instead of the brown of the linoleum floor we had left only a short time before, we now walked on a layer of thick mud. The water had destroyed everything, leaving us with a huge mess to clean, and a house not worth saving.

The house being flooded

We prayed for God to do mighty things. He showed his mighty power in the flood waters that destroyed much of what we loved. The moving of God had started. We prayed for God to move. He did.

One week later, devastating news rocked our little church fellowship. One of the strongest, most faithful members of our church family was dying. Josephine had a tremendous love for her family and those around her stood as a great testimony in the community. She wanted to see her people turn to Christ and follow Him. She encouraged us greatly. Now, doctors diagnosed her with pancreatic cancer. Her prognosis was grim. They did not give her much time.

How was this happening? God was supposed to do great things. We prayed for God to move. We wanted to see lives changed because of OUR prayers. Where were the salvations? The baptisms? The changed lives? The changes we saw looked nothing like what we asked God to do.

Oh! We did see lives get changed. Our family of seven now slept crammed in a twelve-foot-by-eighteen-foot room while we looked for a house. The family from our fellowship saw their beloved wife, mother, grandmother, and spiritual mentor die two months later. Our lives and the lives of those around us changed. God worked in ways we never fathomed. God changed lives.

For months our children struggled with what had happened to their home. The loss of the house bothered them, not the house as much as the loss of sentimental things that can never be replaced. The loss of journals, letters from friends, birthday cards from grandparents and other personal items caused pain and questions. They questioned the goodness of God and why He could allow such loss.

God worked in a way much different than we planned, but He still worked. He worked in our children's lives. God worked even in their grief. They developed friendships and relationships they have carried to this day.

We saw God come through in amazing ways. He provided people to help with the cleanup. He provided the funds and teams to help rebuild. We saw God take us from a mold infested house where Gwendy had trouble breathing to a more efficient home. He took us from a house where our feet were almost always cold in the winter and gave us a house with well-insulated, heated floors.

Our church and community continue to recover after the death of our beloved church member, Josephine. Her commitment to the Lord and to her family stood as a testimony to the Lord and what He can do in a life turned over to Him. Her commitment to First Nation culture while standing strong as a Christian helped others realize they could be Christians and not lose their cultural identity. Yet, two months after her diagnosis, she entered eternity, in the presence of her Lord and Savior.

We all struggle to this day with "*WHY?*" We do not know why God chose to act in the way He did, but we know His will and His plan is perfect. We know while we only see a small fraction of time, He sees the whole picture.

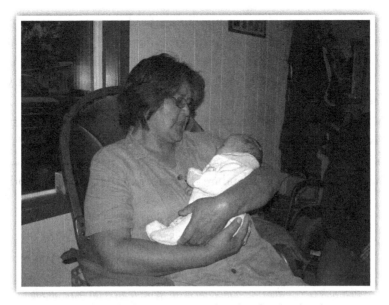

Josephine holding our son shortly after his birth.

I do not doubt God's sovereignty even a little bit, but I have trouble with his methods. Sometimes I have no idea what He is thinking. I do know "all things work together for good to those who love the Lord, to those who are called according to his purpose," Romans 8:28. I know in the difficult times He is right beside me to carry me and my family through.

I hold to the promise given in Psalm 23:4, "Yea, though I walk through the valley of the shadow of death, I will fear no evil: for thou art with me; thy rod and thy staff they comfort me." Whatever hardship or challenging time I go through, God proves to be faithful.

I learned that what we consider to be good is not always God's definition of good. Was it good to lose a house? Was it good to lose a Godly woman, whom we loved? Do we think it is good to go through adversity? Most of us seek to avoid any pain we can.

I remind myself of what the Lord said to Paul when he pleaded with God to remove the "thorn in my flesh" with which he struggled for a long time. God responded to Paul by saying, "My grace is sufficient for thee: for my strength is made perfect in weakness." Paul responded by saying, "Most gladly therefore will I rather glory in my infirmities, that the power of Christ may rest upon me." (2 Corinthians 12:9)

No matter what we go through in life, God's grace and strength are exactly what we need. It is not just the great, big, good things which show me His work in my life and ministry. The storms of life may come upon us. There may be times we question God's will and His plan. It is God who gets us through each trial of every day.

My trust is not in circumstances and situations being to my liking. My trust is not in the fact that God will shelter me from anything going wrong. My trust is in the Lord who will bring me through the difficulties and give me the grace and strength to endure each day with the challenges it brings.

> "Count it all joy, my brothers, when you meet trials of various kinds, for you know that the testing of your faith produces steadfastness. And let steadfastness have its full effect, that you may be perfect and complete, lacking in nothing. If any of you lacks wisdom, let him ask God, who gives generously to all without reproach, and it will be given him. But let him ask in faith, with no doubting, for the one who doubts is like a wave of the sea that is driven and tossed by the wind. For that person must not suppose that he will receive anything from the Lord; he is a double-minded man, unstable in all his ways." (James 1:2-8 ESV)

Chapter 22

HOPE FOR A COMMUNITY, PART 1

"Where there is no vision, the people perish..." (Proverbs 29:18)

The summer of 2009 proved to be a pivotal summer for us and our ministry. It cemented in our minds what God had asked us to do way back in 2001 when we moved into Ross River. The events of the summer helped us to be firm in our commitment to stay where God had placed us, even in bad times. The events of this summer deepened our resolve to see God work mightily in our community. The change took place in our view of how we could reach the people.

We moved north with a passion to see the Lord draw people into a deep, growing relationship with Him. We desired to see a church established where there had been none for fifteen years. To see this church established meant training leaders from among the First Nations. The goal to see a strong church continues to be our passion.

During the first eight years of ministry, we tried to get people involved in churchy things. We held Bible studies, special services, and Kids Bible Club. To us, Hebrews 10:25 held an important truth. This verse says, "Not forsaking the assembling of ourselves together, as the manner of some is; but exhorting one another: and so much the more, as ye see the day approaching." Everything we did was done in the hopes of helping people see the need to meet together for fellowship. We felt if we could get a church going, then the hearts of people could be changed.

The change took place in our view of how we could reach the people. Having grown up in the church, we held the church as a high priority.

Church was where I learned most of what I knew about the Bible. It was in church where I saw believers come together to encourage and strengthen one another. It was the church I saw reaching out to a community and making a difference. It had been through the ministry of the church that Gwendy had come to know Christ as her Savior. *If only the people came and saw the difference Christ will make,* is what we thought.

Some of the church folks- Rachel, Grady, May and myself

The problem was, few people had an interest in attending church. Many had been hurt by so-called "Christians." They want nothing to do with organized religion. How were things ever going to change if the people were not going to come to church or Bible Study? How could the Word of God change their lives if they never got near the truth?

We spent countless hours making frequent visits into people's homes. These visits gave us opportunities to share the hope of Christ with the people. But we were still reaching only a small percentage of the whole community.

Having been in the community for eight years, we talked to many people about their felt needs. We tried to figure out what they felt would bring about true transformation in the area and how what they felt could bring change. We sat in community meetings as people opened their hearts and shared the pain they felt.

The people wanted change. They felt they were losing the next generation. They felt like they were losing their culture. There was no place for the older generation to meet and teach the younger generation. The community had no place to gather and enjoy life together.

We had not come to the area to make a community hall. We had come to build a church. We had not come on some humanitarian quest to provide social justice to the community. We had come to offer Christ. While we knew the power of Christ could solve many of the social ills in the community, we had come as church planting missionaries. Proclaiming the name of Christ to the people of our community stood central in all we did.

We came with a strong belief that only God could heal the wounds that had long inflicted pain on the community. Was God asking us to do more? Could we help meet the people's felt needs and still build the church? We had to answer one question before the Lord helped the ministry to grow for His glory.

"Why do you do what you do?" The words from one of our Summer Missionaries in 2009 caused me to stop and think. I knew why we were in Ross River. I knew what our goal was. But, why do we continue on when we saw such little fruit?

The Lord used the answer to this question to help direct us into where He desired us to go. First, we needed to settle in our own minds who Christ was before He could use us more effectively for His glory. We knew the power of God could change lives, but we did not realize the change He needed to make in us. The Lord asked us to radically live out the truth of God's Word so others could see the truth of the Gospel.

Only a couple years earlier, Josephine had given us 2 Chronicles 7:14. Her desire was for her people to follow the truths of this verse which says, "If my people, which are called by my name, shall humble themselves, and pray, and seek my face, and turn from their wicked ways; then will I hear from heaven, and will forgive their sin, and will heal their land." She wanted to see her people calling on the name of Jesus. She wanted to see God heal her land as her people humbled themselves and cried out to Him. In the Bible we read,

"For whosoever shall call upon the name of the Lord shall be saved. How then shall they call on Him in whom they have not believed? And how shall they believe in Him of whom they have not heard? and how shall they hear without a preacher? And how shall they preach, except they be sent? As it is written, 'How beautiful are the feet of them that preach the gospel of peace, and bring glad tidings of good things!'" (Romans 10:13-15)

The message is clear: any who call on the name of the Lord shall be saved and, to that end, there must be someone preaching the truth. We had the truth. We knew God could make the difference. We had faith in Him, but were we willing to step out in complete trust?

As we mulled over these truths in our mind, I continued to see the great need of our community. The Lord started laying a burden on our hearts. I read a book by Matthew Barnett, a pastor in California, who had a desire to have a "church which never sleeps." His premise was that most churches sit vacant many hours of the week. There are people who are in need and seeking truth more than just the hours the church is open. His desire was to have a church that was always open and offering help to his community.

Gwendy and I began thinking and praying with this in mind. *What would it look like to have a "church which never sleeps" in Ross River?* Sure, we wanted people to gather on Sunday for worship and Wednesday for Bible Study, but was there more? The Lord gave us a vision of such a place. It would be an extension of His church, not something other than His church. His church would reach out to the needs of the people around it. It would be a place of Healing & Overcoming Problems Everyday (HOPE).

Two verses were firmly etched in our minds during this time. Those verses were, 1 Peter 1:3 which says, "Blessed be the God and Father of our Lord Jesus Christ, which according to his abundant mercy hath begotten us again unto a lively hope by the resurrection of Jesus Christ from the dead," and Romans 15:13 which says, "Now the God of hope fill you with all joy and peace in believing that ye may abound in hope, through the power of the Holy Ghost."

God gave us His hope at the moment we had trusted Christ as our Savior and received His gift of salvation. He now asked us to share His hope with the lost, dying, and hurting around us in a physical way. Church services were a part of sharing His hope, but He asked us to do more. As we contemplated what His hope offered to the people of Ross River looked like, He opened our eyes to the possibility of a multi-purpose Drop-In Center.

The Center would be open every day. People could come anytime the doors were open and get a warm cup of coffee and encouragement from the Bible. It would provide them with a safe environment and give us the opportunity to help them learn the truths of God's Word.

For months we struggled with various ideas of what such a place could look like. What should we have included in it? What was our main purpose in developing such a place? The more we prayed about it and the more we talked to people about ideas, the stronger the conviction within us grew. It was as if God was speaking in an audible voice saying, "This is My will, trust Me." God did not speak in an audible voice, but He continued to grow the burden in our hearts to do more. He continued to open doors and lead us forward. He gave us His peace.

We had never been a part of something this big. A project of this magnitude took money – lots of money – that we did not have. If we were going to go ahead with such a project as this, we had to do it without incurring any debt. If God wanted us to move ahead with building a multi-purpose Drop-In Center, He had to provide for it each step of the way.

People have asked me many times over the years, "How do I know the will of God for my life?" I have to admit, I have wished more than once for God to write His will in ink across the sky. Then I would have no doubt in my mind what I am to do. During this time, there was not once when God spoke audibly to me in a voice like I talk to my children. I will say though, there were many times when He spoke to us through the still small voice of His Holy Spirit within us. You may be thinking, "You are not making sense," Does He speak or doesn't He?

Proverbs 3:5-6 was written by my parents on one of the first Bibles they ever gave me. These verses say, "Trust in the Lord with all thine heart; and lean not unto thine own understanding. In all thy ways acknowledge Him, and he shall direct thy paths." It is my belief that the more we trust the Lord, the more He opens our eyes to what He wants for our lives.

Sometimes people say, "God never speaks to me." I have learned in my life that it is not that God is not speaking to me as much as it is that I do not want to hear what He is saying. I like to do what is easy or comfortable more than I like to have to step out in trust. It is easier to ignore Him rather than surrender to His will in faith and blind trust.

I have seen this lived out in the lives of people who came to the north saying God led them through circumstances to be a missionary there. After a few years, when the going gets rough and the "stars are no longer aligned," they bail and go where life is easier. God uses many things to make His will clear to us. We have to be very careful, though, about using circumstances to dictate what we do. If what we do is only based on circumstances then when the circumstances are not right, we feel we made a mistake. We may even begin to question whether we are in God's will. God can use circumstances to get our attention, but we must base life-altering decisions on the truths of God's Word and the peace of His Holy Spirit.

God uses His word to speak to us. In 2 Timothy 3:16-17 we read, "All scripture is given by inspiration of God, and is profitable for doctrine, for reproof, for correction, for instruction in righteousness: That the man of God may be perfect, thoroughly furnished unto all good works." I firmly believe God's Word has what we need to give us instructions for how to live and what to do.

Also, God has given us His Holy Spirit. In John 16, Christ promised to send the Holy Spirit. He says in verse 13, "...when he, the Spirit of truth, is come, he will guide you into all truth..." The Holy Spirit speaks into our lives what is true and what the will of the Father is for our lives. Again, I have found in my own personal life, it is not the Holy Spirit who is not speaking; it is I who is not listening.

If we are unsure after reading His Word and listening to the Holy Spirit's promptings in our lives, we can seek Godly counsel. God gives us those who are older and wiser to give us counsel, if we listen to them. In Proverbs 24:6, we read, "For by wise counsel thou shalt make thy war: and in multitude of counselors there is safety."

There is much to be said about seeking the wisdom of those who have been "around the block" a few times. This is not to say that seeking advice from anyone is a good idea - a person can always find friends who will tell him what he wants to hear. In seeking counsel, we must seek those who are Godly and who are willing to speak the truth whether it is what we want to hear or not.

To hear God's voice, we sought answers from all three of these sources. We meditated on God's Word, sought the direction from the Holy Spirit, and consulted with Godly leaders. Each time we did, the still small voice of God kept saying, "Do you trust me enough to step out in faith?" The more we prayed and wrestled through the Scriptures, the stronger we felt we needed to move ahead. Stepping out in faith is difficult to do.

Chapter 23

HOPE FOR A COMMUNITY, PART 2

"For whosoever shall be ashamed of me and of my words, of him shall the Son of man be ashamed, when he shall come in his own glory, and in his Father's, and of the holy angels." (Luke 9:26)

There are people who look at us and think we never have fears about sharing Christ with others. While we do try to be bold in making the most of every opportunity, there are times when we do so in fear. I often feel like the Apostle Paul; he asked the Colossian believers to pray for him to have boldness to speak "as he ought to speak." (Colossians 4:3-4) I know I have a message to give; I need the boldness to keep proclaiming that message as God wants me to.

It is so easy to let fear dictate when we speak or do not speak. Fear is the tool the Devil uses to keep many Christians from speaking the truth. He knows a fearful tongue is a silent tongue.

As I shared in the last chapter, God gave us a burden to reach people with the life-changing HOPE of Jesus Christ. We desired to have a place where people could come to experience the grace, love, peace and joy of Christ. We have experienced the abundant life Christ has promised in John 10:10. We wanted others to experience it as well.

The plan around the design of the HOPE Centre took months of praying, research, planning, and many meetings with community members. We had ideas after years of living in Ross River, but wanted to hear from the people themselves. The thing which came out again and again in conversation was the need to have a gathering place. People wanted a place where they could gather as a community. With this in mind, we developed the following purpose statements.

"Our Purposes

- To provide a fun facility that is drug and alcohol-free.

- To provide a wholesome alternative to existing recreation and entertainment.

- To empower lives to change, by focusing on Jesus Christ as the source of one's foundational needs of identity, acceptance, security, and significance.

- To cultivate friendships and respectful attitudes and behavior toward others.

- To promote community service, not out of compulsion, but from appreciation.

- To promote drug and alcohol abuse prevention, sexual abstinence until marriage, and to build positive self-esteem.

-To engage volunteers who commit themselves to mentoring the virtues and character of Jesus Christ in their public and private lives."3

As we developed a plan and purpose statement, we were careful to communicate with our community. This involved several meetings where we asked for continued input from the people. We knew if the project was going to succeed, it needed to have the support of the local people.

There was no way we could go ahead with such an ambitious project with only the support from our local people. We did not have the finances or the man-power needed to complete such a project. A project of this size needed God's provision and working. It was more than we could handle. We knew God had placed the vision in our hearts, but He was going to have to do a mighty work if it was going to happen.

Our first appeal for help went to our mission leadership. I approached our director, Barry Rempel and shared our idea. When we shared the idea with him, he told us to move forward and see how the Lord opened doors. If God wanted it to be a reality, He had to provide. How was God going to provide? This project would take more than the idealistic dreams of an overzealous missionary couple. It would take many willing hands and deep pockets if it was going to succeed. Only God had the power to bring everything together to accomplish His purposes.

Before we could start raising the necessary funds for the project, we needed a clear statement as to the necessity of having such a center in the community. With this in mind, we developed the following statement, which we shared with anyone who expressed an interest.

"Why does Ross River need a Drop-In Centre?

Our answer is simple: There are deep physical, emotional, and spiritual needs that are not being addressed elsewhere. There are single parents who need a place to come and talk about their challenges. There are people who are looking for someone to listen as they share their struggles to stay sober. There are elders who are longing for a place to interact with others to fill their loneliness. There are youth who need a place to get help with homework after school. There are youth that need someone to come alongside them to mentor and encourage them. The lives that will be transformed, the souls that will be saved, the hearts that will be lifted because someone cared enough to help is the answer."4

Armed with a vision, purpose, and the reasons why we were going forward, we began to seek out individuals and organizations who could get behind the vision God had given to us. Gwendy and I were not fundraisers by any stretch of the imagination. Other than going to churches and sharing our passion for the lost, we had little experience in fundraising. We spent a great deal of time committing the project to the Lord in prayer, asking Him to provide as He saw fit.

There were times when the task felt as though it was insurmountable. We even questioned our direction. Had God given us this burden or was it some pie in the sky idea of overzealous missionaries? As we pursued the vision, the more the doors kept opening and God continued to confirm our direction.

After going to the local leadership of SEND North, we had to get the approval of SEND International. We submitted the application, giving the details of the project to the board of directors. After prayerful consideration, the project received the needed approval. We began to send letters out asking God's people to get behind His vision. The funds started to trickle in. God was providing. Most of the gifts were not huge, but were gifts given in faith that God would continue to provide.

As I have done many times in the past, I started to look for people I *thought* could help us, or should I say, who I thought *should help* us. Again, and again, the people I talked with respected what we wanted to do, but could not help. Many made previous commitments to the Lord's work in other places.

The funds were not the only issue on our minds. Because of its intended use as a public facility, the building needed to have a structural engineer stamp of approval on it. How were we going to find an engineer who was, first of all, qualified, but who also had a heart for the Lord and would not charge us an arm and two legs? I heard how much engineers could charge and did not want to see the cost of the building climb any higher. I did not doubt God could provide. I prayed for Him to provide an engineer who would be willing to do the work as a free-will offering to the Lord.

Our contacts in Canada were small, but God was already working in the hearts of individuals and bringing *His plans* together. It was His plan. He did it His way with His bountiful provision.

To get plans certified by an engineer, we needed to have more than a napkin sketch to work with. Both of us had drawn plans before this time. Gwendy took mechanical drawing and had a knack for drawing and designing things. I had grown up working with plans and sketching construction projects on graph paper. Together, we developed a good floor plan.

God took care of the rest. In His divine providence, He led us to a man who could draw the plan in a suitable form for the structural engineer. He was also a man whom the Lord had blessed with the means to help with the project. Until this project, we had never spoken to each other. We did not even know about each other. This ended soon into the project and the bond between Christian brothers developed.

He and his crew spent countless hours making sure that our plan was workable. He was very patient with our countless revisions. He got excited as the project moved forward. He was a man of faith whom God used to encourage us in this huge undertaking. His building expertise in many northern communities proved to be indispensable.

Before the project was over, he gave not only his time, but he also gave his resources to help see the project off to a good start. His time and generous gift added to the other gifts, and the twenty thousand dollars of local money given allowed us to order materials. We had enough to build the shell of the building. The project was going ahead. We moved in faith, trusting God to continue to provide.

God did continue to work. I contacted three structural and mechanical engineers and told them about the project. Only one responded. He was a believer and was willing to look at the plans. He had a job in the nearby town of Faro and was willing to meet with us if we could drive there. With plans in hand, I made the hour trip to Faro to meet with him; all the way, praying for God to work in his heart.

Upon my arrival we got to the business of going over the plans. He allowed me to explain the project as he looked over the plans. I waited for his response. Would he help us? If so, how much would he charge? He did not live in the Yukon, but in Alberta, two day's drive away.

The Lord was again working in a mighty way. The engineer looked at the plans and said, "I'll do it, all you have to pay is my time to come up from Alberta." Since the Lord already gave him work in the territory, he could inspect our project when he came to the territory. God had not only provided an engineer; He provided one who saved us tens of thousands of dollars.

Getting the drawing for free, and the structural and mechanical designs for almost nothing had been a big help. But still, the building estimates were three times higher than expected. Much of this was due to the high cost of material in the Far North. Another reason for the extra cost was the amount of insulation needed to keep the building warm. It was one thing to build a building. It was yet another thing to build something efficient. We did not want to be sending limited resources up the chimney in smoke. This did not catch God by surprise. He knew the costs already and He had it under control.

While we trusted God, we did not sit on our hands and wait for His provision. We continued to pursue avenues of revenue so we could keep moving forward. We heard about a fund that was available to Yukon organizations engaged in projects to help their community. In our minds, this was the solution to our problem. *We would get the remaining funds from this organization and everything would be good.*

In life, we are often guilty of this. We commit our way to the Lord, then we take it back and try to come up with our own solutions. This is not what God is looking for. He wants us to "Cast our burdens" (1 Peter 5:7) on Him and leave them there. We had given the project to the Lord to provide for, but we were still trying to figure out how He was going to provide.

Now I do not want to be misunderstood. I do not think God asks us to commit our way to Him and then sit back and do nothing. What I am saying is this, God wants us to give our problems to Him and not take them back. We do not need to worry or be anxious about it once we have given it over to Him.

We began the process of applying for extra funding. As part of the process, two individuals met with us to go over the application. After lunch one afternoon, they came to our home and interviewed us to get a better idea about the HOPE Centre. Together with Rachel Burkhart, our co-worker in ministry, we told them everything.

We proclaimed Jesus as the HOPE. We let them know that He was the One who we would be preaching and teaching about. We did not want any surprises about the use of the building.

Their words still echo in my ears. "In your application, it would be best to keep out any reference to God. The Yukon Government, who would be helping to provide the funds, does not like such projects." We responded by letting them know, Jesus was the only reason we were doing the project. We did not feel it was right to take Him out of the picture so the application looked better. If they did not support the project, God could still provide through another means. Our faith was to be in Him, not in some fund.

We submitted the application and clearly stated our purpose. We explained our commitment to the people of Ross River in the following statement.

"HOPE Centre Commitment-

The Ross River Hope Centre is committed to creating a space that is welcoming, healthy, and safe for all people of Ross River. We strive to actively engage people in our community, so they feel a strong sense of belonging, by helping them find their God-given purpose in life.

'My purpose is that they may be encouraged in heart and united in love, so that they may have the full riches of complete understanding' (Colossians 2:2).

Healing and
Overcoming
Problems
Everyday

With the transforming power of Jesus Christ."5

In Psalm 20:7 we read, "Some trust in chariots, and some in horses: but we will remember the name of the LORD our God." We can say this verse. We can even sing the song that goes along with it. But, do we really trust in the name of the Lord our God? Does He have our total trust, or are we trusting in what we can control? We could have applied for the funding with a hidden agenda. God already knew the reason behind the project. Did the people we were asking for help need to know our true purpose behind the building?

We laid it all on the line, trusting God to take care of the rest. One of the members of our church often quotes the verse in Luke 9:26, "For whosoever shall be ashamed of me and of my words, of him shall the Son of man be ashamed, when he shall come in his own glory, and in his Father's, and of the holy angels." We knew if we were ashamed to share Christ now, what was going to keep us from being too fearful to share Christ once the project was complete?

Even with the boldness to lay it all on the line, I have to admit our trust was not in the Lord as much as we were trusting in the organization to provide for us. Sure, we said we were trusting God. We even prayed for God to work in the hearts and minds of those who were reviewing our application. In reality, our trust was in how the organization could help us. God had to strengthen our faith even further.

Chapter 24

HOPE IN NEED OF A SPARE

"Then he answered and spake unto me, saying, this is the word of the Lord unto Zerubbabel, saying, Not by might, nor by power, but by my spirit, saith the Lord of hosts." (Zechariah 4:6)

For months, Gwendy and I prayed for the Lord to provide the tools needed to build the HOPE Centre. We knew He is able to do "immeasurably more than we ask or could imagine." (Ephesians 3:20) Gwendy looked at the classified advertisements in every edition of the Yukon News as soon as we could get our eyes on them. Weeks went by and we did not see anything of interest. We knew there was no way we could afford all the tools we needed.

One night, as Gwendy looked over the classified advertisements in the Yukon News, she found a series of ads that piqued her curiosity. It looked as though someone was selling off a whole woodshop. In the listing were many of the tools that the volunteers needed to build the HOPE Centre. There were saws, painting supplies, hammers, drills, a table saw, ladders, saw horses, and some small hand tools. It looked like every carpenter's dream. It seemed too good to be true.

With the excitement of a six-year-old on Christmas morning, I called the number on the advertisement. It only took a few minutes for me to realize the older gentleman on the other end of the line was selling what had been his livelihood for many years. He had run a small renovation business and was retiring. He hoped to keep everything together and sell it all to one person, but if he could not sell it as a lump sum he would have a garage sale the following weekend. He named his price and offered to email pictures of everything.

In a day or two the pictures arrived. It was clear the man took great pride in his tools and kept everything neat and tidy. He had everything meticulously organized in a skidoo trailer that he had transformed into a traveling workshop complete with an eighteen-drawer organizer and enclosed table saw. The pictures made me envious, but while there were a wide variety of tools, the price he wanted was twice what we could afford. Had God shown us this as a provision or was God testing our faith in Him again?

After a couple of days of prayer and consulting with my dad, who knew tool prices much better than I did, I called the gentleman and explained my dilemma. While I wanted the tools, we could not pay the price he wanted. During our conversation, the older man shared with great joy how much of his work the past many years had been at one of the local churches. The Lord had been working on his heart as He was asking us to trust Him. It was clear the man was letting go of something which was near and dear to his heart, but he had to sell it.

With the shyness of a kid asking for the last piece of candy, I told him the meager amount we could pay for his workshop. We had received some money to buy tools and we had saved some other money, but would that be enough? The man said that was the amount he had hoped he could get for it all. He was happy and we were overjoyed. God supplied the basics of what we needed. Now, how were we going to get the traveling workshop home? We arranged to meet with him the following weekend. The workshop would be ours.

That Saturday morning was a beautiful late fall day, the ground had already been dusted with a light coating of snow. Soon the road into Ross River would be covered with snow and remain that way for the next six months. Early in the morning, I pulled out of the driveway and began the five-hour, two-hundred-and-fifty-mile drive to Whitehorse. I planned to drive in, do a quick turn around and get home before it got too late so I could get rested for church the following morning.

The drive to Whitehorse was uneventful. I took one of the men of the community with me to help make the long drive go by faster as talking to him is better than talking to myself. I often invite someone to ride with me when my family is not able to come with me.

On this particular morning, I took a young man whom the Lord had laid on my heart as one who might need some encouragement. He had struggled with feelings of anxiety and depression after a close family member had passed away. It was trips like this one that have given me many opportunities to share the hope of Christ with others.

The five-hour trip seemed to go by fast and soon we had located the address where we were to pick up the trailer. With excitement, the retiring man showed us the various perks of his traveling workshop. He thought of everything in its design. The trailer itself was a metal snow machine trailer. The workshop was a five-foot-by-eight-foot box made of half-inch plywood painted with a thick gray paint and fastened to the top of the trailer. The paint showed signs of years of weathering, but still protected most of the wood. The ends were solid except for a twelve-inch-by-eighteen-inch slide which came out of each side. This was to allow for long materials to slide through and cut with the table saw mounted inside. Each of the sides were on hinges and opened to make a roof over the workbench. It was a thing of beauty.

Workshop on wheels

With all the tools and extra equipment, the trailer held more weight than it was designed to carry. I looked at the tires on the trailer; they looked like tires on a matchbox car compared to the load they were hauling. Besides the heavy load in the trailer, I knew we still had the Robert Campbell Highway, which still had gravel patches on it. I asked the owner if he had a spare. He gave me a brand new one and said with a smile on his face, "You'll be good." Content with the spare, we headed back toward Ross River.

Only fifteen minutes into the trip, the spare became a necessity. A look in my side mirror revealed the passenger side tire had gone flat and was coming to pieces. We had only begun the trip and had a flat. Praising the Lord for the spare, we went to work changing the tire. It only took us a brief time to change the tire and be on our way again. The trouble was, we still had almost five hours of driving and the last forty-five miles was on gravel road.

I began praying and asking the Lord to get us home without any further trouble. The only way we were getting home with these tires was by the power of God. They were made for hauling a three to five-hundred-pound skidoo or four-wheeler, not a half ton of tools.

A short stop in Carmacks – two and a half hours from home – allowed us to fill our empty stomachs and inspect the trailer. The tires looked like they were wearing well, so we could continue our arduous drive. The road got rougher the closer we got to home. I tried to maneuver around the bumps the best I could, but at times it was like avoiding rain drops in a downpour. There were more bumps than smooth patches! My prayers continued for God to get us home on the tires we had.

As I made the turn from the Robert Campbell Highway onto the access road heading into Ross River, I began to feel confident. We were going to make it home. The tires had delivered us safely on the first two hundred and forty-four miles of our journey. They would not fail us now.

We had only driven about one mile into the six-mile road when I said to myself, "I got this." Those words still ring in my ears like the echoing of a siren. How could I say that? Had not the Lord delivered us to that point in the journey? My great driving skills had not made the tires last. The tire company may have made good tires, but they are not the ones who delivered us to our home. God's power and might helped us to get where we were and He was the reason we were still driving on those weak, flimsy tires.

No sooner had the words echoed in my ears when I heard the sound I dreaded to hear. The driver's side tire on the trailer had popped under the heavy load. There I was, six miles from home and I could not go any further. We unhooked the trailer and went in to see our local mechanic. After rummaging through various sizes of tires he found one to fit the trailer.

It was close to eleven by the time we got the trailer hooked back up to the van and started moving again. We drove another mile and the other side blew. There is no doubt in my mind God was saying to me, "Really, Tim, you have this. I thought I was in control; I am the one who made you. I am the one who brought you this far. I am the one who will help you. Rely on Me."

I was stuck. I had taken the only tire from the mechanic. How were we going to get it the rest of the way home? We made one last trip into town to grab two six-inch square blocks of wood that were two feet long. We went back to the trailer and jacked the axles and put the wood underneath so we could skid the trailer home. By the time we reached our driveway the sparks were flying. The wood had worn down to the point the wheel was being eaten away by the gravel left on the road. We were home, finally!

God showed me again, He is worthy to be trusted. It was not by my might. It was not by my power. It was not something I could do. It was all Him. So many times, we get proud like Nebuchadnezzar who said, "Is not this the great Babylon *I* have built as the royal residence, by *my mighty power* and for the glory of *my majesty*." (Daniel 4:30, emphasis mine) God's desire is to get all the glory.

In Isaiah 42:8, He says, "I am the Lord: that is my name: and my glory will I not give to another." He is the one who deserves my praise and adoration. This lesson of trusting God and not myself is one I continue to have to remind myself about. When complimented for a good sermon it is easy to say, "Thank you," when in reality, we should be saying, "Praise the Lord." He is the one who gave me the words. When we get home from a long drive it is easy to say, "My skill has gotten us home." In reality, it is God whose "mighty hand and outstretched arm" is working. *Always in everything.*

The lesson God taught me with those blown trailer tires was one that we needed as we stepped out in faith to do the impossible. God was showing me that I can plan, but He will make things happen. I can try to raise funds, but He is the One who will supply. I can labor, but it is He who builds. "The heart of man plans his way, but the LORD establishes his steps." (Proverbs 16:9)

Chapter 25

HOPE FOR A COMMUNITY, PART 3

"But without faith it is impossible to please Him: for he that cometh to God must believe that he is, and that he is a rewarder of them that diligently seek Him." (Hebrews 11:6)

In Bible School, one of my professors said the first thing we do to please God is when we place our trust in Jesus Christ as our Savior. We can go to church, give to the poor, help old ladies across the street, and even tell others about who God is. But, until we put our faith and trust in Him as the One who deserves our devotion, we are not pleasing Him. "All our good deeds are as filthy rags." (Isaiah 64:6)

Many times, God puts us in situations where, if we allow Him, He will strengthen our faith. He is continuing to stretch our faith beyond what we think is possible. I do not think we ever "arrive" at the one hundred percent faith mark here on earth. Our flesh gets in the way.

In the fall of 2010, we began preparing the site to begin construction as soon as the snow melted in the spring of 2011. This meant digging down to good gravel (approximately four to five feet in most places) and then filling the hole with compacted gravel. God provided a local contractor to haul all the junk dirt away and bring in the close to one thousand yards of gravel needed to make a stable foundation. God provided beautiful weather. It was cool, but not freezing. A wet snow fell on some days, giving us the moisture needed to compact the gravel like concrete.

This compaction was important to keep the building from shifting. In the area where we live, many times permafrost (frozen ground that never thaws) lays beneath the top of the ground. When the ground warms, after a building is built on top of it, the ground becomes unstable and starts to sink. By digging down and placing gravel, we help prevent the permafrost from melting.

With the site ready, we set out to recruit work teams to help us start building on May 2, 2011. The Lord continued to provide. Soon, we had teams scheduled for the whole month of May and others who were making plans to come and help later in the summer.

Churches and individuals got excited when they heard what was happening in Ross River. Many wanted to come and help with this God-sized project. They were calling us asking when they could come and help us. Each team came for a one to two-week block of time. Even though we had less than half the funds needed to build, we had teams on the schedule. We stepped out in faith believing God would provide everything and everyone we needed to complete His work.

In April, I received a call in regards to the application for funding our project. The caller said, "I am sorry to inform you, your application was not approved." Our plan fell flat. The money we had counted on was not going to be coming.

I sat in my office in disbelief. How could they turn down such a great proposal? Did they not know what God was trying to do in Ross River? I did not tell them how I felt, but said, "That's ok. We are going ahead anyway." They seemed bewildered and did not understand. How could we be going ahead? They had denied over half the funding. I told them we had people coming and supplies on the ground.

God gave us His peace about moving ahead. We did not know how it was going to work out, but God would make it happen. We were not going to take out a loan; we believed in some way, God was going to come through.

Our first team of volunteers to start
building the HOPE Centre

On May 2, we started as planned. The day was bright and sunny. We could not have asked for a better, sunnier day. Except for a few skilled carpenters and a couple tradesmen, most of the volunteers who helped on the HOPE Centre had little or no experience in building. They were believers in Jesus Christ, whom God had given a desire to help. They came with willing hearts to see God do great things.

There are so many individuals I could write about. Everyone who came to help build has a special place in our hearts. Each one made great sacrifices to come and give their all in seeing the building go from a gravel pad to a beacon of hope in Ross River. Some swept sawdust around the saw table. Others carried water for the workers. Some carried lumber, shingles, and insulation. Each served "wholeheartedly as unto the Lord." (Colossians 3:23)

Words seem small as we express our gratitude for the countless hours (over six thousand) these volunteers gave. They came and fought the Yukon Airforce (the mosquitoes), when they could have gone somewhere nicer. They battled sickness, sore muscles, fatigue, cold rain, hot summer days, and a lack of sleep. They gave vacations and time with their families.

Everyone came with one purpose, to see God's plan to completion. I cannot mention them all by name in the pages of this book. They worked with devotion, sacrifice and humility, and we appreciated every one of them.

In a building this large, there needs to be a boss or project manager. Without someone to be in charge and looking ahead, the progress is slow and directionless. God gave my dad a burden for the project. He donated his time and spent the first month with us helping to be sure the building got off to a great start. Every boss needs a white hard hat. He wore it well even though he never demanded the title of boss. But, his servant leadership was a blessing not only to the project, but to everyone who worked with him. He usually arrived first in the morning and was one of the last to leave at night.

Another person who had an immense impact on the building was Bob, who for years had owned his own plumbing and heating business. When he heard about the HOPE Centre, he designed an energy efficient system and installed it for us. This system, along with how the walls were designed, has saved us a great deal of money. Having walls close to twelve inches thick and having the heat in the floor has saved us thousands of dollars in heat each winter. When the thermometer outside plummets to minus sixty degrees Fahrenheit (-51 Celsius), we are thankful for both.

Bob and his wife Esther

Working alongside these men were college students, senior saints, teenagers, even some of our kids' friends from town. Every person came to do a job and did it well. Everyone left their mark on us and on the building. Some could not swing a hammer, but came and carried shingles. Some could not carry a piece of lumber, but made great food for us to eat.

Even today, almost ten years since the start of the project, I get teary-eyed thinking about the ones who gave all they could for the Lord. Without them, we would not have the HOPE Centre. Each person took us steps closer to seeing the building completed. Every person came because of God's leading and working in their lives and served for His glory.

What good is it to have willing workers if they have nothing to work with? As I stated earlier, we knew the teams needed tools to get anything done. What good is it to have a team of eight to ten people, but not have the equipment to keep them working?

God was stretching our faith, again. As we prayed, planned, and scheduled teams, God worked behind the scenes. He made sure everyone who came to work had the tools they needed.

We received a phone call from Temple Baptist Church in Ontario. The Lord gave them a desire to provide every single tool we needed to see the building to completion. God provided right down to the carpenters' pencils. Every power tool, square, tape measure, level, drill bit, and more, He provided. We trusted God and He provided more than we could have ever imagined.

One of two teams from Temple Baptist
Church; Sarnia, Ontario

What good is it to have tools and quality people, but not have the lumber to build what was in the plans? With energetic and eager workers, the pile of lumber does not last very long. By the end of May, we had the shell of the building built. The windows and doors all in their proper places. The roof was on and the floor insulated. The teams had worked hard. The piles of lumber which once dotted the job site were now almost gone and so was the money.

Did God intend for the building to go this far and then stop? Had not God told us to go ahead? During this time, Luke 14:28 came into my mind. In it we read, "For which of you, desiring to build a tower, does not first sit down and count the cost, whether he has enough to complete it?" (ESV) Were we foolish to start before we had the funds? What was God doing?

As we took one of the teams back to the airport in Whitehorse at the end of May, we faced another bump in the road. We still had volunteers coming. They need supplies in order to work. We could not write a rubber check, yet God was telling Gwendy to write a check for the next supply run. God kept telling us to go forward. Every logical part of us was saying, "How can we move forward?" How could we order another shipment of lumber when we knew the money needed to cover the cost was not in the account?

The Lord was saying again, "Trust me. I got this." We knew He had everything in His control. We knew He could provide, if He wanted to. We did not know how He was going to do it or when He was going to do it. We believed He had not sent volunteers for us to tell them we had run out of materials.

As God always does, He provided things at the right time. He was not early and He was not late. I was standing in Whitehorse when my phone began to ring. It was the person who one month earlier had said, "We will not support your project." This time the phone call was different. "We changed our minds," she said, "We have reconsidered your proposal and have agreed to provide you with the funding you requested."

To this day, I believe God worked it out for two reasons. He desired to see our faith grow much more than we thought was possible. He also wanted us to put our trust only in Him, not anything else. The project was going to go forward as He saw fit; in His time and with His provision. It was not by our words in a proposal. It was not by our fundraising skills or lack of skills. It was not with skilled laborers. It was going forward because He provided. He was at work doing things as He saw fit.

The HOPE Centre today- A beacon
of HOPE for Ross River

Chapter 26

HOPE FOR A COMMUNITY, PART 4

"Take therefore no thought for the morrow: for the morrow shall take thought for the things of itself." (Matthew 6:34)

For me, building the HOPE Centre was an emotional roller coaster. Each time a team left, I rejoiced at what they had done in the limited time they had. Each individual poured his or her heart into the task at hand. They gave it their all, leaving behind blood, sweat and a few tears when they boarded the planes to leave the Yukon. Each one blessed our family, the project, and our community.

After each team left, I looked at the long list of things that had to be finished. I started to fret and say something like, "I do not know if we can do this." Gwendy would look at me and say, "Hasn't God provided so far? Don't you think God will continue to provide for what is yet to come?"

I'd like to share what we learned about God's provision during the process of building the HOPE Centre. He provided for us way before we started. He provided every day we were building, giving us the strength we needed. He continues to provide for us today! This chapter is not so much a chronology of time as much as an overview of where we saw God working.

On the first weekend, a few of us started early on Saturday morning to put plywood on the bottom side of the floor. A group of volunteers had already insulated the floor. The underside needed a layer of plywood to keep the mice and squirrels from stealing the insulation for their nests.

Three of us crawled around like babies on our hands and knees, moving sheets of plywood and nailing them to the bottom of the floor joists. Two people held the sheet above their heads, while I came along and nailed the sheet into place.

Once we got a system down, the four-foot-by-eight-foot sheets started to go up quickly. I was running the air powered nail gun and sliding across the ground on my back. With the nail gun in my right hand I could slide along and with a pop, pop, pop the sheet was up in no time. The two and a quarter-inch nails had no problem holding the half-inch plywood.

We had not been working very long when I got in the way of myself. As I went to slide on my back, I brought my right arm toward my left knee. As the right arm moved down with the air gun, the left knee came up. Now, I was doing what many carpenters do when they are nailing right along. I kept my finger on the trigger so every time the gun hit the plywood, it sent a nail deep into the wood. At least the wood is the intended target.

Instead of wood, this time the gun came down at the top of my knee cap. Pop, I heard the noise. At the very instant, I felt no pain, only the mental realization of what had happened. I had put one of the two and a quarter-inch nails into my leg. Did it hit my knee cap? I gingerly crawled to where I could sit up. Slowly, I wiggled the head of the nail to see if it was stuck in the bone. I praise the Lord even today; it did not stick right in the knee cap. Because I had my knee bent, the nail went in on a diagonal toward my hip. I sunk deep into the muscle. Only the top half inch of nail showed me what I had done.

I did another thing which I learned not to do in first aid. I pulled on the head of the nail and extracted it from where it lodged. Thankfully, it did not hit any blood vessels or arteries.

This five-second mistake of nailing myself meant I had to rely on the Lord to an even greater degree each day. Every time I took a step for most of a year, I suffered from the damage caused by the nail. It was my "thorn in the flesh." The pain was a constant reminder of my need to trust God daily for His strength. I, like Paul, found God's grace and strength were sufficient for each day. (1 Corinthians 1:8-9)

We also saw God provide the needed supplies for each day. Dad and I went through the materials list with a fine-tooth comb. We spent hours going over each item. We went through every step of the building to make sure we had all we needed. Since it was a ten-hour round trip to the hardware store, we needed to make sure everything was on site when we needed it. We did not want volunteers who had come to accomplish great things, sitting with nothing to do because we ran out of materials.

On the day we went to put the roof on we realized that even with all our attention to details, we had forgotten one very important item. Neither of us had remembered to put the drip edge on the list. For those who are not familiar with building, the drip edge goes around the whole perimeter of the roof under the shingles. It helps keep the rain from running back under the shingles and rotting the plywood along the edge of the roof. To start laying shingles we needed to have the drip edge. Yet we had ordered none of the thirty pieces we needed!

What were we going to do? We could not drive to Whitehorse. We had eight to ten people waiting to help put the shingles onto the roof. Where could we find that much drip edge in Ross River? God had known what we needed long before we started. One of our local builders had ordered a large box of it and had it in their storage shed. They not only let us take the box, they also charged us nothing for the material. They had everything we needed. God had again provided.

From the day we started in May until we moved into the Centre in December, God supplied help day after day after day. In the fall, when many of the volunteers had left, we got a call from a couple traveling through the Yukon. God gave them a desire to serve Him wherever they could. They knew nothing of the building. They had only heard our name from another SEND missionary. The time they arrived was exactly when we needed extra help. God provided.

Again, and again, we had a need and God met the need. Some days it was through our Catholic lay minister. Other days, one of the elders from our community came and helped. Sometimes the assistance came by way of one or two of the young men from town. It did not matter who they were or how old they were, God used them for His purpose.

God provided for the thousands of miles people traveled to come and help. People came from Pennsylvania, New York, Michigan, Ontario, Alberta, Alaska, and around the Yukon. They came in campers, on airplanes, in trucks and cars. Everyone had God's hand of protection.

God kept our two fifteen passenger vans going and gave safety to Gwendy in the many trips she made back and forth to Whitehorse to pick up teams. Every one to two weeks she drove in with a load of people. She dropped them off at the airport for a morning flight. She had only a few hours to rush around town and get groceries and the pages of supplies I asked for to keep the next team busy. The next team usually came in the afternoon and then she made her way back to Ross River, often getting in late in the evening or early morning. We thanked the Lord for the long hours of Yukon summer sun.

This building project has been one of our greatest highlights in ministry. Seeing God come through in ways so tangible, we could not help but notice. I tend to lose sight of God's working in the humdrum of everyday life. Yet, I know even in the normal everyday life stuff, God is still working things out for His glory. He has been working on me and through me for over the past forty years and will continue to work with me until He calls me home. I am reminded of 1 Thessalonians 5:24. In this verse Paul writes, "Faithful is he that calleth you, who also will do it." God called us to serve Him many years ago and with His call He promised to never leave us or forsake us. He is faithful and we have seen His faithfulness time and time again.

Many hands make for lighter work
Pictured below are a few of the over one hundred volunteers
who helped build the HOPE Centre. In total they put in over
six thousand hours to make our God-sized dream become a
reality. To God be the glory. Great things He has done.

Second team from Temple Baptist Church, Sarnia, Ontario

SEND North Team; Anchorage, AK

Dawson City Community Chapel; Dawson City, Yukon

Faith Bible Church; Oxford, NY

Team from Detroit, MI

Gerald and Caleb Spratt; Edmonton, Alberta, Marty and
Mary Ann Young and family; Cyler, NY with our family

Pastor Ian and Maria; Dawson City, Yukon

Bob and Turdy- Traveling Evangelist

Mary; Whitehorse, Yukon; Dick and Susan; Syracuse, NY

Keith; Whitehorse, Yukon

Sheldon; Teslin, Yukon

James and Kiefer; Community Youth

Robert; Community Volunteer

John; Community Volunteer

Rachel; Co-worker of many years

PART V

TRUSTING GOD EVEN WHEN IT HURTS

"Therefore, my beloved brethren, be ye stedfast, unmoveable, always abounding in the work of the Lord, forasmuch as ye know that your labour is not in vain in the Lord." (1 Corinthians 15:58)

"Let us not be weary in well doing: for in due season we shall reap, if we faint not." (Galatians 6:9)

Chapter 27

TRUSTING GOD WHEN I AM PERSECUTED

"Ye have heard that it hath been said, An eye for an eye, and a tooth for a tooth:

But I say unto you, that ye resist not evil: but whosoever shall smite thee on thy right cheek, turn to him the other also." (Matthew 5:38-39)

There are a few verses of Scripture which sound good in theory, but to practice them, well, we hope we never have to put them into practice. Verses like Matthew 7:12, "Therefore all things whatsoever ye would that men should do to you, do ye even so to them" and the above verse having to do with turning the other cheek if you get slapped on one side sound good when we tell them to others. They make for powerful sermons with easy applications, but do people live that way today? Does God expect me to offer my other cheek if someone slaps me? I may be a Christian, but how can I let someone walk all over me? Don't I have the right to self-defense?

I have considered the phrase, "turn to him the other..." and wondered, if push came to shove, could I abide by what Jesus was asking of me? I do not consider myself to be a violent person, but if someone slapped me on purpose, I think I would boil over with anger.

Having grown up in a strong Christian home, I never saw abuse. And while my sister, brothers and I fought on occasion, love and forgiveness abounded in our family home. When I left home, I went to a Bible School where most people showed love and kindness to each other. I worked with Christians in my workplace. Some say I lived a sheltered life or that I never had to face the real world. This all changed one night.

The night began like any other spring evening in the Yukon. The ground was still covered with snow. The air was warming, but still had a nip to it. The HOPE Centre was a blur of activity. The shoes of children and adults who stopped in for coffee and hot chocolate lay strewn through the entryway.

Over the past couple of hours, young people wandered in and out. Some stayed and visited with the handful of adults who were milling around. Others decided to go out and see what excitement they could generate. Inside the Centre, there were fifteen to twenty kids. They played with Legos or board games. Some of the younger ones played house with the baby dolls.

Friday evenings are full of activity at the HOPE Centre.

Gwendy and I sat visiting with various community members as they stopped by. Our desire, when the HOPE Centre is open, is to show the love of Christ and engage people in meaningful conversations about the Lord. Oftentimes, small talk leads to deeper conversations. On any given Friday evening between thirty and fifty people find their way into the Centre. In reality, we have a chance to engage ten to fifteen percent of the people of our community in one evening each week.

About two hours through the three-hour evening, things began to change from normal to abnormal. Two girls who had been outside walking around enjoying the evening came in and said, "There is someone outside who is acting strange."

It is not uncommon to have people walk by the Centre or even come in who are under the influence of alcohol or drugs. Most are courteous and we have no trouble with them. They come in, we show them the compassion of Christ by giving them a cup of coffee, and they go on their way. Since we had many young kids in the building, I walked out on the front porch to observe and make sure we did not have any surprises.

It did not take me long to see who they were talking about. A young man, whom I will call Bob, came crisscrossing his way down the street past the Centre. I and three others stood quietly observing him as he walked down the snow-covered street. Since he did not look like he wanted to come in, I felt I did not have reason for concern.

Without warning, as if I had called him, Bob looked at me and headed straight toward me. It did not take long before we were standing face to face. He was, without a doubt, under the influence of something that made him unaware of what was going on around him. As he came toward me, he mumbled something I could not interpret. When he was within arm's reach of me, he said three words which came as clear as day, "Preach to me."

Are not these the words every missionary wants to hear; the cry of a lost soul saying, "Preach to me"? At that moment, the only words given to me by the Holy Spirit were, "Jesus loves you." As quick as I said the words, he lunged forward and without saying another word, he slapped me on the left cheek and knocked my glasses to the floor of the deck.

His swing caught me off guard and I stood there looking at him. I will admit, turning the other cheek was not what was going through my head in the moment. I was standing wondering what to do. I was not angry as much as I was in shock. It was as if I was somewhere else looking at what had happened. I stood there frozen, but I was not standing alone. At this time, one of the young men who had dropped in for coffee and had stayed around to visit came outside to see what he could do. He stood near me and two women stood off the edge of the deck by their quad. Each of us wondered how Bob would react next.

As we stood there looking, he proceeded down the front steps of the deck, picked up a twelve-foot two-by-four, which blocked the icy sidewalk, and came toward me. When Jesus said in His Word to turn the other cheek, I do not think He expected us to stand there when someone threatened us with a two-by-four. Anxious thoughts filled my mind. Things were not looking good. Behind us were four, four-foot by five-foot windows. Would he break the windows? Worse yet, what if he hit one of us? He brought the wood to the foot of the stairs and threw it down on the ground. I stood there relieved. God had protected us.

With eyes blurred from substance abuse, Bob bounded up the stairs toward us like a wolf going after a struggling caribou. Determined to get into the building, he headed straight for the door. Like soldiers guarding the fortress, we stood between him and the entrance, trying to protect the children inside. With one quick motion, we grabbed the Allen Key by the door and tried to pull the door closed between us and him. Faster than we could get it closed he yanked the door out of my hand and pushed his way inside. With anger he yelled, "Why did you do that?" and proceeded to slap me on the other cheek.

The situation escalated the more we tried to keep him away from the others in the building. He was angry and not in the right state of mind. The young man and I were the only thing standing between him and the main room. Unknown to us at the time, the police were on their way. One of the people outside had been quick in thought and had called for help. I wiped my forehead and realized I was bleeding – my glasses had cut my nose when he had hit me the first time.

He wound up for another swing. I did not even feel him connect as we, with one motion, took his hoodie over his head. He slid out of his sweatshirt as quick as I had grabbed it and slipped past us into the main room.

No sooner had he passed me than the four of us each grabbed an appendage and laid him on the floor. My friend and I held his arms, while Gwendy and her friend held his legs. At the moment, we had him secure. I grabbed one of his fingers as he struggled to get free. In that moment, I wanted to break it. He caused such personal pain and disrupted the evening. He had scared the kids, young people and adults who had come to a place of safety. But what kind of testimony would I have when word got around the town of the "preacher man" who broke the man's finger? Would Jesus break his finger?

In a matter of minutes, but what felt like an eternity, the police arrived, placed Bob in handcuffs, and escorted him out of the building. We all took deep breaths of relief when he was out of sight. What had happened? As the reality of the events began to hit, I shook with adrenaline. It had happened so quickly.

As the adrenaline began to wear off, I realized the room was empty except for the four of us. Where were the kids? Where was the rest of my family? I was thankful when Gwendy told me our three kids had ushered everyone to the back room and locked the door when they saw Bob enter the building. God protected each one from harm and had prevented them from seeing what had transpired. I was grateful to the Lord for those two girls who were outside to warn me of the coming danger.

After the police left, the children began to return to the main room, filled with questions. When Bob had hit the floor, they had heard it! They wanted to know if we were alright. Who had come into the building? Some shook with fear. We comforted them and assured them we were all ok. Inside I was shaking. I knew the attacker was not in his right mind due to the influence of drugs/alcohol, but still, why had he come after me? Why was he so determined to get into the building?

Two days after the incident we got a phone call from Bob's mom. She was beside herself with what had happened. She apologized many times, letting us know how bad she felt over what her son had done. She listened with a great sense of relief as we told her we had forgiven him as the Lord had forgiven us. In spite of our pain, we were able to extend the love of Christ.

This would not be the last time we saw Bob. Several months later he returned and dropped off his younger brother to play at the HOPE Centre. As he went to leave, I called him back. He looked as though he was unsure of my response. I invited him in while his brother played with some of the other kids. He admitted not remembering anything from that night. Again, I told him we had forgiven him.

In a case of personal harm and attack, the flesh cries out for justice.

Our inner self wants to pounce on the attacker. But is that what the Lord would do? As I reflect on this story over the course of time, I am reminded of how Christ reacted when he was falsely accused, beaten and spat upon. He, of all people, could have been justified in lashing out and seeking justice. He was wholly man and wholly God. The incarnate son of God who came down for us. He did nothing wrong, yet He suffered, bled, and died for me. The Bible says, "Who, when he was reviled, reviled not again; when he suffered, he threatened not; but committed Himself to Him that judgeth righteously." (1 Peter 2:23)

When Jesus could have taken a swing, He resisted. He took the beating and committed Himself to the Father, whom this verse says judges righteously. We have a Father in Heaven who knows what we are going through. He knows our pain and He will judge righteously in the end. One day, "every knee should bow, of things in heaven, and things on earth, and things under the earth; And that every tongue should confess that Jesus Christ is Lord, to the glory of God the Father." (Philippians 2:10-11)

It is only in faith that Christ knows how to handle each situation that allows us to turn the other cheek. It is only in our realization that this world is not our final destiny that we can endure through the challenges of this life. It is only through abiding in Christ that we will be able to suffer for His name.

Chapter 28

TRUSTING GOD WHEN I HAVE TO LET GO

"Train up a child in the way he should go; even when he is old he will not depart from it." (Proverbs 22:6)

We raised our children where some people consider to be the middle of nowhere. Some even say we are at the end of the world. To that, I like to say, we are not at the end of the world, but we can see the end from where we live. I mean, we are five hours from Walmart, we must be in the middle of nowhere. Growing up where they did, our kids experienced things they would not have gotten to experience had they grown up in New York where Gwendy and I were both raised.

They learned many aspects of the traditional First Nations/Native culture of living on the land. This is largely due to the friends we developed over the past twenty years. The older three got to spend hours trapping rabbits and lynx with some of the Native elders. They got to sleep in a wall tent over sixty miles back in the wilderness. They learned how to make a fire in the bush (wilderness). They have also learned the importance of being prepared for anything.

There are things they got to do that many other children their ages have not been able to do. They have seen more of the US than I ever did as a child. Our youngest daughter, Jenna, has a goal of reaching all fifty states. So far, she has only six more to visit.

They learned how to live and work with people of other cultures as they grew up around Summer Missionaries from German, Switzerland, Sweden, United States, and Canada. They have seen interns come and help us in ministry. They have said many sad goodbyes to close friends as they moved to other places.

There are also experiences that they have missed living here. Our children did not grow up going to the mall on Friday evenings for something to do. Most of them have ridden a school bus very few times, if at all. They grew up seeing their birth grandparents, uncles, aunts, and cousins only once every couple of years. They grew up having many adopted grandparents, aunties and uncles who took them in as their own. They never had a high school prom or the opportunity to play in school sports (except for one year of wrestling in our community).

Their experiences have made them who they are. Shopping for groceries once every four to six weeks feels normal to them. They do not understand why a person shops every day. They grew up with our family running a Coffee House/Family Game Night every Friday evening. We start at eight and finish around midnight, then clean-up the HOPE Centre afterward. Our kids thought this schedule was normal and, for them, it was...until they went off to college. Then they thought, "What do 'normal people' do on a Friday Night?"

As parents, we tried to protect them from the sin that is so prevalent around them. There are choices we made as parents that we would not have had to make if we lived somewhere else. Our kids did not know what it was to have a sleepover at someone else's home. They never knew what it was like to walk around town by themselves as we always had them go in pairs. They knew what it was to see a drunk staggering down the street. They knew children whose parents struggled to care for them. They knew what it was like to get picked on because of who they were and for the color of their skin. We did our best to let them see the evil around them, but from a safe place.

When we responded to ambulance calls, we wanted them to learn from others' mistakes. So, we stressed how a person's decisions affect his or her life and the inevitable consequences they faced from those decisions. When I had to spend the night in jail (not as a prisoner but as a guard), I talked openly about why a person ends up in the "drunk tank." They did not have to try the evil to see where it would take them. They saw it lived out on a regular basis.

Gwendy and Jocelyn showing the
ambulance to a group of kids

It was easy to protect our children when they were at home with us under our roof. But what would happen when they left for college? Would they crash under their new-found freedom? We raised our children to the best of our God-given ability, but they still grew up. All too soon, they became adults who wanted to think and act according to their own will.

It is amazing how one day we held Jocelyn in our arms trying to get her to sleep, and the next day it seemed she was going off to college. When she went off to college, we lost more than her. Our second daughter, Jessie went with her. We lost two girls in one year.

As a dad, taking my girls to college was one of the hardest things I have had to face. For almost eighteen years, they were under our care. I got to tell them where they could go, and what was right. God gave me that responsibility the day we welcomed them into the world. I got to teach them how to drive a car. We hunted together, visited together, and ministered together. They were and still are my little girls. We understood the importance of what it meant to "Train up a child in the way he should go: and when he is old, he will not depart from it." (Proverbs 22:6)

Don't get me wrong, we allowed them to make choices to learn about consequences, but we were still responsible for them. If something went wrong or they had a bad day, Gwendy and I were there to help pick up the pieces. We did not dictate their every move, but tried our best to instill in them the principles they needed to make right decisions in the future.

I remember when one of the girls was in grade school and a boy kept picking on her. She came home and told me what was happening. In response, I told her to ignore him and he would lose interest – at least that's what I thought. For several days, she tried to ignore it. Then one day she came home very upset. He had not stopped. She pleaded with me to do something.

The next day, I went to school and had a chat with him. I kindly told him my daughter did not appreciate his bugging her and she wanted him to stop. The picking stopped and he never bothered her again. I found out later, he had a crush on her and tried to show it through his teasing.

Now we had to let them go off on their own. I was not going to be there to help them. Anxiety and questions filled my mind. Were they going to make it? What if they ran into difficulty? Would they be able to make the right decisions? Would they choose the right friends? What if we had not done enough as parents to prepare them for the world in front of them? They were going to college in Alberta, twenty-three hours away. I was not expecting to have them stay home forever, but how did they get this old already?

The day came for us to take them to Prairie College. They were filled with anticipation and excitement. They had researched the school and loved what they had heard. They had been best friends all their lives and were now headed to college together. They looked forward to new friendships. They were ready to be college freshmen.

Their first day of college orientation was a gorgeous one. As we stood in line to register them, they began to meet new people. The college did a great job at putting together a full day of activities to help the new students adjust and feel welcomed. They also did a lot to make sure the parents felt comfortable in leaving their children under their care. We passed through the various stations. Paying their bills. Registering for classes. Picking up their room keys. Going to the library/bookstore for textbooks. And learning where the mail boxes were.

After a full morning, we thought it was time for food. I was feeling good already and now, having a hamburger cooked out on the grill, I was almost sold. I still did not like the fact that by the end of the day, we had to leave our girls. We would be leaving them in a strange, unfamiliar place, by *themselves.* We would be going home without them.

As we sat on the ground in the courtyard of the college eating our lunch, we met more of the new "children" starting college. They seemed normal. They seemed more than normal. They were going to be great friends for our girls. Our girls were going to love being at the college.

The afternoon's schedule was much different from the morning. It had only two activities for the parents. They had a parent's orientation scheduled and then what I was dreading. They scheduled a time for us to say goodbye and leave. The college told us when we were to leave our children! Could I trust God to be with them even though they were close to thirteen-hundred miles away?

The college was telling us as parents to leave our children in their capable hands. I knew they had done the same thing, many times before, during their over ninety years of existence. But, these were my girls we were talking about. They were the ones I had taught to ride a bike and drive a car. The ones I taught to work with their hands.

The new parent's orientation was what I needed. The college designed this special session for those who were letting go of their children for the first time. There must have been fifty or sixty of us gathered in the auditorium. The dorm staff talked about how they kept our kids safe. The dean of education talked about what he expected out of the students. Then the president spoke. He must have written the speech for me. He said, "You do not build ships to keep them in the harbor."

For almost eighteen years, we "built our ships." We did not build them to keep them in the harbor of home all their lives. God had matured them and brought them to the place where they were ready to leave. It was going to be hard. There were going to be tears shed. There were going to be lots of phone calls. They did more than survive; they thrived.

As Gwendy and I walked out of the session, the president's words kept ringing in my ears. I knew I needed to let Jocelyn and Jessie go. We had built our ships to survive the storms of life. We had built them with the future in mind. We did not want them to stay home and be babies all their lives. God entrusted them to us to train and now we needed to trust Him to care for them.

With the job of training coming to an end, we needed to send them on their way to complete their education, find husbands, get married, and start the cycle all over again. Sure, they would need advice. They might need a shoulder to cry on. They still needed us to help them, but they were entering a new phase of life.

With tears in our eyes, but a peace in our hearts, we met with the girls for one last goodbye before we headed out for our long trip back to the Yukon. We exchanged hugs and last-minute requests like, "Don't forget to call," and "Study hard," then we were on our way.

This day would only be the beginning of releasing our grown children into God's care. He gave us the responsibility to train our children and then trust Him as we let them go. Those two girls did more than survive. They thrived in the environment of college. We saw them grow from being our little girls to becoming lovely young ladies who have a love for the Lord. They love coming back home and we love having them. Yet, they also spend time away doing what God has asked them to do. It is still hard to let them go when they move to another state or province. Tears still flooded my eyes as we waved goodbye and as we traveled down the road away from the college. It is not that I want them to stay; it is the bond between a father and his daughters. A bond that continues no matter where in the world they "sail."

Four years later, we returned to register Jaime, our third daughter, at the same college. This time, the flood of emotions was different. No, I was not looking forward to her leaving any more than I looked forward to the first two leaving. But now the campus was familiar. We knew many professors by name. We even knew some of the students. God had brought us through a time of letting go and was bringing us to the same point again. We did not doubt His ability to care for our children.

We trust His care as we are reminded of Matthew 6:26, "Behold the fowls of the air: for they sow not, neither do they reap, nor gather into barns; yet your heavenly Father feedeth them. Are ye not much better than they?" If our God takes time to care for the birds of the air and the lilies of the field, will He not care for us and our children?

We have to remind ourselves to trust our Father. There are days our lack of control in a situation that involves our children leaves us anxious and wanting to be right there with them. Through it all, we know God is worthy of our trust and He will take care of them as He faithfully cares for us. Sure, they will have problems and challenges, but God uses those hard times to show them He can be trusted in everything.

Leaving our daughters at Prairie College

Chapter 29

TRUSTING GOD WHEN I LOSE CONTROL

"But ye shall receive power, after that the Holy Ghost is come upon you: and ye shall be witnesses unto me both in Jerusalem, and in all Judaea, and in Samaria, and unto the uttermost part of the earth." (Acts 1:8)

At some point in our lives, most of us have heard a story about someone who said, "Lord, please do not make me _____ " or they say, "Lord, I'll go anywhere, but please do not send me to_____." After telling about their prayer, the person then tells how God asked them to do the very thing or go to the very place they did not want to. When I was growing up, I had an aunt who prayed for the Lord not to have her marry a farmer. Sometime after the prayer she met the man of her dreams, who turned out to be a farmer. Another person I knew asked God not to have her marry a pastor. She later met and married a pastor. Each of these have been happily married for almost as long as I have been alive.

Why do we pray such prayers? Why does it sometimes seem that God does not answer? Why is it that often the very thing I do not want is exactly what God gives me anyway? For example, why did God send me to Canada, when my desire was to stay and minister in the "land of the free and home of the brave?"

For almost thirty years, I have studied and preached the Word of God. Through this, the Lord has helped me learn some principles about how God answers His children and what God desires from those who follow Him.

The first principle the Lord taught me is *unconditional obedience.* Paul writes and says,

"I appeal to you therefore, brothers, by the mercies of God, to present your bodies as a living sacrifice, holy and acceptable to God, which is your spiritual worship. Do not be conformed to this world, but be transformed by the renewal of your mind, that by testing you may discern what is the will of God, what is good and acceptable and perfect." (Romans 12:1-2 ESV)

God's ultimate desire is for us to be willing to do whatever it is He wants. He does not want conditions of service. He wants a simple, "I'll go where you want me to go."

By understanding the meaning behind the sacrifices in the Old Testament, we learn about unconditional obedience to the Lord. When one of the Israelites brought a lamb to the priest for a sacrifice, they did not expect to take the lamb back home with them. The sacrifice was all or nothing. The lamb did not get up and run away to join its family when the priest got done.

In Mark 8:34, Jesus said, "Whosoever will come after me, let him deny himself, and take up his cross, and follow me." When Christ was on earth, He taught unconditional obedience. He said if anyone desires to follow Him, they must deny themselves.

In my own life, I have found that I often have conflicting desires. I desire to do what God wants, but my flesh desires to live the way I want to live. These two desires are in a constant battle against each other. Only when I have offered Christ my unconditional obedience can I follow Him the way He wants me to.

Another principle I have learned is that *God always knows best.* We see this principle in Jeremiah 29:11. This passage is a prophetic message to the people of Israel. Jeremiah prophesied of coming judgement. The people of Israel were going to be carried off to a foreign land. God says in this verse, "For I know the thoughts (plans) that I think toward you, saith the Lord, thoughts of peace, and not of evil, to give you an expected end." Through Jeremiah, God reminds the Israelites of His knowledge of the big picture,

211

which far exceeds their limited vision. When God asks something of us, He not only sees the present, he also sees the future. He knows His plan is so much better than what we desired.

When I surrendered my life to the Lord at thirteen years old, and then again when I was in my first year of Bible School, I did not worry about whether God was going to take care of me. I did not wonder if He knew what was best for me. God opened my eyes to His desire for me to surrender *one hundred percent* to His will for me *whatever* and *wherever* that will might take me. The road has not always been easy. The path has taken us through some very rough and troubled spots. In these tough spots, God has taught me He always knows best. I only see a limited view of my life. God sees the whole picture.

In Isaiah 55:8-9, we read, "For my thoughts are not your thoughts, neither are your ways my ways, saith the Lord. For as the heavens are higher than the earth, so are my ways higher than your ways, and my thoughts than your thoughts." When God asks something of us, He already knows the whole plan; we only see our part. We can see this in the story of Jonah. Jonah only saw the wickedness of the people and did not see the love and compassion God had for the Ninevites. One could say we are also very short-sighted. God has plans and ways that are much higher than what we think or plan.

Earlier in the book, I shared how I had a desire to serve the Lord only in the US. God gave me a desire to serve Him and see churches planted there and I had limited myself to this geographic location. When I was asked to go to the Yukon, Canada, I was devastated because my thoughts were not God's thoughts. God knew His plan for the Yukon. I only knew my limited view of what I had seen.

A story about our second daughter provides another example of God's work to get us where He wants us. During her first year of college, Jessie enrolled in an outdoor leadership program which developed her leadership qualities. This program also strengthened her trust in the Lord by pushing her beyond what she thought was possible. As she continued on in her education, she felt the Lord leading her to work toward a Bachelor's Degree in Intercultural Studies. This gave her exposure to global opportunities by allowing her to travel overseas for an internship.

We raised our children to seek the Lord and His will, not their own.

On one of her phone calls with us, she said she was considering going overseas for most of the next school year. She shared about needs she heard about in Romania and how she hoped to go there. As she pursued an internship in this far away country, nothing opened up. No matter where she tried, God kept closing the door to any ministry there.

One day she called and told us about a children's home. This home ministered to needy people near the slums of an overseas city. The staff sought to help babies and children whom they found on the streets, dumps, hospitals, and sometimes even on their doorstep. As we listened, we could not help but think, "this is her." This was exactly where we could see her fitting. Its location in Nairobi, Africa was a different story. She felt the Lord was opening the door and leading her to Africa!

Was Africa the best place for our daughter? She was so young. It was one thing to trust the Lord to be with your kids when they are thirteen hundred miles away. It is yet another to trust Him when they are on the other side of the world. We knew the overseas environment might not be as kind and civilized as in North America.

Our minds started thinking of the bad things that could happen. In many ways, we were like the disciples when they were in the storm and Jesus was asleep in the boat. They came to Him in Mark 4:38, "Don't you care we are perishing?" We thought she was going overseas to die. It did not help us when we learned she would be in an area "Unadvisable to visit."

This was the beginning of our having to let go and let God have His way with her. Inside, we knew we could trust Him to care for her, but on the outside, we were anxious. Saying goodbye to her was hard to face. The fact that she was with a wonderful group who would be traveling with her for the first month brought us some encouragement.

But, saying goodbye was also the beginning of lessons God needed to teach us. He taught us much about ourselves and grew our trust in Him during this eight-month internship. Our faith went through times of testing and stretching often during those months.

The home in which she worked stood as a beacon of hope near the heart of downtown Nairobi. She fell in love with the place as soon as she entered. She was responsible to help provide care for six to eight, sometimes more, babies in the "baby room." Eight hours each day, she fed, changed, rocked to sleep, and cared for the little ones. In reality, she was the mom many of them did not have. She worked alongside and lived with Kenya nationals. Her mentors were a couple who, like us, were missionaries. They loved the work the Lord had given them and poured their lives into it.

This gave us peace to see how much they not only cared for the children at the children's home, but also how much they cared for Jessie. Things were going well for about a month until she started complaining about a rash on her head that had not healed. It kept getting bigger and developed into a fever. She did not feel well and did not know what to do. How could she get it taken care of? She was in a foreign country where doctors are sometimes harder to find than fish when I go fishing.

Over the next three to four days her condition continued to get worse. She had little energy and a headache that did not go away. We grew more and more worried about her. What could we do with her so far away? Paul wrote to the believers in Philippi,

> *"Be careful for nothing; but in everything by prayer and supplication with thanksgiving let your requests be made known unto God. And the peace of God, which passeth all understanding, shall keep your hearts and minds through Christ Jesus." (Philippians 4:6)*

We knew God could care for her, and we committed her to do His will asking Him to help her in some way. We could do nothing to help her except trust the Lord, which was exactly what God wanted us to do.

God knew exactly what she needed. During her greatest time of need, God brought her a doctor who knew exactly what to do. He gave her an antibiotic to help with what he believed was a bacterial infection. Within a week, the spot almost completely healed and her strength began to return.

She usually texted every morning as I got ready to go to the office. She shared the highlights of her day, like when one of the children she worked with learned to crawl. Sometimes she shared about kids who were struggling to stay alive. One time it was about a child who did not make it. Even though she was half-way around the world, we were able to communicate with her most every day as she texted, telling us about her joys and sorrows.

One day, we sent texts and there was no answer. "She must be busy," we thought. Later in the day, we texted again. No response. We thought, *maybe she had to go somewhere, but usually she told us if she was to be gone for a day.* How quickly our minds began to worry! I find this true in many areas of my life. God can heal a rash or solve another problem we face and we rejoice. Sometimes only a day or two later, we are right back to worrying again. God says, "I know the way; trust me." We want to worry. God says, "I got this." We say, "Are you sure?" We ride the roller coaster of fear and trust. We know the trust God wants us to give Him, but we also know the anxiety that can take over.

Another day went by and still no communication. We considered calling the missionaries with whom she was staying, but realized the only way we had ever talked to them was through our daughter's phone. We searched the internet to see if there were any headlines about a power outage or lack of internet in Nairobi. We did not see anything to cause us alarm, yet we still heard nothing.

On the third day, we finally heard from her. The area of town where she was living and working had been without internet for three days. Three days does not seem like very long when we are away from the problem. Yet, when we are in the thick of our troubles and we go into worry mode, three days can seem like an eternity.

I am reminded of how the disciples and followers of Jesus lost hope after Jesus' death on the cross. When Jesus met the two travelers on the road to Emmaus (Luke 24:13-35), they suffered from a broken heart and were discouraged. They had plans for Jesus. They wanted Him to deliver them from Roman oppression. Yet, the ones He was supposed to conquer had crucified Him. Their hope was gone. They thought the worst. Their dreams dashed. They lost control of the situation. Yet, He was still in control. He did things differently.

Often, our anxiety and fear come from our not being in control. We desire to control every situation. We want things to be done the way we think is best. God uses our lack of control to teach us that we can rely on Him. He cares for the safety of our children. He can protect them and provide for them even in a foreign country. Even thousands of miles away!

Jessie with some of the children during
her overseas internship

Chapter 30

TRUSTING GOD WHEN IT LOOKS HOPELESS

"What man of you, having a hundred sheep, if he has lost one of them, does not leave the ninety-nine in the open country, and go after the one that is lost, until he finds it? And when he has found it, he lays it on his shoulders, rejoicing." (Luke 15:4-5)

(Some of the details in the following story have been altered to protect the person's identity)

One of the things I have enjoyed most about serving the Lord in the Yukon, has been the variety of ministry opportunities. I would not be a very good factory worker; doing the same thing day after day becomes monotonous to me. In ministry, days are not often the same. Some of this is due to the extreme weather changes in the Yukon. We cannot keep the same outside activities at minus fifty as we can when it is seventy above.

Some of this is due to the culture of the people with whom we work. Traditionally, they were always on the move, traveling with the game they hunted. Their lives revolved around the seasons. They went fishing in the summer. Hunting took place in spring and summer. Berry picking came in the fall. Because of this, they very rarely stick to something for a long duration. They like variety, so if we are to continue to minister to them, we must be willing to vary our methods and approach to ministry. The

Gospel message stays the same, as does the Lord whom we are preaching about, but the way we reach people changes.

Some of the variety is due to the nature of our ministry. We have tried to focus on every age group so we can reach as many as we can with the Gospel of Jesus Christ. One day we run Kids Bible Club for kids ages five to twelve years old. The next day we may be running a youth activity focused on our teenagers. Later in the week, we host our adult Bible Study. By doing this we are able to teach the Bible to the whole family.

Since we built the HOPE Centre and moved in December 2011, there has been more of a schedule to our ministry. We try to stick to a schedule so people know when they are apt to find us at the Centre. At the same time, we still try to be flexible enough to meet people when they desire or need to meet somewhere else.

Each day, Monday through Friday, starts with a morning coffee drop-in time. This has proven successful in giving people a place to come and ask questions and visit with community members. Sometimes these morning sessions turn into discipleship times for believers. At other times, these sessions seem more like the good ol' boys club at the local diner. On those days, politics and town events dominate the conversations.

After school each afternoon we open again for another drop-in time. This is more focused on the school-aged children of our community, but it is open to anyone who wants to stop by. This time gives us opportunities to help teach Biblical principles to the children while they play in a safe environment. The kids enjoy a healthy snack and a Bible story or lesson.

On Tuesday evenings, we host a women's craft night. The women gather together their unfinished projects. This evening is filled with laughter, heart-felt conversations, and a time for the ladies of our community to get away from the home for a couple hours.

Wednesday evenings we have an adult Bible study. This is for people of the community who have a desire to grow closer to the Lord and learn more about His Word. Our studies often take us through a book of the Bible or through a topical series such as discipleship, reaching the lost or Biblical doctrine.

The highlight for the community is what we do on Friday night from eight until eleven. We invite the whole community out for a family game night/coffee house. The coffee and hot chocolate is free. In the summer, the kids enjoy Italian sodas. It is a great time for the community to gather especially when the weather has been cold and everyone is going stir crazy from being in the house all week. There is always great commotion and excitement in the Centre on these nights.

Saturday is a family day. We take time to straighten the house and get yard work done. Some Saturdays we are home bodies, barely leaving for a couple of minutes. On other Saturdays, we take advantage of the nice weather and take a drive.

Sunday begins the week with our traditional morning worship service. Fifteen to twenty people gather together for fellowship and spiritual encouragement. This gives them the boost they need to get through the week. The fellowship continues sometimes an hour or two after the service as members visit and talk with each other. It is one of the highlights of our week.

It was in the midst of this normal routine when an abnormal event occurred. This event taught us to trust God in the midst of dire situations. No one is ever "too" lost for God to find and protect.

I spent a typical morning at the HOPE Centre. People came and went. Some came by for the free coffee. Others came in because they were lonely and needed someone to talk to. For a few moments after everyone left, I worked on the distance education class I had enrolled in. Before I knew it, I heard the noon bell from across the street. Lunch time had snuck up on me again. I headed out the door to go home for the delicious lunch Gwendy had waiting for me. I made a "quick" stop at the post office to check the mail.

It was a typical day for the end of October. The late October air bit at my face as I walked outside. The weather was changing. The long days and warmth of summer had given way to the cool of the coming winter. The nip in the air demanded at least a coat and a hat and gloves. As the nights dipped down below freezing, ice started to build on the puddles and small lakes. Fresh snow covered the nearby mountain peaks. Soon, a blanket of snow would cover the Yukon until the following May.

My kids make many comments about my "quick" stops at the local grocery store/post office. It is never just a trip to get the mail or to get groceries. Each visit is a chance to interact with people who do not visit the HOPE Centre and do not come to church or Bible Study. It is a chance to challenge them to think about their Creator. A "quick trip to get the mail" can turn into an hour event.

Today was no different. As I was about to climb into the car and head home, someone called my name and asked if they could talk to me for a few minutes. The look of anxiety on his face and fear in his voice let me know now was not the time to run home. He needed someone to talk to. He said his son, Bill, left the house for a meeting several hours before. He never arrived for the meeting and no one had seen him since. He had concern for Bill's safety as he thought he may have headed out of town on the family's quad.

His concern also stemmed from his son not having on the right clothing for the weather. Bill left the house with the intention of being gone only a short time. He was not dressed for the cool air of late fall.

Since I spent the morning in the HOPE Centre and failed to see his son, I said I would pray for his safe arrival back home. I assured him if I saw Bill, I would let him know. Saying a quick silent prayer, I climbed into the car and headed home.

I was not too concerned. I figured Bill had decided to go for a drive around town and would be back shortly. *All would soon be well*, I thought. In our small community, people often stop and visit others. What can start out as a five-minute stop can turn into a couple-hour visit. Little did I realize the severity of the situation that was beginning to unfold.

At lunch, we prayed for Bill and went about our day like nothing was happening. In fact, we heard nothing more about the situation until around five when we got a call at the HOPE Centre. Bill was still missing. Some workers had seen him head out of town in the morning but did not see him return the whole day.

The father was worried and starting to panic as he thought about what might have happened to his son. Who would not be? The direction he traveled took him out into remote and rugged wilderness where there were no services. Two hundred and fifty miles of open road lay between where he had started and the next town. It usually took at least five hours to travel by car or truck.

On a quad, it would take much longer if he even had enough gas to go that far. The father guessed Bill could only make it no more than seventy miles on the full tank of gas. If Bill did not watch the fuel level, he would get stranded in the middle of the open wilderness. He had no phone or means of communication and very little to keep himself warm once it got dark. The light sweatshirt and a pair of sneakers were not enough to protect him from the freezing temperatures. The father was letting people know so they could be on the lookout.

After receiving the call, I joined the search. I made my way down the highway looking for any sign of him or the quad on which he had been traveling. Surely, he did not get that far from town. Or did he? We had no idea where to even start. Thankfully, the Yukon has limited side roads on which to turn. There are, however, lots of gravel pits, pull outs, cabins, and camps all along the way he had headed.

Other than the workers who had seen him on the highway in the morning, we had nothing to show us where he was heading or why he had not come home. He disappeared without leaving anything for us to follow. How could a person and quad disappear and leave no sign of where they had gone? In vain, we searched well into the night and found nothing to give us assurance that we were even looking in the right direction.

The next day, several other community members joined the search. They drove up and down the highway, hoping to catch a glimpse of Bill or a sign they were on the right track. They searched every cabin and driveway off the main road. They called out his name. Still, no one found even a track in the gravel.

Gwendy made a hot pot of soup for the searchers. I delivered it to them along the road as we continued to search. The clouds started to move in and the sky turned from blue to gray. It was not too cold, but the soup was well received as people had been looking for hours and were cold and hungry. If they were getting cold, we knew Bill had to be even colder. The search dragged on, but once again, no one had found anything.

Finally, late in the afternoon one of the searchers found his backpack close to forty miles from town. It lay at the edge of the road unnoticed by all but the most observant. It provided the first glimmer of hope since he had gone missing the day before. It was not much, but it showed where he had been. The search started to focus on the area near where they found the backpack.

It was like looking for a needle in a haystack. We needed to search miles and miles of road, as well as hundreds of square miles of wilderness.

Cabins dotted much of the search area. What if he had gone into one of them to seek shelter, realizing the quad was running out of gas? There was so much area to search and who knew how long we had before the weather began to affect his thinking? It was possible he could succumb to the elements.

The weather started to turn miserable. The wind picked up and the temperature dropped. We needed to find Bill and soon. The chances of him surviving were decreasing. History is filled with stories of Yukoners whom the weather crept up on and before they knew it, their story of life on earth was cut short. A person can only live so long in the cold, fall Yukon air. Hypothermia would be setting in. He could lay down and fall asleep, never to wake up again.

Hypothermia affects the body and mind of a person in strange ways. As a person's body begins to cool down, the body starts to pull heat from the extremities to keep the core warm. This rush of heat to the center of the body makes a person feel too warm and often they begin to take off some clothes trying to "cool down."

If a person continues down this path, they are headed for disaster. The blood continues to be taken from the outer parts of the body and even the head in an attempt to keep the organs warm. With the blood goes the oxygen flow needed to provide healthy thoughts. The exposed person begins to feel sleepy and seeks to find a spot to lay down and rest. Many times, the hypothermic person feels like they need a short nap. They think if they can sleep for a few minutes, they will wake up and be able to keep going. Unless someone finds them and gets them to a warm spot, this nap is often the last nap they get. We all knew this and prayed for Bill's safe return.

Late in the evening on the second day, searchers found a sweatshirt that looked like it could be Bill's. The family confirmed it indeed belonged to him. It seemed our fears for him were coming true. Hypothermia was setting in. People began to fear the worst. We needed to find him soon.

Near where searchers found his sweatshirt, an old, abandoned mining road ran parallel to the road. It lay hidden from view of the main road. Built decades ago, only some of the locals even knew of its existence. Those familiar with it took a drive in to see if Bill had gone in that direction.

Their search paid off. Beside part of the old mine road stood a big tree. They found the four-wheeler under the tree. Piece by piece we were getting closer, but we needed to find Bill. A quick inspection showed the quad was almost out of gas. Bill must have parked it there to keep it safe while he went to look for gas.

Search and Rescue set up a command post in a gravel pullout near the old road. Teams of searchers combed the willows and dense brush with flashlights. Some of the locals gathered around a fire, trying to keep warm. We prayed for his safe return as we stood by the fire, shivering.

Believers from the community gathered around Bill's parents seeking to offer comfort and strength during this difficult and stressful time. I told the father often that we were praying for Bill to be found, alive and in a healthy condition.

I pleaded with God to help us find Bill, but I wondered if there was any hope for him to survive. I did not know what God was trying to teach the family. I did know God loved Bill more than anyone else, even his family. I also knew that God often works in mysterious ways to draw people closer to Himself. I had to trust God to do what was best for His glory.

The night dragged on. The mercury in the thermometer dipped into the single digits. Snow blew around us, causing us to shiver. Even with the fire, the searchers could not stay warm. The snow soaked our clothing. We tried to stay positive. No one mentioned it, but we were losing hope. The weather was going to turn the search and rescue mission into a recovery mission if God did not do something.

Most of the searchers left the scene around one in the morning to drive the forty miles back to town. Sadness gripped my heart. I prayed as I looked out at the weather conditions. Somewhere in the dense wilderness sat a young man who needed God's protection. I trusted the Lord to have the ability to protect him, yet doubted very much it was His plan to save him. I shivered even in the car with the heat blasting, due to the hours I searched. How could Bill survive with no sleeping bag, blanket, boots, or a fire going to keep him warm and dry?

One and a half hours later, I sat down on my comfortable couch in our living room as the woodstove poured out the heat. Gwendy and I discussed the situation with each other. A quick glance at the thermometer showed zero. The wind howled, sending the snow swirling in every direction. We needed a miracle tonight. We had done what we could. God had to do the rest. He and only He could keep this missing person alive through the horrible weather.

We awoke the next morning to beautiful clear blue skies, and temperatures below zero. The wind had stopped. What a glorious, sunny, Sunday to worship the Lord! What made the day even more praiseworthy was what happened down the highway.

Two men decided to spend the night along the road instead of coming back to town. Early in the morning, they drove along the highway looking for signs of life in the new fallen snow. Something caught one of their eyes. Fresh tracks wandered through the snow which had fallen through the night. About thirty to forty yards off the highway, hidden from view, lay a clearing. Bill stood next to a stump in the clearing. His mind dulled from hypothermia. He stood hypothermic and hungry, but very much alive.

Even in our doubt, God protected him. He worked in his mind and gave him clarity of thought in the midst of a horrific night. He had realized the symptoms of hypothermia and did not let himself stop to sit down, knowing if He stopped to rest, he might never wake up. He had walked in circles around the little clearing for hours. God reunited the son with his father and mother. God protected him from the bitter cold night. God again taught us what it meant to trust Him completely even when things look impossible.

The parents felt immense joy and gladness when they saw their son. The whole ordeal had taken its toll on them, but the joy and relief radiated from their faces. The joy they felt is nothing compared to the joy we read about in the Bible that happens in heaven when one lost sinner comes to repentance.

Jesus said, "there is joy in the presence of the angels of God over one sinner that repenteth." (Luke 15:10) We read later in the New Testament, "the Lord is...not willing that any should perish, but that all should come to repentance." (2 Peter 3:9) As much as these parents love their son, God loves us with an even greater love.

All the events during this search and rescue mission taught us much about the God we serve and in whom we put our trust. In the Bible we read, "With God all things are possible." Do we actually believe it? For me, I know the impossible is possible, but I often doubt that God will actually do the impossible. I even pray for the impossible, but then doubt God will do what I have asked.

After this incident, I learned that God not only has the *power* to do the impossible, sometimes He even *does* the impossible. He kept one of His precious creations alive when all things were against survival. He showed the father and us how worthy He is of our trust even in the most difficult and impossible situations.

Chapter 31

TRUSTING GOD WHEN LIFE IS UNCERTAIN

"The Lord is not slack concerning his promise, as some men count slackness; but is longsuffering to us-ward, not willing that any should perish, but that all should come to repentance." (2 Peter 3:9)

"I have stage four lung cancer." Gary's words echoed in my ears. He stopped by the HOPE Centre and dropped this bombshell on me. His doctor confirmed what he had already suspected. He felt shocked and devastated. He started to cry. What was he going to do? He did not want to leave his wife a widow. Who would help her care for the house?

As we talked, I was concerned for more than his earthly house and possessions; I was concerned for his eternal destiny. We talked many times over the years. While he supported the work of the Lord and knew about Jesus, I wondered if he had ever put his faith and trust in Christ as his own Savior.

Soon after getting the news of his cancer, Gary was to travel to the hospital in another province to find out how extensive the cancer was inside his body. His wife was not able to go with him and neither were any of his family. He needed someone who could go with him on the flight. He asked me to go with him. A quick look at my calendar revealed he needed me on Easter weekend.

As a believer, Easter is one of my favorite holidays. I love Christmas and all the celebrations, but it is Easter and the events surrounding it that give me hope of my salvation. Because Christ is risen, I know my future is sure. I have no fear of death because, "Thanks be to God, which giveth us the victory through our Lord Jesus Christ." (1 Corinthians 15:57) Because Christ rose, I can live with God in heaven forever someday. I had the hope of Christ and wanted my friend to have the same hope.

After looking into the flight, we found out we could leave on Good Friday and be back on Saturday. If I drove home late Saturday, I could be back for Easter. Was my Easter celebration more important than making sure my dying friend made the HOPE of Easter personal in his own life? I prayed for the Lord to give me the opportunity to have a deep spiritual conversation with my friend and accepted his invitation.

We waited for the day of his test to arrive. He worried about how far the cancer might have spread. I worried about how long he had left on this earth. I did not want him to die. Seeking to give him comfort as he waited, I often told him I was praying for him.

Finally, the day came for us to head to Vancouver, British Columbia for his appointment. The flight was beautiful. Flying at around thirty-six thousand feet, we could look out over the snowcapped mountains below. Of course, the Yukon lay under a thick blanket of snow. The further south we got the barer the ground became. By the time we reached our destination, the flowers were in full bloom. I took off my heavy winter coat and enjoyed the spring breezes blowing off the water. The warmth we felt was something we had not been able to enjoy at home since the previous summer. The welcoming, noisy chirping of the birds filled the air as they sang their good night song.

Our taxi ride through the city made me wonder if my life was in danger. The driver definitely knew the city and was not afraid to take control of the busy streets, swerving in and out of traffic like a seasoned driver. After a half-hour taxi drive, we climbed out of the taxi and breathed a sigh of relief. We were glad to arrive at our hotel in one piece.

The hotel sat along one of the busy streets of the city. The sound of traffic filled our ears, but could not drown out the inner gnawing we both were feeling about the reason for the trip. What would the test show? We both knew the news he heard the next day might not be good, but we made the best of the evening, enjoying the sights and sounds of the city.

The light of the sun turned into the shadows of night. Soon the lights of the city took over, illuminating the night sky. We sat in the room talking about what the future might look like. None of us has a desire to die prematurely. To know we have a limited time on earth gets a person thinking. Gary had worked all his life to establish a good retirement for him and his wife. Now it all meant very little in light of what lay ahead. All he wanted was more time.

The test gave Gary the results he did not want to hear. The doctors said he had two years or less to live. The results floored him. We flew back to the Yukon less than twenty-four hours later; his thoughts were on what he was facing. Sitting in the airplane, I asked him if he was ready to meet Jesus Christ. His words said yes, but still I wondered. I knew I could not know any man's heart; only the Lord knew the state of this man's soul. I had to trust God to keep working in his heart and to give me more opportunities to speak Christ's love and grace to him.

Over the next one and a half years I made frequent visits to Gary's home. We talked often about the end of his life. We all knew it was coming. He kept getting weaker and weaker. With each trip to the hospital, we wondered if this might be his last.

Time and time again, he came back determined to live. He and his wife planned for years to build a cabin. He finally built the "weekend getaway" he wanted. He loved to spend time in the bush (out on the land). He looked forward to what he would do in the months to come. We looked on as the cancer sucked the life out of him. He never lost hope that he was going to keep living.

We celebrated that Gary had made it through each holiday that passed. He continued to deteriorate. His afternoon naps turned into all-day dozing. As death drew closer, we continued to encourage him to look to Jesus to help him through.

About four months before his death, our family needed to go back to New York for our home service and visit supporters and prayer partners. I hated to leave him and his wife during this challenging time in their lives. I knew the chances of me seeing him alive again on this side of heaven were slim.

The months dragged on as we visited church after church in our home state. I called him to see how he was doing. Every time we talked, he was optimistic about how long he would be around. He talked about what we would do together when we got back. The last time I talked to him he promised, "I'll be here when you get back." He said he would take our family on a "wiener roast" as soon as it was warm enough to do so in the spring.

Shortly after that phone call, he left his home and went to the hospital. It looked like the end was near. We sat four thousand miles away unable to do anything but pray for the man and his family. We had to trust the Lord to be with him as he drew his final breath.

His time on earth came to an end. We never did get to see him again in the Yukon. We never did get to have that wiener roast. He took his final breath on earth and began his eternity. When we returned to the Yukon a couple months after his death, his wife said the last song he had on his lips before he died was one of the Gospel songs he had heard many times in his life.

I knew Gary had heard the Gospel many times. I knew that he knew of Jesus. I knew the peace of Christ was what helped him in his final days. What I did not know is the condition of his heart when he took his last breath.

Only the Lord knew the condition of his heart at the time of his final breath. We read, "Man looketh on the outward appearance, but the LORD looketh on the heart." (1 Samuel 16:7) With each person we minister to, we must share the Good News that God used to change our lives. We must allow God to work and trust that he will bring about the result.

Gary loved the outdoors. Used with
permission from Dorothy Dick.

Chapter 32

TRUSTING GOD WHEN IT IS DIFFICULT

"And all things, whatsoever ye shall ask in prayer, believing, ye shall receive." (Matthew 21:22)

The verse above is one I still do not understand. There are times when I have asked for something in prayer, believing God can do it, but I get a no as my answer. I firmly believe there are times when what I pray for is not what God wants for me. He, in His infinite wisdom and knowledge, knows what I need more than I know myself. I have learned to pray saying, "If it is pleasing to you Lord, please_____."

Because we are missionaries, we travel back to New York around every four to five years for a period of three to six months. This helps us connect with supporting individuals and churches, and it gives us a change of pace and a rest from our day-to-day ministry. It is not so much a vacation as it is a change in assignment. For the whole time we are away, we are on the road. It is not uncommon for us to put fifteen thousand miles on our van in the months we are visiting churches and supporters.

We have gained many great memories and experiences during each of our four home service assignments. These trips allowed us to see many of the states. During one trip back to New York, we traveled for three weeks around the US and put on seven thousand miles. Stops in California, Arizona, Colorado, and Georgia made the trip memorable for our children as they each got to choose something special for us to do. It is not uncommon for one of our children to say, "I remember when..." and talk about one of their memories. Each trip holds a special place in our minds, and each in their own way. They do not come without challenges though.

Our children grew up knowing only life in a small community. Life in the community has a certain rhythm, a stability to it, and they like that stability.

Every time we get ready to head out for our home service trip, there are grunts and groans from our children. It is difficult when we pull them away from home. As much as they enjoy seeing their grandparents and other relatives in New York, New York is not their home. We travel every weekend, which gets tiring for them. Over the years, though, our kids have made friends and memories in each of the churches we have visited.

As we prepared for one of our home service trips, the Lord placed on my heart to be praying for our youngest daughter, Jenna. She struggled with leaving the Yukon and wondered why she could not stay with her sister in Ross River. One evening I asked, "What do you want to be able to do while we are in New York this next time?"

Without even thinking much at all she said, "I want to go to a youth group." During a previous trip, we spoke at a youth group meeting at one of our churches. Our daughter loved it so much she wanted to be able to attend a youth group every week while we traveled.

My heart sank. I knew the difficulty of being able to go to a consistent youth group because of our constant travel on weekends. Many youth groups met on Sunday evening and our schedule did not allow us to be in one area consistently. We always ministered as a family and we did not want to start leaving our children back with their grandparents so they could attend a youth group.

I sought to encourage her by letting her know we would look for one, but I wondered how it was going to work. We prayed about it, leaving it for the Lord to work out. I did not see how it was going to be possible, but I prayed for the Lord to make it possible. She may be able to visit a couple of times, but to attend every week seemed unlikely to me.

We continued to pray about her desire to have a youth group as the time drew closer for us to leave. We looked at a few online, but they were either too far or gathered together on the wrong night. I knew God had this under control, but as a dad who likes to fix everything, it seemed hopeless.

When we arrived in New York, her cousins invited her to attend the youth group they attended. I thought, "Good, she can go there and she will get her answer." She came home the first night and said, "I do not want to go back." How could she have us pray for something and then reject God's answer? The youth group had not been what she was looking for. The music was too loud and the message was not to her standards. As a dad, I had a choice; I could tell her not to be picky and take what she could get or I could join her in prayer and trust God to meet her needs. In her heart, she knew what she needed to help her grow spiritually.

She did not let her prayer request go. She kept looking and I kept praying. Little did I know how God was working to answer the prayer request by not giving her just any youth group. He had something bigger in mind. He wanted to give her one where she could flourish and grow as well as develop friendships that lasted longer than a few months.

One evening, she came to me and said, "I found where I want to go, I found a youth group on the internet." What???? I did not say it, but I was thinking, "Yeah right, on the internet." I must confess, I was suspicious. When I was growing up we did not find churches on the internet; we looked down the street. Who finds a youth group by looking online?

Even so, she found one she thought would be what she wanted. Better yet, it met on a day when we could take her. We dropped her off at West Windsor Baptist Church for their youth group. Our reluctance was not in the church. From the time we entered until the time we left, the members of that church were welcoming and friendly. We were reluctant because we wanted to make sure she had a good experience. Of course, God already knew what she needed and wanted.

As she exited the church that evening after her first night, her face beamed as she said, "I want to go back." The group was exactly what she had wanted, what we had prayed for, and what she needed. She loved the games and fun times with the other teens. But, the games are not what made her consider coming back. She wanted to return because of how the church did the Bible study. The youth pastor, Pastor Christian, gave a Biblical challenge and then the youth broke into small groups. She loved the small group interaction. The group was exactly what she had longed for and we had asked God to give her.

We prayed and asked God to give us something she needed. God worked everything out. For almost four months she attended that youth group. She met wonderful, Godly people who cared for her and encouraged her spiritual walk. They included her in their weekly activities. They invited her to attend their special events. The bond that was built continued long after we left NY. It continues to this day.

I ask myself again, "Why do I doubt God?" We read in Matthew 6:8, "Your Father knows what you need before you ask him." (ESV) God knew even before Jenna and I prayed about a youth group. He was working things out for His glory.

In my mind, I confess, I am a skeptic. I could blame it on being a father who does not want to see his children hurt or disappointed. I could say I am skeptical because I do not know what God's plan is and what I pray for might be different than what God wants to do. But, ultimately, it comes down to this fact: I am a doubter at heart. Even though God continues to show me how trustworthy He is, I continue to be a "Doubting Timothy."

Chapter 33

TRUSTING GOD WHEN HE SAYS, "NO"

"Blessed be God, even the Father of our Lord Jesus Christ, the Father of mercies, and the God of all comfort; Who comforteth us in all our tribulation, that we may be able to comfort them which are in any trouble, by the comfort wherewith we ourselves are comforted of God. For as the sufferings of Christ abound in us, so our consolation also aboundeth by Christ." (2 Corinthians 1:3-5)

None of us likes to say goodbye to people we love. The First Nation people, with whom we have worked for over twenty years, have it right. They never say goodbye because "goodbyes" are said when a person dies. Goodbye is final. Instead they say, "see you."

Over the years, I've done many funerals. The days before and the day of the funeral are some of the most emotionally draining of anything we do in ministry. Being able to offer comfort and hope to hurting families and individuals is something we enjoy being able to do. It is taxing to see the grief of those who have lost a loved one. It has been during these times that the Lord has given us the ability to have deep conversations about spiritual matters.

During these times, we do our best to show the same compassion Jesus showed while He was on earth. We know Jesus felt the grief of those around Him because of what we see in John 11. He was called to the home of three of His closest friends, Mary, Martha, and their brother Lazarus. Lazarus had gotten very sick and had died before Christ had made it to their home. As He goes to the tomb, it says, "Jesus wept." (John 11:35)

Jesus lived His life full of compassion for those in need. Another time, we read in the Bible, in Luke 19:41-44, how Jesus wept over the city of Jerusalem. It was the week before He gave His life for all mankind. He looked over the city and wept as He prophesied about the coming judgement of the city. He wept because His heart was not bent on destruction, but on a desire to see men and women, boys and girls have a growing personal relationship with Him.

In the beginning, God created a perfect world. The Bible tells us everything was "very good." (Genesis 1:31) God made a garden so beautiful it would make even the greatest botanical gardens of today look like trash heaps. Adam and Eve, the first man and woman, had everything they needed to survive and be happy. The greatest thing about the garden was the fact that God Himself walked with the man and woman in unhindered open communion and fellowship. Nothing but peace and harmony reigned in the Garden of Eden.

Even though the garden was perfect, God gave Adam and Eve one rule. You may eat of every tree in the garden, except for the tree in the center of the garden, the Tree of Knowledge of good and evil. God said, "But of the Tree of the Knowledge of good and evil, thou shalt not eat of it: for in the day that thou eatest thereof thou shalt surely die." (Genesis 2:17)

It has intrigued me over the years what people say about humanity. Some people say, "If you give a person a good environment they will come out good. The reason we have so many bad people is because they grew up in a bad environment." If we gave everyone perfect living conditions, we could have a perfect world.

Yet, with everything going for them, how did Adam and Eve respond? The Bible says, "And when the woman saw that the tree was good for food, and that it was pleasant to the eyes, and a tree to be desired to make one wise, she took of the fruit thereof, and did eat, and gave also unto her husband with her; and he did eat." (Genesis 3:6)

Even with everything going for them and living in perfect harmony with the Lord Almighty, they still felt they needed more. We could blame Eve like Adam did. We could blame Adam because he knew better. But would we have been any different? How many of us would have done the same thing?

I realize I sometimes live my life worrying about missing something the world has to offer because I follow God and His desires. But, God has given us everything we need. He promises to care for us even in our greatest needs. (Philippians 4:19) He promises He will never leave us or forsake us. (Hebrews 13:5) He promises to be with us always even to the end of the ages. (Matthew 28:20) Yet, with all those promises, we still feel like we are missing something.

When God says no, it hurts. We are like a three-year-old who wants a stuffed animal in the store. They cry and cry. They scream and raise a ruckus until their parents give in and buy the toy for them. I did this as a child. I remember as a youngster, crying and sobbing through Kmart because my parents had told me no. I knew what I wanted and did not think my parents knew best. I thought I had to have the toy and have it *Now*!

The sooner we learn to trust God when He says, no, the better off we will be. As I write this chapter, this lesson is very fresh in my mind. God has been teaching me to trust Him during the times He tells me no. It is not as though He is keeping something from me or taking something away; He is doing what is best for His glory and my good. When God answers with a no, He answers seeing the whole picture. He does so with infinite knowledge and understanding of every situation and circumstance.

When I started this book, I said I was the oldest of four. I have two brothers and one sister. My youngest brother and I were seven years apart, but we were the closest. This was true in our growing up years and even after we moved to the Yukon.

My youngest brother, Ben, and I loved to do things together. I remember one of the things he loved to do with me as a boy was to play Legos. We built houses, trucks, cars, and whatever else came into our active imaginations. We spent hours around the Lego bin. In fact, we even played Legos in the middle of the night. One night around two in the morning as I slept, my brother woke me. He wanted to play Legos and play it *now*. We sat there on the bed for around half an hour before Mom heard us playing and put a stop to it.

Ben traveled with Gwendy on her first visit to the Yukon before we got engaged. He spent hours with Gwendy and me when we were dating. He loved to buy gifts for our kids for Christmas each year.

He looked up to me. I loved to have him as my "little/big brother."

I called him that because once he graduated from high school, he could cradle me in his arms. He was as big as I was small.

Due to the age difference, we got married about the time he finished high school. He went on to college to become a videographer. With a skill for technology like no one else I've ever seen, he excelled in his field and was soon working for the local news station. He loved what he was doing. He sometimes sent us pictures or emails about the stories he got to cover.

His professionalism landed him jobs in Florida, Arizona, New York, and other places. His love was holding the camera. His attention to detail and organization caused him to climb the corporate ladder. He became supervisor of close to thirty other camera operators. He edited their work and prepared it for the news each day. He loved his work and loved the people.

As we grew older, we began to differ on lifestyle choices. We never argued about things. He knew where I stood and I knew where he stood. I did not preach to him. He did not put me down for my beliefs. The barrier between us grew bigger. He never denied the Lord or said he wanted nothing to do with Him. He wanted to live according to what he thought was good. I prayed often for the Lord to get a hold of his heart.

In the midst of his success, he had an unfortunate incident. One night after going out for the evening, the car he was riding in collided with another car. He came out of it all with a severe back injury. This injury made it difficult for him to carry the camera for work.

Pain overwhelmed his body all the time. He pursued surgery, but the pain continued. He cried for relief from the pain. He continued his profession as a videographer by day but at night, he tried to deal with the pain, which crippled him. He was hurting and we were hurting with him. We prayed for God to do whatever it took to bring him back to the way Jesus wanted him to live. We prayed for the Lord to give him victory and heal his pain.

In early 2020, he started calling me. He said he knew things were strained and he wanted to restore our broken relationship. I was overjoyed. For years, I wanted to restore the childhood closeness we had early in life, but did not know how to bridge the gap that had developed between us. As we talked, I noticed a change in him. He did not seem to be the same person he had been. Hurt and grief filled his words. He needed help. I encouraged him the best I could and continued to pray for the Lord to give him the help he desperately needed.

In March, he started showing signs that things were not ok. He started getting sick. Was it COVID-19 or something else? His body turned yellow and began to swell. He went to the doctors and looked for answers. He got no answers, and went home frustrated. He called, letting us know how he was feeling, upset with his situation and not being able to work. We prayed for his health and for the doctors to be able to cure him.

In April, his problems got worse. He went into the hospital a very sick man. The doctors tested his gallbladder. He had gallstones and his kidneys and liver were compromised. What was going on?

He could hardly talk or pick up his head. For days, he laid on the hospital bed with doctors trying to figure out what was causing the problems. For days, we prayed, "Lord heal Ben, for your glory and honor; do not let him die." We prayed as a family. We prayed as individuals. We prayed out loud around the dining room table. We prayed in silence on our beds at night. We knew God was the God of miracles. We could trust Him. After all, did He not raise Lazarus from the dead in John 11?

In May, we rode the roller coaster of doctors giving us little hope and them telling us not to give up hope. His numbers told us his liver functioning was improved one day and failing the next. Our prayer was, "Lord restore him to health and to that relationship you desire with him." We got people around the world to pray for him. We prayed over the phone for him. We had faith in God and trusted Him.

Even when the doctors said there is little hope, we clung to the miracles of Jesus in the Bible. God could not be done with him as long as he was breathing. God was in control. The battle belongs to the Lord, we told each other.

Then one night, the phone startled me awake. Mom's words came out in sobs. "The nurse just called and said Ben's organs are shutting down. We are headed to the hospital." All night I prayed like I have never prayed before. I was not ready to have only two siblings. I wanted him to live and be a great testimony to what God had done by healing him and bringing him back to full health.

The hours went by. The texts kept coming. There was no good news. I still held on to hope. God could still come through. He had done it before for others; He could do it again for us. I begged God like that young boy begging for the stuffed animal to my parents. "God, we do not want it to end this way."

Around five-o-clock in the evening the call came. My little brother, the one whom we had loved, laughed with, played with, and kept our mother up all night with, had slipped into eternity. God did not do a great miracle. Sickness had overcome his body. He was in the hands of His Savior.

God said, no. How could He get the glory by taking a life that seemed to be getting back on track? How could He say no to the prayers of so many people? Why did He let my little/big brother die?

I wish I knew the answers to each of these questions. This is one of those times when I want God to write in the sky what He is doing. I know I can trust God. He never lets us down. His Word tells me He never will. Paul writes, "Faithful is he that calleth you, who also will do it." (1 Thessalonians 2:24) I firmly believe He knows what is best. I look forward to finding the answers as He continues to teach us what it is to trust Him completely.

I know that to question God is like a boy questioning his grandfather on things too high for his understanding. Who am I to question the God who made the world and sustains it daily? I do not know the plans God has for us. I do not know what He is trying to do. I know He is able to do "immeasurably more than we ask or think or can imagine..." (Ephesians 3:20)

"Who has measured the waters in the hollow of his hand and marked off the heavens with a span, enclosed the dust of the earth in a measure and weighed the mountains in scales and the hills in a balance? Who has measured the Spirit of the LORD, or what man shows him his counsel? Whom did he consult, and who made him understand? Who taught him the path of justice, and taught him knowledge, and showed him the way of understanding? Behold, the nations are like a drop from a bucket, and are accounted as the dust on the scales; behold, he takes up the coastlands like fine dust." (Isaiah 40:12-15)

My "little" brother- May 14, 1979- May 20, 2020

Chapter 34

TRUSTING GOD WHEN THERE IS A NEED

"But when ye pray, use not vain repetitions, as the heathen do: for they think that they shall be heard for their much speaking. Be not ye therefore like unto them: for your Father knoweth what things ye have need of, before ye ask Him." (Matthew 6:7-8)

The week following my brother's death was tough on my family and me. The distance between my family in New York and our home in the Yukon had never seemed greater. Oh, how I wished I could board a plane and close the distance between my parents and me.

My brother knew we were on the mission field. In his final wishes, he asked that a service time be held only when it was convenient for all of the family to get together. He had no idea when he wrote those wishes how important his words would be to us, especially since the government had declared such gatherings as "non-essential" due to COVID-19 concerns. I still wanted to be with them all. I wanted to be able to hug my dad and mom and let them know I cared and we were going to get through this. We all had to rest in the Lord and the timing of the events.

The whole ordeal was hard on Dad and Mom as they were still in Florida, trying to take care of his belongings. They knew very few people there. The ones they did know they had only met in passing as they had been visiting my brother. They longed to be home and my desire was to be with them in New York. We all wanted to be able to sit together and cry. Little did we know how quickly things can change.

There are times when I am thankful for technology, then there are other times I am *very* thankful for technology. This was one of those times. It was such a blessing to be able to open my cell phone and talk with Dad and Mom like they were right beside me in the Yukon. In reality we were over four thousand miles away.

Six days after Ben's death, I called Mom. She was getting ready to turn in for the night, but like she always did, she took time to talk to me. I could hear the grief and distress in her voice as we talked. The battle with the hospital during my brother's last week and his death affected her and took its toll on her. She shared some of her struggles in having to go through my brother's things.

I can only imagine the pain she felt at having to sort through his household items. Many of his items were gifts that she and my dad had bought for him. We talked for around forty minutes. I told her I was praying for her and Dad. Together, we knew God could handle the situation. Mom had done this for as long as I could remember. Whenever a burden was too much to bear, she turned it over to her Lord, knowing He could handle it all.

The next day, she and Dad spent the day together trying to make the most of the time they had in Florida, but wishing they could leave and travel back to New York. She mentioned several times to Dad how her heart felt so heavy. As a mother who figured her children would bury her, I wonder if she was thinking about how she was going to be able to go on. Even though he had been in Florida for several years, there was still a strong bond between her and Ben.

That night, Dad and Mom ended the day as they had for almost fifty years. They got in bed together, opened their Bibles and prayed for their children, grandchildren, great-grandchildren, and others whom the Lord brought to their mind. Little did we know what lay ahead.

Early in the morning, Dad awoke out of a deep sleep. Something did not seem right. The light on the nightstand lit the room. The book Mom had been reading lay beside her. But, she was no longer with us. She closed her eyes on this earth with its sorrow, pain, and agony, and opened them beside her Savior. In her youth, she trusted Jesus as her Savior. In her life, she trusted Him to give her strength for each day. Now Christ has welcomed her into His presence.

The shock waves of this loss are still felt as I write this chapter. It has only been a short time since this dreadful night. Dad, my brother and sister and I all know that God never works without a purpose or a plan. His ways are perfect, though they are not our ways.

The urge to get to New York welled up inside of me, stronger than ever. How could I get there? The US was not allowing commercial flights in from Canada. My kids joked with me saying that I should find a pilot friend. We did something better than that; we talked to our Friend who sticks closer than a brother. We laid it at the feet of Jesus and said, "Lord, please work out the details." Never before had I felt so helpless. I felt trapped in another country with borders closed and a great need to escape.

It is easy to trust God when things are going well, but could I trust Him when things were going horribly wrong? The Holy Spirit inside of me said I could trust God to work everything out. Still, I wondered how this situation was going to resolve itself, or rather how God could work everything out for my good and His glory.

We contemplated ways to get back. I considered driving to Alaska and getting a plane in Anchorage. This meant an eighteen to twenty-hour drive. Besides that, Alaska required any outsiders to quarantine upon arrival. I could not wait fourteen days to leave Alaska after arriving. We checked about flying to Toronto and then renting a car. Could we cross the border into the US? We only had valid Canadian Passports; our US Passports expired many years ago. A quick phone call to the border crossing in New York lightened our anxiety. The immigration officer told us as long as we could prove our US Citizenship we could enter the US.

I still had one big problem in leaving Canada. Upon returning to the Yukon, we would have to be in quarantine or self-isolation for fourteen days. Losing a month in the already short summer seemed like a huge thing to commit to. Already, I had a long list of things that I needed to do before the end of our three-month summer. Besides this, I'm a people person. I did not like the idea of having to spend two weeks locked in one place, by myself, especially at a time when I needed people around me. I had to trust the Lord. He knew when Mom would enter His presence. He knew the effect COVID-19 would have on travel. Nothing caught Him off guard. Not Ben's death, not my parents traveling to Florida, not my mom's sudden death; nothing caught Him unaware.

God gave me a wonderful travel agent when He gave me Gwendy.

She is great at finding tickets at the best available price. But, how could we afford the tickets given such short notice? I heard about what airlines charge when a ticket gets booked at the spur of the moment.

We did not have an extra five thousand dollars laying around for the whole family to go. Gwendy and I decided that Jenna would go with me. She wanted to see her cousins and then I would have someone to quarantine with when I got back. Gwendy located tickets. They were over one thousand dollars each. She booked them, trusting the Lord to provide for what we needed.

Next, she had to find a rental car and make sure we could drive into the US. She found one with a reliable company. They charged over five hundred dollars for the twelve-day rental. We had to take it and pray, again, for the Lord's provision. We did not know how we could afford all the expense, but we knew God could handle it.

The day came for us to fly. I was thankful to be leaving, but anxious about the border crossing. Though the immigration officer had told me I could get across if I could prove my US citizenship, I was also told it was up to the customs and border patrol officer at the time of my entry. I had dealt with the border patrol countless times over the years crossing between Alaska and the Yukon and any time we flew back to the US. Most of the time they were reasonable, but sometimes they come across as ones who seemed to love to make life miserable, or at least prove they had the power. We placed this into the mighty hand of our God, trusting Him to move in the heart of the border patrol officer.

The two flights across Canada were uneventful. We arrived in Toronto after one in the morning. By the time we found our luggage and picked up the rental car, another hour had passed. We decided to go for the border in the cover of darkness, hoping there would not be any traffic to contend with. The roads were almost empty. As we got close to the border, we saw signs stating the borders were closed. They said, "Non-essential travel is not allowed." I did not let our daughter see it, but my insides tied themselves in a big wad of knots.

A few miles from the border, we prayed and asked the Lord to help us be able to get through without any problems. It looked like a ghost town as we pulled to a stop before the gate. There was hardly any sign of life. I began to wonder if the border was even open. We waited for someone to motion us forward. After what seemed like minutes but in reality, was only a few seconds, a gentleman reached out, moved the cone blocking the lane, and motioned us forward.

The moment I had been dreading and worried about had come. I shut off the vehicle while handing the officer our expired US Passports and our valid Canadian Passports. Seeing the two passports, he asked where our citizenship was. At times I have joked with the officers trying to lighten the mood, tonight was not the time. I told him we were dual citizens.

Next, he asked why we were trying to enter into the US. I explained to him about our family's losses. He asked to see my documentation. I may have been a bit groggy from flying all day, or this could be the fact that I can be a little slow to understand things, but I said, "What documentation?" I had handed him our passports; what more could he want? He wanted proof of the deaths.

The day before we left, Dad sent me a copy of both death certificates. To begin with, I saved a copy on my phone and thought that would be good enough. Hours before leaving, the still small voice of the Lord spoke to me and said, "Print them out." Sitting there in front of that border patrol officer early that morning, I was thankful I had listened.

There are times when I pass off what goes through my head as my being overly anxious or trying to be over prepared for whatever comes my way. We had committed this trip to the Lord and even before we left, He cleared the path of the minefields that could keep us from getting to our destination.

After receiving the documents, he asked the typical border questions, said, "I'm sorry for your losses," and sent us on our way. I have never been happier to be across the border. God cleared the way. God gave us a sympathetic and compassionate border guard. God answered our prayers. God had worked out all the details long in advance. He organized who would be working the night shift. He planted in my mind to print the documents off. He paved the way as only He could do.

I have found this in so many areas of life. God is constantly at work behind the scenes for His glory. We saw this some years ago. Our family took some of our Summer Missionaries to a Yukon community to introduce them to village ministry. During the visit, our son Joe, who was only four at the time got attacked by a dog. The dog latched onto his face and tore open his nose and very close to the eye.

We rushed him to the nearby health center and were surprised at who we found. The nurse, a retired nurse who had been in Ross River, was working. She was exactly what Joe needed. With the skill of a seamstress, she meticulously sewed his face. She knew what she needed to do and did not get rattled by the severity of the situation. God put her in that health center for the time we needed her most. We praise the Lord today for His perfect timing.

I am reminded of what is written in Esther 4. Esther, a Jew, served as queen. The problem was, Hamman, the king's official, hated the Jews. He wanted to destroy them. Esther's uncle, Mordecai, found out about the destruction plan and asked Esther to do something about it. Esther was scared for her life. She may have been queen, but the power still rested in the King's hand. She did not want to get on his bad side. Mordecai spoke these words of encouragement and exhortation,

> "Then Mordecai told them to reply to Esther, 'Do not think to yourself that in the king's palace you will escape any more than all the other Jews. For if you keep silent at this time, relief and deliverance will rise for the Jews from another place, but you and your father's house will perish. And who knows whether you have not come to the kingdom for such a time as this?" (Esther 4:13-14 ESV)

I do not think we are aware of all the times God works things out ahead of time. We do not know how many animals He keeps off the road as we travel and transport kids to Bible Camp each summer. We do not know how many times He works in the hearts of lost people before we talk to them to prepare them for the words He gives to us. We do not know how He orchestrates everything in His sovereignty. But when we see His mighty provision and guiding hand, we should be filled with praise and adoration for all He provides.

The day we arrived in New York, someone came to us and gave us a check which, after converting it to Canadian Funds, covered the cost of our airline tickets, down to the very penny. Several other gifts came a few days later. By the time we arrived back in the Yukon almost two weeks later, God provided for every penny of the trip. The tickets, the rental car, the travel, *everything*. God had provided for our needs in our time of sorrow.

God answered our prayers for the border, our prayers for a way to get to New York, and our prayers for our financial need even before we asked. He faithfully worked ahead of our need to provide.

I have found this to be true in so many areas of life, and God has laid burdens on individuals before we even knew we had a need. Sometimes it is a financial need. Other times it is a material need, like supplying drip edge on a building as I referred to in an earlier story. At other times, it is preparing a person's heart to hear the message that he laid on my heart earlier in the week.

It says in Matthew 6:8, "Your Father knows what you need before you ask Him." When I see things happen like this, I wonder why I have such a hard time trusting Him completely. He has never let us down. He has always taken care of us and provided what we needed, when we needed it, how we needed it. His provision has come through gas in the tank, strength for the ministry He has given us, money to pay the bills, volunteers to help complete a task and much, much more. I have to ask myself, "When will I quit doubting Him?"

My mother- May 17, 1951- May 27, 2020

Chapter 35

TRUSTING GOD WHEN IT MEANS SAYING, "GOODBYE."

"But they that wait upon the LORD shall renew their strength; they shall mount up with wings as eagles; they shall run, and not be weary; and they shall walk, and not faint." (Isaiah 40:31)

As I look back on my mom's life, I do not see a perfect individual. I see one who, despite her humanity (sinfulness), lived her life for God's glory. As I shared early on in the book, she and Dad were faithful to teach us the things of the Lord. I dedicate this chapter to her memory in hopes it will inspire those who feel like they lack the energy or faith "to mount up with wings as eagles." (Isaiah 40:31)

Mom was the third child born to my Grandparents, Vernon and Ruth Travis. She was born with a congenital defect. She had no hip sockets. After several operations and wearing a cast for months at a time, she walked without a whole lot of difficulty until later on in her life.

She grew up learning to love the Lord. At a youth rally with YFC (Youth for Christ) as a teen, she committed her life to Jesus as her Lord and Savior. From the day of her salvation to the day of her death, she tried to live her life completely as the Lord wanted her to live. In high school, when kids were out partying and enjoying the pleasures of sin for a season, she served as summer help at Letourneau Christian Camp.

Upon high school graduation, she attended Practical Bible Training School. She attended part of one year, but dropped out due to having mono. She made friends with Dad's sister and one weekend she came out to the farm. It must have been love at first sight because they both said within two weeks they knew they loved each other and would get married.

In her years as a young mom, she lived to support and help us kids. Before the public school provided transportation for us to go to the Christian School, she drove us and our cousins to school. This trip took over an hour round-trip, twice a day, several days of the week. She helped with VBS by teaching crafts. She loved to give of herself to see others have joy in life.

One of the areas where I saw her giving of herself the most was in choosing to teach us at home. When I finished eighth grade, she and Dad pulled the three of us older kids out of school. She now had four to teach: one in fifth, seventh, ninth grade, and our youngest brother was starting kindergarten. She never complained. She took it upon herself to make sure we had a good education.

In the days we started homeschooling, many people thought that those who chose to homeschool were those who could not make it in real school. They said it led to socially challenged individuals. Mom faced ridicule and scorn, even from those close to her. People told her we would be socially sheltered and might not make it through college. Her faith stood not in what she could do for us, but in the Lord, who gave her the strength for each day.

Day after day, she roused us out of bed and had us ready to start school at nine o'clock. There was no sleeping in at home with her as the teacher. She always started the school day by reading "Keys for Kids" or another devotional. Even in school, she made God the priority.

As we got older, evidence of mom's lack of hip sockets began to show. She walked bow legged, causing pain in her legs, knees, and feet. She developed arthritis and was in constant pain. In all this, she very rarely let anyone other than her close family know the pain that plagued her.

At a younger age than is usually recommended, she had her first hip replacement surgery. Because of her lack of sockets, the first few operations did not work. She would have surgery on the one hip, and as it healed they would do the other hip. Because of the way she had to walk, by the time one hip healed the previous hip replacement would come loose. This happened several times until finally a doctor from Canada operated. He performed the surgery in such a way that it held.

Even with so many hip replacements, each with excruciating pain, she did not complain. She kept a cheerful attitude, helping others where she could. Her mobility began to be a problem the last two decades of her life. She walked with crutches at home and used a wheelchair out in public when she had to go a long distance. Toward the end of her life, her shoulders were wearing out from the constant strain the crutches had put on them. Yet she still complained very little. Her trust was in the Lord to give her the strength not only for each day, but also to keep helping others.

Her ministry was one of the greatest ministries of the church. She was a constant prayer warrior. She knew the God who had helped her through her pain was the One who could help others.

This ministry became hers at her grandmother's funeral, my great-grandmother Hazel Battles. At her funeral, a missionary stood and told how Great-Grandma prayed for her and her ministry day after day, week after week, for many years. She wondered who would take her place. Mom said, "I will." From that day forth, she developed an ever-growing prayer journal. When she heard a name of someone who needed prayer, she wrote it in her book. When God answered the prayer, she put the date in the journal. She spent one to two hours in bed, praying each morning, asking God to touch lives. She prayed for healing. Salvation. Financial help. Her children. Her grandchildren. And her great-grandchildren. She prayed for whatever the Lord brought to her mind.

She could do this because she knew she was talking to the Creator of the universe. She talked to the one who said, "Let your request be made known." (Philippians 4:6) She knew there was no problem beyond God's infinite power.

One person she prayed for was a wayward teen who wandered away from their parents and from the Lord. Mom committed to pray for this person. She trusted God to work in the person's heart and soul. The teen returned to the Lord and follows Him to this day. Only God knows how many lives were changed because of her faithful prayers.

The legacy she left is not one of money, fame, or a great education (although every one of us kids went on and succeeded in college). Her legacy was not in the crafts she made with countless kids and even adults. Her legacy was not in her knitting, though she made hundreds of knitted blankets, vests, sweaters, mittens, stockings, and more. Her legacy was not in sewing, which she also loved to do.

No, her legacy was a life spent in whole-hearted trust in the Lord. She trusted when things were good. She trusted when things were horrible. She trusted when she was standing alone. She trusted when she barely had the strength to stand on her own two feet. When she died prematurely, she knew where she would open her eyes. She knew the God who had been with her during all her days of pain on earth would be the One to welcome her home for eternity.

The pain of losing her is sometimes more than I want to bear. As much as I wish she were still here, how could I ask God to send her back? I know she found those eagles wings we read about in Isaiah 40:31, to those who "wait (trust) in the Lord." She is running and not weary. She is walking and not growing tired and worrying about her legs giving out. She is walking with Jesus, who loved her every step of the way.

It is a day-by-day process of continuing to trust the Lord to do what He has always promised. He said He would never leave me or forsake me. (Deuteronomy 31:6, 8; Hebrews 13:5) On the days I miss Mom so much, I have to remember He is still with me. He has promised never to give me more than I can handle. (1 Corinthians 10:13) He has given me His all sufficient grace. (2 Corinthians 12:9) Even in the midst of the adversity and grief He has shown He is worthy of our trust. I may not always agree with what He does, but I know "All things work together for good to them that love God, to them who are the called according to his purpose." (Romans 8:28) He uses the challenges of life to show us how worthy He is to receive our unaltered, undivided, unwavering trust.

Chapter 36

TRUSTING GOD WHEN IT SEEMS NOTHING IS HAPPENING

"Therefore, my beloved brethren, be ye stedfast, unmoveable, always abounding in the work of the Lord, forasmuch as ye know that your labour is not in vain in the Lord." (1 Corinthians 15:58)

It would be another sleepless night in the Yukon for me. At around eight, one of our local police called and requested I come into the RCMP (Royal Canadian Mounted Police) detachment. As a minister, I am called on a regular basis to "guard" prisoners who need a safe place to sober up.

This was the second night this week I had to stay overnight. I must say, I am not feeling as young as I used to. I used to be able to do an all-nighter and then work the next day. It takes longer for my body to recover from the lack of sleep.

Over the years, this job has given me many opportunities to share Christ with people whom I otherwise would not be able to. It is when people are at their worst that they begin to think about where their poor life choices have brought them. I have been able to pray with many who realized they needed freedom from the addictions that sought to destroy their lives.

I have had this position for almost as long as we have been in Ross River. It was never something I aspired to do. I got involved after one of the corporals asked if I would like to speak to "a captive audience." He had a deep respect and love for the work of the Lord and desperately needed guards. I guess I looked desperate for someone to listen to me preach.

In the past four months, we have seen a rise in the number of prisoners. With the world on high alert because of the pandemic, an abundance of free stimulus money has given many the means to spend more on leisure activities. One might think, there are better ways to "stimulate the economy."

One of the saddest things about this ministry is seeing the same people over and over again. Each night I am called to guard brings about its own excitement and adventures, as Gwendy likes to say. I never know who I'll have or what they'll need. Everyone I see in the "cell block" as it's called, is a person who is looking for something.

Many have found themselves in the cell because they were "trying to numb the pain." Years of physical, sexual, emotional, and verbal abuse have caused them to turn to drugs and alcohol to numb the pain. Most of them did not intend to become addicts. In fact, many of them put down their parents for the same behavior, swearing they would never live in the same trap. Yet, the cycle continues as more lives get hurt in the process, leading to more victims who need to "numb the pain."

It is when people are at their worst and find themselves unable to control themselves or the situation, that they are more receptive and begin to listen to the message we preach. I wish they would do more than listen to the message of Christ. I wish they would let it sink into their hearts and souls, letting the Holy Spirit take residence in their lives. Some let me pray with them and even say they feel good afterwards. As soon as they leave, they go back to old habits and seem to forget the message they heard.

It does not matter the culture or race; every person is the same. They come in with hearts full of pain and emotional baggage. They feel trapped, not so much by the cell which holds them, but by the lifestyle they have found themselves living.

On this night before coming to work, I prayed. I had no idea who I was going to meet. I prayed for the Lord to give me an opportunity to share the hope we can have through Him to the person I would be watching all night. It is a prayer I often pray before heading out of the house. For me, this is more than a job; it is ministry.

What hurts me is the downward spiral I have seen many people take.

The ultimate end of many is premature physical death. Even greater is where they will spend their eternity. Not wanting to surrender to what Jesus wants, they hold on to the "control" they have in their lives.

I can put them down and say, "Why don't you change?" In reality, I am the same way. As I have spent hours writing the words in this book, I have realized how many times I have failed in putting my total trust in the Lord. I am like the drunk who returns to his bottle and like the drug addict who returns to his drug of choice. I know what God wants, but I find it so hard to put it into practice. After God answers a prayer or comes through in an amazing way, I see how much more I should have trusted Him. It is not long, though, before I am right back to the worry and anxiety that come from carrying my own burdens.

God continues to ask us to trust Him; to trust Him to do His purpose. He asks us to trust Him to do what is right and good in His good time. I hear him say to me, "Oh ye of little faith."

That night was one of those nights. I had just finished talking to an individual who had had enough of life. A recent break-up, a family tragedy, and an uncertain future had led this person to feel like there was not much left to live for.

As I listened to their concerns, I asked if I could pray for them. They agreed and I thanked the Lord for never leaving us and asked Him to give the person peace. This person was like many all over the world who wanted to end it all. They want the pain to stop so much, they are willing to do anything to make it stop. Sometimes this means taking their own life.

I find myself wishing, praying, hoping the Lord will do something. It seems the longer I am in ministry, the worse the situation is getting. I know in Scripture, we read,

> *"...in the last days there will come times of difficulty. For people will be lovers of self, lovers of money, proud, arrogant, abusive, disobedient to their parents, ungrateful, unholy, heartless, unappeasable, slanderous, without self-control, brutal, not loving good, treacherous, reckless, swollen with conceit, lovers of pleasure rather than lovers of God..." (2 Timothy 3:1-4)*

It is hard to watch as people ruin their lives. Their pain wells up inside of us like the surge of an angry ocean. The sinful choices of many are destroying their lives. Seeing the youth get so skinny there is nothing left of them due to the insatiable desire to be high saddens our hearts and causes us deep emotional pain. I find myself crying to the Lord to do something. I wonder, "Are we doing something wrong?"

Why do so many choose to turn and walk away from God after listening to the truth? Why is it that more people are not coming to Christ for the answer to life's difficulties? Does this mean God has lost control? Does this mean God does not care anymore? There is hope in all the hopelessness!

I find myself realizing, even in this, I must trust the Lord and His timing. I must wait on the Lord with great patience. Trusting is a lot of waiting. I am waiting for God to do what He deems best. Even as much as we love the people around us, God loves them even more.

"The Lord is not slack concerning his promise, as some men count slackness; but is longsuffering to us-ward, not willing that any should perish, but that all should come to repentance." (2 Peter 3:9) God is waiting for people to turn to Him. He is waiting for people to repent and turn from their destructive behaviors.

We must trust Him enough to keep carrying the light to the lost of this world. We must trust Him to bring about the harvest "in due time if we faint not." (Galatians 6:9) I pray we continue to be steadfast, unmovable, always abounding in the work of the Lord.

PART VI

TRUSTING GOD IS YOUR CHOICE

*"Now therefore fear the Lord and serve him in sincerity and in faithfulness. Put away the gods that your fathers served beyond the River and in Egypt, and serve the Lord. And if it is evil in your eyes to serve the Lord, choose this day whom you will serve, whether the gods your fathers served in the region beyond the River, or the gods of the Amorites in whose land you dwell. **But as for me and my house, we will serve the Lord.**" (Joshua 24:14-15 ESV, emphasis added)*

"The way of Christ is a NO to the former things and YES to a new life." (Pastor Alvin Bueckert)

Chapter 37

YOUR JOURNEY AWAITS

"And as it is appointed unto men once to die, but after this the judgment." (Hebrews 9:27)

Several years ago, our third daughter, Jaime, got sick. It did not seem like much at the time. It appeared to be a bit of a fever and nausea. She thought she might have caught some bug. Her body though, never recovered. And now, for some reason even unknown to medical professionals, her mind does not communicate very well with the rest of her body. Any of the normal tasks that the body regulates on its own are not normal anymore. She lives in a constant state of cold (not only because she lives in the Yukon). Her blood pressure is extremely low. And she ends up with brain fog which causes her to struggle with normal thought processes.

She has always been an energetic, outgoing person. Very little seems to bother her. Since the development of Postural Orthostatic Tachycardia Syndrome (POTS), her condition, she has to watch what she does. She needs to eat frequently and consume large amounts of water. With this she needs to consume more salt than a normal person should have to. All this to keep her blood pressure up.

With all this, she still maintains her energy and zest for life. Even in her difficulties, she maintains a sense of humor that catches even me off guard at times. I wonder where she comes up with some of the things she says. Even in her brain fog, she is wittier than I am.

With her condition, she is one of the "vulnerable sectors." All this has made us very aware of the brevity of life, not that we expect her to die anytime soon. It has however, made for some interesting conversations during meals. There are some days when she feels like she is going to die and we talk about what we want our funerals to be like.

Our children have grown up knowing the harsh realities of life. Death comes to everyone, sometimes sooner than we imagine it will. They have seen more death than they should have. They have lost friends, classmates, adopted grandmas, and many more. They know death comes to all. None of us likes to think about death being just around the next corner.

Whether we like to admit it or would rather avoid the topic, we are all destined for the same end. In the verse at the beginning of this chapter, we read that we all have an appointment with death. Unlike a doctor's appointment or an appointment for a meeting, we do not schedule this appointment. In reality, none of us knows the day of our death. None of us knows whether we will live to be forty-five or one hundred and five. We do not know whether we will die of old age or die of a crippling disease. We have no idea what God has planned for our life or our death.

When I was younger, death scared me. I was afraid of what faced me at the end of life on this earth. Would I end up in heaven or would I end up in hell? I was afraid of God's judgment.

When I became a teenager, I did not want to die. I wanted to get married and be able to have children. I wanted to experience life. I was not afraid to die; I just wanted to live and enjoy the fullness of life.

As I have gotten older, I realize death is coming. It does not scare me. It does not make me concerned, except for the way I die. I do not like the idea of suffering at the end. As much as I hated to lose my Mom without warning, I think she died in the best possible way. She laid down in her bed and awoke in glory.

Now don't get me wrong, I am not looking for a way to die. Neither am I suicidal, looking for a way to end it all. What I am saying is death's coming is not something I dread or fear. I look forward to being in the presence of the One who loved me and gave Himself for me.

Death is coming unless the Lord returns first to take His followers with Him. The apostle Paul writes,

"For the Lord himself shall descend from heaven with a shout, with the voice of the archangel, and with the trump of God: and the dead

in Christ shall rise first: Then we which are alive and remain shall be caught up together with them in the clouds, to meet the Lord in the air: and so shall we ever be with the Lord. Wherefore comfort one another with these words." (1 Thessalonians 4:16-18)

Death or the coming of the Lord does not have to be something that causes us to fear. Paul said we could take comfort in knowing we will face Christ someday.

This comfort I have in death and its certainty only comes because of the relationship I have chosen to have with Christ. It was when I put my faith and trust in what Christ did for me on the cross that He gave me His peace. I now look forward to my home going. I look forward to joining my Savior and walking hand-in-hand with the One who has stood with me and guided me through all of life's adventures.

There are many who say, "I will wait and see." They approach death and getting prepared for it as something they will do in the future. "When I see my life coming to an end, then I will make sure I am ready." The problem is that none of us know the day nor the hour we are going to face our eternal destiny. We may not have any warning. We may die peacefully in our sleep. We may get into a severe accident going to work one day. Our last breath could be on the operating table for a routine surgery.

I do not write this to scare people into the Kingdom of God or to raise fear in my readers. But whether we like it or not, death is coming. God desires us to trust Him NOW. He does not want us to wait until our dying breath to place our trust in Him. He desires an ongoing relationship with us. He desires us to live daily in reliance of Who He is and in an understanding of our need for Him.

As I look back on my life, I can see how there have been times when I have missed out on what God was trying to do, because I failed to open the door and allow God to do what He wanted to do in my life. I have also seen where God has blessed me as I have trusted Him. I don't feel blessed because of bountiful riches, though God has given us what we need for every day. I don't feel blessed because of the things I own here on earth. While I enjoy what we have, I know we cannot take it with us to glory. His blessing has not come through me always getting the things I want. As you have read, there have been many times when God has said no.

The blessing of peace I have from God is not because of my upbringing. While I praise God for the parents, grandparents, and even great-grandparents He gave me, I am not blessed because of them. I am not blessed by God because of any of the good things I have done with or in my life. (Ephesians 2:8-9) In the Bible it says, "Without faith, it is impossible to please Him." (Hebrews 11:6)

I do not receive God's blessing of peace because I have made conscious choices many times in my life to follow the Lord's leading and step out in faith. I am not blessed because I gave the past twenty years of my life to serving the Lord in a remote community. No, God's blessing is not felt by the things we have or do.

God's blessing of peace is all because of His goodness and grace. The Apostle Paul, one of the greatest missionary leaders of all time wrote,

"He saved us, not because of works done by us in righteousness, but according to his own mercy, by the washing of regeneration and renewal of the Holy Spirit, whom he poured out on us richly through Jesus Christ our Savior." (Titus 3:5-6)

God's blessing of peace for me is all because of Him. He is the One who deserves the praise. He is the one who gave His Son, Jesus, so I could have peace with Him. This peace is the greatest blessing anyone can ask for.

This blessing of His peace is available to anyone. I started my life living in fear and doubt. I was afraid of facing the judgment of a holy God. I knew I was undeserving of God's blessing. I knew the things I tried to get peace led only to more fear and uncertainty. As I trusted in the Lord Jesus Christ and what He did for me on the cross, my fear and doubt left.

Trusting the Lord is not only what missionaries, pastors, and people who are said to be super-spiritual do. Trusting the Lord is what God asks of each one of us. Proverbs 3:5 says, "Trust in the LORD with all your heart, and do not lean on your own understanding." The Lord created us to have a deep and growing relationship with Him.

Romans 10:13 says, "Everyone who calls on the name of the Lord shall be saved." Saved from separation from God. Saved from fear and doubt. Saved from eternal punishment. Saved from the destruction the Evil One wants for us.

God is inviting each one of us into a personal relationship of trust. In the Bible, Jesus says, " Behold, I stand at the door and knock. If anyone hears my voice and opens the door, I will come in to him..." (Revelation 3:20 ESV) God does not stand outside the door and beat on it. He does not demand that we let Him in. He stands outside, waiting for us to open the door.

Like the stranger in New York City who said, "I know the way, follow me," we face two choices. We can try to go through life stumbling and wandering aimlessly, or we can trust the Master of the Universe, the King of Glory, the One who knows and understands it all.

We need to trust God with life's ultimate decision – where we will spend eternity – but we also need to trust Him every day. Trusting God is not just something we do when life gets too bad for us to handle on our own. We do not trust God only when we do not know what else to do. Our trust is to be in God, *always*.

We need to trust God for the words to say to our co-workers who need Jesus. We need to trust God enough to be willing to go to the far reaches of the earth if He leads in that direction. We need to trust God to help us raise our kids. We need to trust God for our everyday provisions. We need to trust God as we help others. We need to trust God in everything, all the time.

A life lived on my own yields only heartache. A life lived trusting in the Lord reaps the blessing of peace with the Lord.

"Blessed is the man who trusts in the Lord."

Verses on Trusting God

All verses are quoted from English Standard Version of the Holy Bible

Joshua 1:9- Have I not commanded you? Be strong and courageous. Do not be frightened, and do not be dismayed, for the Lord your God is with you wherever you go.

Psalm 9:10- And those who know your name put their trust in you, for you, O Lord, have not forsaken those who seek you.

Psalm 13:5- But I have trusted in your steadfast love; my heart shall rejoice in your salvation.

Psalm 20:7- Some trust in chariots and some in horses, but we trust in the name of the Lord our God

Psalm 28:7- The Lord is my strength and my shield; in him my heart trusts, and I am helped…

Psalm 32:10- Many are the sorrows of the wicked, but steadfast love surrounds the one who trusts in the Lord.

Psalm 37:5- Commit your way to the Lord; trust in him, and he will act.

Psalm 40:4- Blessed is the one who trusts in the Lord…

Psalm 56:3- When I am afraid, I put my trust in you.

Psalm 62:8- Trust in him at all times, O people; pour out your heart before him; God is a refuge for us. Selah.

Psalm 118:8- It is better to take refuge in the Lord than to trust in man.

Proverbs 3:5, 6- Trust in the Lord with all your heart, and do not lean on your own understanding. In all your ways acknowledge him, and he will make straight your paths.

Proverbs 29:25- The fear of man lays a snare, but whoever trusts in the Lord is safe.

Isaiah 26:4- Trust in the Lord forever, for the Lord God is an everlasting rock.

Jeremiah 17:7, 8- Blessed is the man who trusts in the Lord, whose trust is the Lord. He is like a tree planted by water, that sends out its roots by the stream, and does not fear when heat comes, for its leaves remain green, and is not anxious in the year of drought, for it does not cease to bear fruit.

Philippians 4:6, 7- Do not be anxious about anything, but in everything by prayer and supplication with thanksgiving let your requests be made known to God. And the peace of God, which surpasses all understanding, will guard your hearts and your minds in Christ Jesus.

Hebrews 13:5, 6- Keep your life free from love of money, and be content with what you have, for he has said, "I will never leave you nor forsake you." So we can confidently say, "The Lord is my helper; I will not fear; what can man do to me?"

1 John 5:14- And this is the confidence that we have toward him, that if we ask anything according to his will he hears us.

Biblical Examples of Trust

Noah- Building the ark- Genesis 6-9

Abraham and Isaac- Offering Isaac on the altar- Genesis 22

Rahab- Forsook her people to protect God's people- Joshua 2

Israel- Crossing the Jordan River- Joshua 3

Israel- Marching around for 7 days- Joshua 6

Ruth- Left her land and people to follow the True God- Ruth 1

David- David and Goliath- 1 Samuel 17

Widow of Zarephath- Gave her last oil and flour to cook Elijah a meal, 2 Kings 4:1-7

Esther- Trusted God to risk her life for her people- Esther 1-10

Shadrach, Meshach, Abednego- The fiery furnace- Daniel 3

Peter- Peter walking on water toward Jesus- Matthew 14:22-33

Thief on the Cross- Trusted Christ for his salvation- Luke 23

Mary- Mother of Jesus- Luke 1

Hebrews- Faith Hall of Fame- Hebrews 11

Other Good Books

Books that have encouraged my faith and
challenged my relationship with Jesus:
The Holy Bible- Jesus, the Author and Finisher of our faith
Mover of Men and Mountains- R.G. LeTourneau
"Open the Sky"- The Story of Missionary
Pilot Dwayne King- Mark Winheld
Brought To A Place of Abundance- Leander Rempel
Alaskan Bush Adventures- Lessons from the Land,
Lessons from the Lord- Don Ernst
Into the Copper River valley: The letters and ministry of Vincent
James Joy, pioneer missionary to Alaska- by Faye E. Crandall
Hope When Your Heart is Breaking- Ron Hutchcraft
Your God is Too Safe- Mark Buchanan
A Tale of Three Kings- Gene Edwards
The Church That Never Sleeps: The Amazing Story That Will
Change Your View of Church Forever- Matthew Barnett

GET IN CONTACT WITH THE AUTHOR

If this book has been an encouragement to you or helped you
in any way, pass it on to someone else who could benefit from
it. You can connect with me using any of the following:

Email- blessedishewhotrustsinthelord@gmail.com.
Instagram at _blessedishe_
Facebook at Timothy Colwell@blessedishewhotrustsintheLord
Mail- Timothy Colwell, PO Box 118, Ross River, YT Canada, Y0B 1S0.

Endnotes

1 "Definition of Blessed". Oxford University Press. Lexico.com. 22 Jan 2021. https://www.lexico.com/definition/blessed.

2 From the book, *Mover of Men and Mountains*, bibliography on the life of R. G. LeTourneau

3 Taken from "The Ross River HOPE Centre" brochure, 2009

4 Taken from "The Ross River HOPE Centre" brochure, 2009

5 Taken from "The Ross River HOPE Centre" brochure, 2009

Scripture Index

Special thanks to Gracelife.org for their scripture indexing
tool which made the scripture index possible.

Old Testament

New Testament

Printed in the United States
by Baker & Taylor Publisher Services